1996

A Guide to Research for Educators and Trainers of Adults

Second Edition

by

Sharan B. Merriam
University of Georgia

and

Edwin L. Simpson
Northern Illinois University

KRIEGER PUBLISHING COMPANY
MALABAR, FLORIDA
1995

A Guide to Research for Educators and Trainers of Adults

Second Edition

First Edition 1984
Second Edition 1995

Printed and Published by
KRIEGER PUBLISHING COMPANY
KRIEGER DRIVE
MALABAR, FLORIDA 32950

FROM A DECLARATION OF PRINCIPLES JOINTLY ADOPTED BY
A COMMITTEE OF THE AMERICAN BAR ASSOCIATION AND A
COMMITTEE OF PUBLISHERS:

This publication is designed to provide accurate and authoritative information in regard to the subject matter covered. It is sold with the understanding that the publisher is not engaged in rendering legal, accounting,
or other professional service. If legal advice or other expert assistance is
required, the services of a competent professional person should be
sought.

Library of Congress Cataloging-in-Publication Data

Merriam, Sharan B.
  Guide to research for educators & trainers of adults / by Sharan B.
  Merriam and Edwin L. Simpson.—2nd ed.
      p.   cm.
  Includes bibliographical references and index.
  ISBN 0-89464-849-7 (acid free paper)
  1. Adult education—Research — Methodology.   I. Simpson, Edwin L.
  II. Title.
  LC5225.R47M46   1995   93-47936
  374'.0072—dc20   CIP

10 9 8 7 6 5 4 3 2

CONTENTS

LIST OF FIGURES

LIST OF TABLES

PREFACE TO THE
SECOND EDITION

When the original edition of *A Guide to Research for Educators and Trainers of Adults* was published in 1984, we wrote in our preface that the need for competent teachers, administrators, trainers, and counselors of adults had accelerated with the growth of the field. As we go to press 10 years later with this second edition, the demand for competent practitioners is even greater. So, too, is the need to better understand our practice so that we can be even more effective in our various adult education and training roles. To know more about our practice we need to step back from it, look at it, ask questions about it, reflect upon it. We can formalize this process by conducting research on and within our practice.

As with the original edition, it is the intent of this book to provide guidance in the process of systematic inquiry, or research. Through our style of presentation and the organization of material, we have tried to demystify research and allow readers to feel comfortable in attempting to "systematically inquire" about their practice. To this end, we have preserved many of the features of original edition.

The order of the chapters remains basically the same, except for the addition of a new chapter on the important issue of ethics in research. We begin with an introduction and overview of the research process, followed by chapters on how to shape a research problem and conduct a review of the literature that will help to inform and structure one's investigation. Chapter 3, which explains the purposes and functions of a literature review and how to go about doing one, still remains one of the few resources available on this important part of the research process. Many readers have conveyed to us their appreciation of this chapter in particular. The middle four chapters are on various methodologies. Chapter 6 on qualitative methods has been completely rewritten to incorporate new developments within this paradigm. The last four chapters are on data collection procedures, writing up your findings, ethical dilemmas in doing research, and graduate research. The new chapter on ethics and the research process we feel is an important contribution; most other research design texts allude to ethical issues, but rarely address them in a substantive way. All of the other chapters have been revised, some substantially, to facilitate understanding of the research process. Our revisions reflect our own growing competence and understanding of the research process, as well as the many things we have learned within the last decade of directing graduate student research and teaching research courses. Further, we have added up-to-date examples of research studies from adult education and training to illustrate important points. Readers are encouraged to consult these studies for even greater knowledge of the research in the field.

As with the original edition, we want to acknowledge those who have contributed in various ways to this edition. Mary Roberts, editor at Krieger Publishing Company, was particularly helpful in shepherding this project through to completion, including copyediting the entire manuscript. Many of our colleagues and students have contributed to the development of this book through their encouragement and comments. They have our thanks. We would like to give special thanks to Mary Risseeuw who deftly deciphered our editorial notes and typed both numerous drafts and finally the entire manuscript. The work of Nan Zhang and Vivian Mott, graduate research assistants, is also much appreciated. The authors hope this book continues to be a helpful resource for designing and conducting research.

PREFACE TO THE
FIRST EDITION

As the demand for educational and training opportunities for adults has accelerated within the last decade, so too has the need for competent teachers, administrators, trainers, and counselors of adults. In addition to the fields of adult education and human resource development which have traditionally dealt with adults, other areas of social practice—vocational education, allied health, social work, and counseling—have begun preparing people to attend to the needs of a growing adult clientele. Within the last decade, the number of graduate programs in adult education and human resource development and the number of adult-focused courses in other social science programs have increased dramatically.

Academic programs that train practitioners to work with adults also strive to produce graduates who not only understand but will perhaps contribute to the theory and knowledge base of their field. In order to realize this goal, those involved in the education and training of adults must know something about research, for it is through research, or systematic inquiry, that the knowledge base of a field expands. The development of research skills in most graduate programs has the two-fold purpose of training persons (1) to be consumers of research—that is, to be able to understand, interpret, and apply research findings to their practice, and (2) to be researchers themselves, to initiate and implement investigations.

There are, of course, numerous books available on research design and statistical procedures. However, most texts on educational research methods present only the most commonly used research designs and draw supporting material from school-related studies. The authors of this book have attempted to address the shortcomings of other educational research texts by presenting a full range of methodology for doing research, and by supporting points with examples from research studies done with adults in adult settings. The traditional experimental, descriptive, and historical research methods are presented in Chapters 4 and 5. A discussion of ethnography, case study, and grounded theory can be found in Chapter 6. Also presented are philosophical inquiry (Chapter 5), interactive, ecological, and futures research (Chapter 7).

To provide an organizing framework for discussing these methodologies, the common processes found in all research approaches are used as a guide: (1) types of research problems, (2) assumptions underlying methodology, (3) ways the research phenomenon is delineated, and (4) use of data gathering procedures and techniques. Throughout the discussion, examples of actual research studies will be used and strengths and limitations of each method pointed out.

The text also contains two chapters not commonly found in other research texts. Chapter 3 explains the purposes and functions of a literature review and offers a step-by-step procedure for conducting and writing a review of the literature. And since much of the research in applied fields dealing with the education and training of adults is done by graduate students, Chapter 10 is devoted to the process of graduate research and the procedures unique to that process.

The authors hope this text will be a helpful resource for conducting and understanding research. Decisions about what to include and what to leave out were guided by our overall purpose of providing an overview of the research process and the alternative methodologies one might choose from in conducting a research study.

Many of our colleagues have contributed in different ways to the development of this book. We would like to give special thanks to two people—William Russell, author, doctoral student, and a former editor who put in long hours editing and critiquing the entire manuscript, and Dorothy Jossendal, who deftly typed numerous drafts and finally the entire manuscript. We would also like to acknowledge help from colleagues Peter Abrams, Ronald Cervero, Sean Courtney, Suzanne Davenport, John Niemi, Jeffry Simpson, and Harold Stubblefield who read and critiqued individual chapters. Finally, we want to thank our families and the Adult Continuing Education Program at Northern Illinois University who provided support throughout the project.

CHAPTER 1

THE NATURE OF RESEARCH

Research is central to the development of any field of study. Research activity is largely dependent upon the curiosity and energies of individuals who are attracted to practice and study in the field. Some people imagine research as the job for a well-trained scientist engaged in an important but somewhat mysterious activity in a laboratory. Though this perception may have been accurate at one time, it no longer is true. Today research is conducted by many people in many settings. All fields, including applied areas of social sciences (e.g., education, counseling, social work, human resource development), recognize the need for and the value of research. It is the means by which a discipline expands its knowledge base; and in applied fields, it informs and enhances practice. This text is intended for those persons engaged in an applied field of social practice and, in particular, areas of practice dealing with adults.

Because the practice of educating and training adults is diverse, research interests and pursuits of researchers in the field also are diverse. Such fields as business, political science, health, religion, industry, and vocational education all deal with educating and training adults. The daily work lives of persons engaged in any one of the above-mentioned fields entail problem solving, decision making, planning, instructing, and evaluating. As additional experience is gained in doing these tasks in our work, knowledge accumulates, decisions improve, better planning results, and so on. Hence, more experience and knowledge lead to more "professional" practice.

How do practitioners get the experience and knowledge to handle problems and make decisions? There are both informal and formal ways of enhancing practice. For instance, if you are the one who determines what training courses to offer company employees, informally you could ask your friend in another company what has been successful there, or you could ask for some suggestions from the employees themselves. You could do some casual reading in the latest issues of *Training and Development Journal*. You could also use your common sense and guess what might be relevant to the employees, given the particular business. Finally, you might employ a trial and error approach, offering some courses and seeing which ones the employees select.

However, more systematic ways exist for approaching the same problem—ways that are more effective and more efficient in the long run. First, you could read in an organized fashion, using indexes to pinpoint articles that are relevant to the problem. Second, rather than asking a friend, you could consult with an expert or authority on the topic. You could also take a course in program development or attend a workshop on how to assess needs. Finally, you could conduct a systematic investigation to determine what is needed and when and how it should be offered. This systematic investigation might entail interviewing certain employees, administering a paper and pencil survey, searching company records of course offerings, and so on. In using this last method to handle to problem you would be engaging in "research." The purpose of this book is to acquaint those in applied fields with this particular systematic approach to enhancing practice—that of doing research. We especially hope that those who deal with adults will not only discover the importance of conducting research in their field, but will also consider the ways in which they themselves can engage in the process.

THE MEANING OF RESEARCH

As many definitions of research exist as there are books on the topic. Some see research as "systematic investigation to increase knowledge and/or understanding" (Page & Thomas, 1977, p. 290), as "disciplined inquiry" (Good, 1973, p. 494) or as a discipline guided by both the technique and the philosophy of science (Kaplan, 1985). All of these conceptualizations have one idea in common—research is a systematic process by which we know more about something than we did before engaging in the process. Several questions are important to the understanding of research. First, where does knowledge come from? Second, what is meant by *systematically* searching for knowledge? Third, how and by whom will the knowledge be used?

Knowledge can be accessed through the four processes we have come to accept as part of the human experience-what we believe, what we think, what we sense, and what we feel (Royce, 1964). We may use belief as the avenue to knowledge if we are told something by some trusted individual, or if we have always found something to be true in the past. When we have confidence in what others say or we have consistently experienced something in our day-to-day happenings, we may say that we *believe* it to be true. Thinking also is one of the most commonly accepted paths to knowledge. If we use reason to sort out the truth, we may claim that we *think* it is true. Systematic use of mental processes is the source of our knowledge in this instance. Using our five senses to arrive at truth also is a typical approach to gaining knowledge. We *sense* something to be true when we experience it through one or more of our senses—seeing, hearing, tasting, touching, smelling. One of the traditionally less trusted but equally valid avenues to knowledge is through our feelings. Knowledge is interpreted as true if we have a positive, affective response to the knowledge, if we feel good about what seems to be true or have insight as to the correctness of the knowledge. Individuals accept or reject what they interpret to be true through the use of one or more of these four ways of knowing.

Knowledge is frequently categorized by the sources of truth used in our quest to know. It is determined by which one of the four processes is used for accessing knowledge. For example, when personal belief is the source of truth, the result is referred to as *authoritative* knowledge. In this instance, knowledge is based upon the acceptance of an ideology. Knowledge based upon thinking, on the other hand, is termed *rational* knowledge. Logical or rational, as opposed to illogical or irrational, thinking is the test of reason as the source of knowledge. Knowing through one of the five senses is classified as *empirical* knowledge. Here, one's senses are trusted to reveal truth. The use of feeling as the source of knowledge, in contrast, is cast as *intuitive* knowledge. Intuition is judged by the degree of insight or revelation we possess in determining what is true.

Although all sources of knowledge have been used throughout human existence to help explain and adapt to life, certain sources have been used more at particular times than others. In pre-literate societies, for example, effective patterns for adapting to life were learned by watching other people and passing on traditions from one generation to the next.

Authoritative knowledge greatly influenced the interpretation of truth and reality throughout early human history. Truth was often accepted by virtue of the role assumed by the appointed individuals, such as priests, witch doctors, or soothsayers, who espoused certain special abilities. Belief, usually conveyed through cultural or religious tradition, is still a principal conveyor of truth. Documents such as the Bible or the Koran represent knowledge that is authoritative. Also, individuals representing cultural or religious traditions, such as Jesus Christ or Mohammed, are used as authoritative sources of knowledge. In a contemporary sense, dictionaries and legal documents are authoritative sources, as well as delegated individuals in society such as Supreme Court judges and religious leaders.

Rational thinking gained acceptance as a pathway to knowledge during early Greek civilization and again in 17th and 18th century Europe. Emphasis was placed upon logic and the elements of the rational process. Use of deductive Aristotelian logic and inductive thought, proposed by Francis Bacon in the 17th century, helped develop thinking as a way to knowledge. Deductive reasoning, which involves applying general observations to specific cases, and inductive reasoning, wherein observing individual cases leads to generalizations, are the primary modes of thinking in conducting research today.

Two approaches commonly used to solve the problems of everyday life involve gaining access to knowledge through sensory experience and through intuition. In using our five senses we are trusting our sensory experience above other sources of truth. An example of sensory-based knowledge is the way we know the sun rises and sets. If a resident of the United States were asked about the regularity of the sun each day, the response probably would be that the sun rises each morning and sets every evening. This, of course, would not be the same experience as a Finnish Laplander living in the land of the midnight sun where the regularity of the sun is in terms of months.

Knowledge resulting from the use of feeling, or *a priori* knowledge, as explained by Kerlinger (1986), is intuitive knowledge. Intuition is a self-evident way of determining truth. By using feelings as the pathway to knowledge, the researcher jumps from the known to the unknown, and the responsibility for the validity of that knowledge belongs to the individual. Some researchers characterize intuition as the pursuit of hunches, while others, such as Bruner (1967), refer to this source as the "educated leap." Artistic or creative expression also is an example of intuitive knowledge. By blending contrasting colors from the palette into a provocative synthesis on the canvas, for example, the artist is demonstrating a way of knowing. Likewise, the novelist's woven tale of fiction or the jazz musician's improvisation on a Dixieland tune is a form of knowledge.

An assumption that supports the types of categorical descriptions of knowledge acquisition discussed here is that all humans generally experience knowing in the same ways. However, a body of research developed during the last part of the 20th century calls attention to the possibility that humans as individuals may be quite different in their ways of knowing (Belenky et al., 1986; Reinharz, 1992). Various psychological and sociocultural influences may play an important part in how we individually experience the pursuit and outcome of knowledge.

An important aspect of research is discovery. However, the phenomena of discovery alone should not be confused with the process of research. Truths are discovered by individuals in their everyday lives. These discoveries may be coincidental or may be the result of being curious about common occurrences. Daily personal discoveries, indeed, may also lead to more productive or satisfied lives. The process discussed in this book, which we call research, pertains to the ways in which those engaging in the process prepare for their task, pursue it, and become responsible for the results of their efforts. The process is fundamentally a process of "re-search"—systematically looking at a situation or phenomenon, not occasionally or causally, but again and again until certain previously stated criteria, goals, or guidelines of inquiry are met. When we are doing research, we are committed to systematically searching the breadth and/or depth of a situation or phenomenon, often from numerous vantage points. When we are engaged in research, it is not a casual episode of discovery that results in having our curiosity satisfied. Doing research is to search in ways that not only may produce the desired outcomes, but also may be clearly discernable to other scholars and practitioners (both present and future) who may be interested in how our investigation was conducted, in addition to learning of our results. Research also requires those pursuing it to be ethically responsible to those participating in the research. Researchers have a commitment as well to those who may be consumers of their findings. These parts of the process of research are discussed in more detail in Chapters 8, 9, 10, and 11.

The defining characteristic of research is that it is a systematic, purposeful, and disciplined process of discovering reality structured from human experience. Research is a matter of process as well as outcomes. The results of research efforts may not be what are expected. Whether or not an investigation leads to uncovering truth is only of immediate concern. For example, the alchemists of the Middle Ages seriously undertook the task of determining what sort of matter made up the world. While they failed to find an answer to their question, alchemy was a scholarly process of inquiry. And through alchemy "hard facts were learned about the behavior of metals and their alloys; the properties of acids, bases, and salts were recognized; the mathematics of thermodynamics was worked out; and, with just a few jumps through centuries, the helical molecule of DNA was revealed in all its mystery" (Thomas, 1982, p. 35).

Since each type of knowledge is unique, different "systems" or methods have been developed to access different types of knowledge. For example, logic has been developed to help access rational knowledge and the scientific method structures an investigation of empirical knowledge. Historical methods are in part used to investigate authoritative knowledge, and intuitive knowledge can be accessed by methods of naturalistic inquiry.

Until recently, researchers have made more use of rational and empirical knowledge bases than those of authority or intuition. During the Renaissance there was a great desire to interpret the so-called laws of nature. Experiments were conducted, for example, on the speed of objects falling through space in relation to their weight and the density of air (Santillana, 1953). Systematic though these early experiments were, it was not until Charles Darwin combined inductive and deductive reasoning with observations that research became "scientific." Realizing that direct observation of various species of animals alone was not leading to productive ends, Darwin formulated a tentative explanation about the extinction and continuation of animals. In so doing he posed a hypothesis of natural selection which he could then test through additional observation and data collection.

Darwin's approach, which was considered "scientific," came to characterize much of the research that was done after the mid-nineteenth century. The term *science* itself came to mean knowledge that is accurate, verifiable, and organized. It no longer only referred to specific subjects such as physics, chemistry, or biology. The scientific method in research involves inductive and deductive reasoning, testing hypotheses, and observing empirical phenomena. It is a highly refined, systematic approach to rational and empirical sources of knowledge.

It was not until the mid-20th century that a source other than rational and empirical knowledge was thought suitable for systematic inquiry. In contrast to the objective, rational approach of the scientific method, humanists make the point that all science is grounded in the subjectivity of human experience (Kockelmans & Kisiel, 1970). Based in phenomenological philosophy, this approach added an intuitive or inner perspective to social research and theory. That is, research in this mode involved "direct investigation and description of phenomena as consciously experienced, without theories about causal explanation and as free as possible from unexamined preconceptions and presuppositions" (Encyclopedia Britannica, 1967, p. 810). The influence of phenomenology and humanism has resulted in a different emphasis in the research process. "Qualitative" or "naturalistic" research, as this approach has come to be labeled, rests upon different assumptions about knowledge and the nature of reality (Lincoln & Guba, 1985). Consequently, research techniques other than the scientific method have also been developed with which to access this type of knowledge. In the opinion of some researchers who have keenly observed this recent development in social science research, two distinct research subcultures seem to be represented by the two research paradigms—quantitative and qualitative (Palys, 1992, p. 3).

PURPOSES AND TYPES OF RESEARCH

Typically, persons in applied fields of practice are overworked and underpaid. Taking the time to learn about the research process and to carry out a study requires a commitment that not many are able to make. Many professionals, however, realize the value of research to the field and are able to involve themselves in various ways. In addition to actually conducting research, they are in positions to utilize research results and to identify problems needing study.

Ultimately the value or purpose of research in an applied field is to improve the quality of practice of that discipline. The improvement of practice can come from various types of research endeavors, but the most common are basic research and applied research. *Basic* or pure research is motivated by intellectual interest and has as its goal the extension of knowledge. *Applied* research is directed toward solving an immediate practical problem. Kidder and Judd (1986) comment on the role of basic and applied research in the social sciences:

> Applied research, which really subsumes evaluation research, is any social research designed to answer practical questions. Applied researchers may also be testing theories while they are answering practical questions, and they may be more or less directly involved in a practical or real-world setting, but ultimately they are interested in answering some question with practical implications. (p. 396)

Applied social researchers generally are interested in speaking to a different audience than are basic researchers; for example, they hope their work will be used by legislators, judges, and administrators to change social policy. While more applied research is carried out in fields dealing with the education and training of adults, both forms—basic and applied—can have an impact upon practice. The results of basic research may have very practical applications, and applied research may lead to the building or testing of theory. For example, applying Piaget's theory of cognitive functioning could lead to specific curriculum materials and instructional practices when working with learners at various levels of cognitive functioning. On the other hand, if one were to test the levels of cognitive functioning of adults and find that many have not achieved formal operations (said by Piaget to develop at adolescence), then Piaget's theory would be challenged.

A form of applied research widely used in fields of social practice is evaluation studies. The difference between evaluation and research, which are both forms of systematic inquiry, lies in the questions asked, not in the methods used, for the methods in each are essentially the same. Evaluation research collects data or evidence on the worth or value of a program, process, or technique. Its main purpose is to establish a basis for decision making. "Such decisions might pertain to selecting the most effective procedure, material, or organizational structure. Evaluation studies may also address such questions as 'Does this technique (material, treatment) work?' " (Drew, 1985, pp. 16–17). Evaluation is considered a type of applied research because it is involved in immediate problems and is likely to have an immediate impact upon practice.

In business and industry, applied research often deals with the development of a product and is thus referred to as "developmental" or "product" research. Companies may have research development (R&D) divisions devoted exclusively to product development. Borg (1981) discusses the relationship of R&D to applied and basic modes of research. Too often, he maintains, basic and applied research studies have little effect upon practice; thus, one of the more promising developments in education is the emergence of programs of research and development.

> Educational R&D programs typically differ from educational research in that the objective of most research is the search for new knowledge. The outcome of this search is usually a report that appears in a scholarly journal. In contrast, the objective of educational R&D is a finished product that can be used effectively in educational programs. (p. 221)

Thus, practitioners have many options open to them if they choose to make an active contribution to their field through research. Searching for new knowledge for its own sake or refining available knowledge may prove as important in the long run as using research to solve an immediate practical problem, evaluate a program, or develop a new product. The type of research done will be determined by the questions raised as a result of being engaged in a particular field of practice. Whether one's motivation is primarily theoretical or practical, however, the process of research is essentially the same.

THE RESEARCH PROCESS

The process of planning and conducting research can be divided into the tasks of (1) identifying a concern or problem, (2) establishing a conceptual framework, (3) delineating the research phenomenon, (4) determining research methodology and using appropriate data-gathering procedures and techniques, and (5) analyzing and reporting data. As authors of this book, we have chosen this research process as the organizing structure. We realize, however, that the process is not always sequential and that variations in the sequence are not only possible, but at times appropriate. Judgments about appropriate methodologies and data-gathering techniques are greatly influenced by what is being researched and the background and skills of the individual doing the research. The reader is advised to treat the book as a reference, using those portions that fit the need for assistance in planning and conducting research as it arises.

Identifying a problem or concern occurs at the very beginning of most research. Problems in applied fields such as adult education and training are usually taken from practice. Problems or concerns of a conceptual nature, on the other hand, typically guide basic or fundamental research. The research problem statement describes variables and/or concepts around which research activity will focus. The problem statement is a paragraph that identifies the research topic area and ends in a broad general question, such as "What is the influence of training on adult performance on the job?" or concludes in a hypothetical statement such as "There is a difference in patient wellness after leaving a hospital that provides programs of patient education." Some statement of a problem, no matter how general in description, is established in order to guide further activity. The research problem is discussed in more depth in Chapter 2.

A second task in the process of research is establishing a conceptual framework. Recognizing and discussing theories, concepts, and factors that are part of the study are essential to planning research; however, when and how these are clarified depends on the type and purpose for the study. Studies that are based on theory that is to be tested, for example, require definition of the theory and related concepts at the initial stages of planning. Research that is intended to discover new theory and concepts will focus much less on definitions at the early stages of research planning. In this instance, the literature review will serve to better delineate the area of study or to determine the parameters where the research will focus. The process can be compared to baseball. The conceptual framework in research outlines the "ball field" or topical area where the game (research) is to be conducted. A thorough review of literature usually leads to a more focused study and better use of research energies; in other words, a winning "game plan." Developing a conceptual framework involves the progressive discovery of the exact problem or concern to be studied. As the problem or concern becomes clearer, related theories and concepts are clarified. In a reciprocal way, delineation of the problem statement also assists in identifying and clarifying important concepts and factors to be studied. Once the research problem has been identified, it is helpful to discover what concepts and procedures other researchers have used in pursuing the same or similar lines of inquiry. Knowing the variables and methods that others have identified in their research can also give direction and warn against pitfalls in planning research. These functions and other aspects of the literature review are discussed in Chapter 3.

After describing the problem and reviewing literature to develop a conceptual background or to explore the topical area for the study, the researcher begins the third task of identifying the specific research phenomena—that is, the variables that will be investigated. Careful identification of phenomena to be studied is accomplished by (1) defining terms, (2) delimiting the scope of the study, and (3) specifying the assumptions upon which the study is based. For example, if a researcher planned to study training as it influences job performance, terms such as *method, influence,* and *performance* would require definition. Also, characteristics of the adults participating in the study would need to be described (e.g., age range, sex, and socioeconomic status). Defining and delimiting the study help establish boundaries of the inquiry and bring into focus the particular variables and interrelationships that are important in the investigation. Assumptions the researcher is making about training, as it is related to performance, would be another consideration in developing an adequate conceptual framework.

As the conceptual framework for the particular problem is being developed, one identifies the research methodology that would be most appropriate in conducting the study. This fourth task, the selection of a methodology, depends upon the source of knowledge being accessed and the assumptions underlying the nature of research. It also is influenced by the background, experience, and skills of the researcher. Attributes of the researcher need to be assessed as part of the planning process. Testing theory or describing phenomena involves sampling, hypothesis testing, and so on, which are common to experimental, ex post facto, and descriptive research designs. Building theory or interpreting phenomenon will most likely involve qualitative or naturalistic approaches such as those found in ethnography, grounded theory, and historical or philosophical inquiry. Chapters 4, 5, 6, and 7 are devoted to explaining various research designs that one might use in conducting a study.

As part of settling upon an overall methodological approach, one must also select appropriate data collection techniques. Using the training study as an example, the researcher might use a questionnaire or interview protocol in collecting data. Or, if observation is to be used, a rating scale might be incorporated. Specific data collection techniques are discussed in Chapter 8.

The fifth part of the process that all research has in common is data analysis. If research is carefully planned and conducted, an analysis of data will produce descriptions and inferences about the phenomenon being studied. Research findings eventually lead to conclusions pertaining to the original concern or problem, or they serve as a guide to reconceptualize the problem in the event conclusions cannot be drawn. Analyzing data depends to a large extent upon the particular methodology being used. Therefore, general considerations in the handling of data according to the type of methodology being employed are found in Chapters 4 through 7.

Once the research investigation is completed, it is important to report the results. Only through reporting and disseminating findings can research contribute to the knowledge base of a field and be available for use to enhance practice. Chapter 9 offers suggestions on how to report and disseminate research. In addition, the reporting and dissemination of research results may involve ethical considerations regarding the identity of participants and other repercussions of publicizing findings. Ethical concerns involved in all phases of the research process—from problem formation to dissemination—are discussed in Chapter 10.

In the experiences of the authors of this text, much of the research in an applied field is done by graduate students employed in the field who are also pursuing (usually part-time) a master's or doctoral degree. While the actual research process is the same regardless of the

Table 1.1 The Process of Graduate Research

	Chapter 1 The Nature of Research	Chapter 2 Framing the Research Study	Chapter 3 Reviewing the Literature	Chapter 4 Experimental and Descriptive Designs	Chapter 5 Historical Inquiry and Philosophical Inquiry	Chapter 6 Meaning and Interpretation; Qualitative Methods	Chapter 7 Action, Participatory, Critical and Feminist Research Designs	Chapter 8 Data Collection Procedures and Techniques	Chapter 9 Writing Up Your Findings	Chapter 10 Ethical Dilemmas in Doing Reasearch
A. Selecting a Topic	■	■								■
B. Forming a Committee										
C. Presenting a Proposal										
#1. The Problem or Concern*	■	■								■
#2. Review of Literature			■							
#3. Methodology				■	■	■	■	■		■
D. Completing the Research								■		■
#4. Findings								■	■	■
#5. Discussion and Implications									■	■
E. Defending the Research									■	■

*Note: Numbers 1 through 5 reflect the chapter divisions of a typical dissertation and the sections of the standard research report.

role one is in, there are some formalized procedures characteristic of graduate research. Writing a proposal, forming a committee, and holding an oral defense are three procedures most students need to deal with as part of their graduate research experience. Chapter 11 deals with the practical aspects of doing graduate research. Table 1.1 presents a matrix that displays the parts of the graduate research process in conjunction with the book's other ten chapters. The table highlights where fuller discussion of each part of the graduate research process can be found.

Finally, at the end of the book, readers will find a comprehensive glossary of commonly used research terms. It is our hope that all parts of the book will assist researchers in meeting the challenges of conducting research effectively.

REFERENCES

Belenky, M., Clinchy, B., Goldberger, N., & Tarule, J. (1986). *Women's ways of knowing: The development of self, voice and mind.* New York: Basic Books.

Borg, W. R. (1981). *Applying educational research: A practical guide.* New York: Longman.

Bruner, J. S. (1967). *A study of thinking.* New York: John Wiley and Sons.

Drew, C. J. (1985). *Introduction to designing and conducting research.* St. Louis: C. V. Mosby Co.

Encyclopedia Britannica. (1967). Chicago: Encyclopedia Britannica Inc.

Good, C. V. (Ed.). (1973). *Dictionary of education* (3rd ed.). Chicago: McGraw-Hill.

Kaplan, A. (1985). Research methodology: Behavioral science. In T. Husen, & T. N. Postlethwaite, (Eds.). *The international encyclopedia of education* (Vol. 7, p. 4293).

Kerlinger, F.N. (1986). *Foundations of behavioral research.* (3rd ed.). New York: Holt, Rinehart & Winston.

Kidder, L. H., & Judd, C. M. (1986). *Research methods in social relations.* New York: Holt, Rinehart & Winston

Kockelmans, J. J., & Kisiel, T. J. (1970). *Phenomenology and natural sciences: Essays and translation.* Evanston, IL: Northwestern University Press.

Lincoln, Y., & Guba, E. (1985). *Naturalistic inquiry.* London: Sage Publishers.

Page, G. T., & Thomas, J. B. (1977). *International dictionary of education.* New York: Nichols Publishing Company.

Palys, T. (1992). *Research decisions.* Toronto: Harcourt, Brace & Jovanovich.

Reinharz, S. (1992). *Feminist methods in social research.* New York: Oxford University Press.

Royce, J. R. (1964). *The encapsulated man.* Princeton, NJ: VanNostrand Company.

Santillana, G. de. (Ed.). (1953). *Dialogue of the great world systems.* Chicago: University of Chicago Press.

Thomas, L. (1982). On alchemy. *Discover, 3,* 34–35.

CHAPTER 2

FRAMING THE RESEARCH STUDY

The process of designing a research project begins with identifying a particular topic of interest or area of concern. Most people can pinpoint a broad area of interest. The difficult step is to perceive a problem within the area of interest that is significant, of manageable size, and is systematically approachable. After identifying something specific to investigate, a problem must be fashioned or shaped in order to guide the study. "Shaping" is done by delineating the problem's relationship to theory and previous research, by defining terms and concepts, and by developing research questions or hypotheses. In this chapter we will present considerations involved in identifying and shaping a research problem. Specifically covered are selecting a topic, shaping the problem, assessing the significance of the problem, and situating the problem within a theoretical framework. Also discussed are how to define key concepts and how to write questions and/or hypotheses.

WHAT TO STUDY?

How do you figure out what to study? First, consider your own daily life. What about your work, your family, your friends, your community? Look around. What interests you? Does something at work puzzle you? What are you curious about? In an applied field such as adult education and training, a great many research topics come from the work setting, but they can just as easily arise from attending to events or people that make up your everyday world. Following are several examples of how our daily lives can generate a topic area:

- Working on a grant to provide continuing education for lawyers and judges, Pat became interested in what kind of training judges received in order to know how to be a judge. Discovering

15

that most judges receive no formal training at all, she became especially curious as to how some judges become acknowledged experts on certain issues (Stein, 1990).

- In her spare time, Betsy volunteered to work in the town's homeless shelter. She became interested in the process by which some homeless adults are able to move out of the shelter and achieve a stabilized housing situation.

- At midlife Dan was able to make a major career change within the company for which he had worked for 15 years. This experience led him to wonder how other employers respond to the career-changing needs of their employees.

A research topic can come from other sources. Current social and political issues offer numerous possibilities. Boshier's study (1992) of the ways in which the discourse around AIDS has been framed and the consequent implications for educators is an example. A topic might come from the literature, especially previous research or theory in an area. Something you read in your professional journals, for a course assignment, or even casual reading may be the source of a question that can evolve into a research study. Further exploration of topics from any of the above sources leads to identifying and shaping a research problem.

WHAT IS THE PROBLEM?

No simple formula exists for identifying a researchable problem within an area of interest. As Guba (1978, p. 45) observes, "problems do not exist in nature, but in the *minds of people.*" What becomes identified as a problem depends upon an individual researcher's notion of the nature of a problem. Some have defined it as a situation demanding a solution. Others, like Kerlinger (1986, p. 16), define it as "an interrogative sentence or statement that asks: 'What relationship exists between two or more variables?' " But not everyone defines a problem as a specific situation needing a solution or as a question needing an answer. Dewey (1933), for example, observed that a problem arises out of some felt difficulty; a person is puzzled, dissatisfied, unsure about something. Dewey points out that "there is a genuine problem or question if we are willing to extend the meaning of the word . . . to whatever . . . perplexes and challenges the mind so that it makes belief . . . uncertain" (pp. 12–13).

A problem, then, might be best defined as something that "perplexes and challenges the mind." The research problem is a catalyst for transferring one's general curiosities into a workable tool for planning and guiding research. The process of problem identification involves refining and narrowing the topic of interest. This process can be helped along by reading widely on the topic, talking with other people, especially those who are familiar with the area, observing closely situations pertinent to the problem, taking notes as thoughts on the topic occur to you, and so on.

Typically, a research problem exists when there is a gap in information or knowledge about the topic. We don't know how judges become expert, how homeless people reestablish themselves, how companies respond to employees wanting to make a career change. We don't know from our daily experience (if we did, we wouldn't be curious or perplexed about it); nor has this problem been directly addressed by previous writers or researchers. Other aspects of the problem may have already been studied, but not what we are particularly interested in. Following are two examples of problem statements where a gap in our knowledge base is identified. The first study is on the broad topic of power relations in adult higher education classes:

> Power relationships are present everywhere in society. There is a power disparity between racial minorities and the white majority, between the poor and the wealthy, the uneducated and the educated, and women and men. To some extent, these power relations are reproduced and maintained through the educational process . . . The power of both the hidden and overt curriculum to contribute to the maintenance and reproduction of existing power relationships is operative at every level of formal education from nursery school to graduate school, even in higher education settings where critical thinking skills are promulgated and valued, and emancipatory educational theories are developed and discussed . . .
>
> While there is a body of literature that discusses the nature of power relations in adult education (Collard & Law, 1989; Cunningham, 1988, 1992; Hart, 1985, 1990), *there has been a lack of data-based research* [italics added] that specifically examines power relations in the learning environment based on gender or race, or interlocking systems of privilege and oppression, such as gender and race, or gender and class. The purpose of this study was to determine how power relations predominantly based on gender, but including other interlocking systems of privilege and oppression, such as race or ethnicity, class, and age, are manifested in classrooms composed of adult students. (Tisdell, 1993, pp. 203–204)

In the second example, the general topic is participation in adult education and, more specifically, deterrents to participation:

Beginning with Houle's seminal work published in 1961, theoretically-oriented research on participation in adult education has strongly emphasized identifying learning 'types,' motives, or 'motivational orientations' (Boshier, 1971; Burgess, 1971; Grabowski, 1972; Morstain & Smart, 1974, Sheffield, 1964) . . . Although Houle's typology of adult learners and the subsequent factor-analytic studies of motivational orientations have enhanced our understanding of participation phenomena, they have not been successful in predicting participation behavior (Ordos, 1980). Specifically, motivational orientation factors have not proved useful in distinguishing participants from nonparticipants.

Strangely, despite all the attention focused on what impels participation, *few studies of comparable sophistication have examined what deters it.* [italics added] This lack of attention to deterrents is particularly disturbing in that the construct of deterrent or barrier occupies a central place in theories of participation . . . The general purpose of the present inquiry, therefore, was to explore the underlying structure of the multitude of reasons adults give for not participating in continuing education. (Scanlan & Darkenwald, 1984, p. 155–156)

In the first, the researcher points out that there have been studies about power relationships in higher education classrooms, but none were found that studied *adult* students. In the second example, the authors point out that we know quite a bit about what motivates adults to participate in formal learning experiences, but we know little if anything about what deters them.

SETTING UP THE PROBLEM

The problem statement is couched within a carefully crafted essay that lays out the logic of the research study. Fashioning a problem statement "involves both a progressive sharpening of concepts and a progressive narrowing of scope" (Selltiz, Wrightsman, & Cook, 1976, p. 55). Consider the funnel shape. It is wide at the top and gets progressively narrower as you move to the bottom. Similarly, in setting up the research problem, the essay begins broadly, identifying for the reader the general area of interest. Is it judicial education, homelessness, midcareer change? What is this topic all about? What has already been studied with regard to this topic? What are some of the key concepts and how are you defining them? Why is this an important topic? Why should we care about it?

Once the stage has been set by identifying for the reader what the topic is all about and why it is of interest, the next step in the narrowing process is to identify specifically what *aspect* of the topic you are particularly concerned with. This is also where you might point out the lack of information on this particular aspect of the topic. There is a gap in our knowledge base. Or, there may be some research on this aspect, but for reasons you make clear, the research to date is inadequate or flawed in some important way.

You have essentially led your reader along to the point where it is obvious what needs to be done. What needs to be done is stated as the *purpose* of your study. A purpose statement is a direct response to the problem that you have carefully identified. Purpose statements are just that—a statement beginning, "The purpose of this study is to. . . . " Below is an example of a problem statement (in abbreviated form) ending with a purpose statement.

> For American businesses to remain competitive in an increasingly global economy, some are calling for drastic measures to be taken with regard to training and developing the workforce. Business and government leaders continually lament the lack of motivation, education, and job skills of the American workforce but yet offer few concrete suggestions as to how to remedy these problems.
>
> The manufacturing sector, in particular, seems most at risk for losing its competitive edge (Mark, 1987). Increased automation, while stepping up production, has at the same time increased the demand for workers who can read and interpret technical instructions, instantly perform calculations, and use computers. These demands are set against a workforce that is less prepared in basic literacy and numeracy, is more demographically diverse, and is increasingly aging (Carnevale, 1988; Mikulecky, 1988) . . .
>
> More than 30 years ago, McGregor (1960) noted that many managers believe that the effectiveness of their organization would be at least doubled if they could discover how to tap the unrealized potential present in their human resources . . . Subsequent studies have continued to underscore the key position that human resource development plays in increased performance, increased wages, reduced turnover, and worker satisfaction . . .
>
> Most studies of successful organizations have been conducted in large corporations with well-established human resource departments . . . The vast majority of U.S. businesses, however, are small to mid-sized having annual sales well under $10 million (Lee, 1991) . . . Small businesses (those which employ 100 or fewer people) constitute 98 percent of America's businesses (Dumaine, 1992) . . . Little is known about human resource development in these small companies.
>
> The purpose of this study was to delineate the role of human resource development in successful, small to mid-sized manufacturing businesses in the Southeastern United States. (Rowden, 1993, pp. 159–160)

Note the "funnel" shape of the problem statement. Although in abbreviated form, the "logic" of the above problem statement is as follows. At its broadest the topic is identified as businesses in the United States and concerns retaining a competitive edge (first paragraph). The topic is narrowed a bit by identifying manufacturing businesses in particular as being at risk (second paragraph). Getting even more focused, the author tells us that what can be done about the problem is tied up in developing the human resources of companies (third paragraph). He then identifies the gap in the knowledge base in this area—there is research about the role of human resource development in large Fortune 500 companies, but none in small manufacturing companies, and it is these companies that constitute more than 98% of America's businesses (fourth paragraph). He then concludes with a purpose statement, clearly delineating what is to be investigated.

It might be pointed out here that defining terms and concepts is an important step in shaping the problem. Concepts represent a constellation of ideas used to explain and describe the phenomena being studied. Concepts are abstractions; they represent phenomena understood to exist but which cannot be observed directly. Selltiz, Jahoda, Deutsch, and Cook(1959) point out that:

> The greater the distance between one's concepts, or constructs, and the empirical facts to which they are intended to refer, the greater the possibility of their being misunderstood or carelessly used, and the greater the care that must be given to defining them. They must be defined both in abstract terms, giving the general meaning they are intended to convey, and in terms of the operations by which they will be represented in the particular study. The former type of definition is necessary in order to link the study with the body of knowledge using similar concepts or constructs. The latter is an essential step in carrying out any research, since data must be collected in terms of observable facts. (p. 41)

In the problem statement example above, human resource development would need to be defined. Also, the author needs to clarify what constitutes "small" and "successful" manufacturing businesses. Definitions of key concepts and terms are often integrated into the narrative as "small" is above (employing fewer than 100 workers). In a research proposal (in contrast to an article) a section of definitions might be included. However you choose to handle defining concepts, it is important that the reader know how you are using them. When concepts are to be measured, you must also provide an operational definition, that is, specifying exactly how the concept will be measured.

RESEARCH QUESTIONS AND HYPOTHESES

The purpose statement is often followed by research questions and/or hypotheses. Both are designed to guide the inquiry; both determine how data are to be collected. Research questions are derived from the problem statement and reflect the researcher's judgment of the most significant factors to study. Using the above comparative case study of the role of human resource development in small, successful manufacturing businesses, the researcher structured his inquiry around the following research questions:

1. What formal and informal activities related to employee training and development, organizational development, and career development to improve individual, group, and organization effectiveness take place in the company?
2. How is human resource development, broadly defined, viewed by the company and its employees?
3. What links can be established between human resource development, management, organization behavior, and other functions of the organization, and the various measures indicative of a successful business? (Rowden, 1993, p. 3)

As in this example from a comparative case study, research questions, not hypotheses, guide qualitative studies (see Chapter 6).

Other types of research may have both research questions and hypotheses. The primary difference between questions and hypotheses is the greater precision and predicted direction of change that is included in many hypotheses. Hypothesis statements assist not only in the gathering of data, but also in the measurement and analysis. For example, one might hypothesize that fewer incidents of absence from work by trainees will occur after the trainees have learned a new technique on the job. Occasionally, positive and negative degrees of relationship between variables are also predicted in the hypothesis statement (a greater positive relationship between worker attitude and work productivity will exist following on-the-job training, for example).

Certain characteristics are present in well-constructed hypotheses (Ary et al., 1985). Effective hypotheses should:

1. have explanatory power
2. state expected relationships between variables
3. be testable
4. be consistent with the existing body of knowledge
5. be stated concisely

Having explanatory power means that the hypothesis provides a plausible answer to the stated research problem. Incongruence between the problem and the answer supplied in the hypothesis statement is of little or no help in gathering and analyzing data. For example, if one were seeking an answer to the problem "What kind of continuing education is most useful to professionals in carrying out their professional roles?" the hypothesis "There is greater job success among professionals graduating from universities than among those graduating from technical schools" does not provide a plausible answer. Though there may be a relationship between pre-service education and job success, the hypothesis does not address the question about continuing education inherent in the problem.

The statement of expected relationships indicates what the researcher anticipates or does not anticipate (null hypotheses) will come from the study. In the previous example, "greater job success" is the expected relationship. Words such as higher, lower, negative, and positive often are used to indicate expected relationships.

A testable hypothesis is one that can be verified. That is, empirical observations can support or not support any deductions, conclusions, or inferences drawn from the hypothesis (Ary et al., 1985). If a hypothesis is stated in such a way that it can stand scrutiny through empirical observation, it is testable.

Finally, simplicity or conciseness in stating hypotheses is necessary to make them of maximum value in guiding research. Long, wordy statements make identification of variables and expected relationships difficult to sort out. If a hypothesis cannot be expressed concisely, it may contain more than two variables to be investigated; having more than two variables requires making multiple hypotheses.

IS THE PROBLEM IMPORTANT?

Besides identifying some gap in our knowledge about a particular phenomenon, it is important to make it clear why we need the knowledge. Of what value is it to know the answers to your questions? How will this knowledge make a contribution in the world? Who will benefit and in what ways? Establishing the significance of the research is usually handled at least to some extent in the setting up of the problem. That is, as part of the "funnel" movement in your narrative, you create, through the use of pertinent quotes and other supporting data, a sense of urgency surrounding this issue. Dissertations usually have a separate section in which the significance of the study is addressed; however, references to the importance of the topic are still made in setting up the problem.

A study might be significant in a number of ways. The study can contribute to the field's knowledge base. All research does this since the purpose of research is to expand the knowledge base in some way. The gap that is identified in the problem formation is a gap in knowledge about the phenomenon of interest. However, the fact that some information is lacking does not mean we need this knowledge. A case has to be made as to why it is important. How will this new knowledge advance the field? How will it advance our thinking about the phenomenon? Part of the knowledge base of a field is the theories or models that have already been developed. A research study can also contribute to theory development through testing or building theory.

Another major way a study can be significant is what it contributes to practice. Especially in applied fields like adult education and human resource development, research is often undertaken for the expressed purpose of improving practice. How might someone make use of the findings of your study? Who in particular would be most interested in your research? Will your research help someone make better decisions, plan programs, teach, develop policies?

Finally, a study might be significant if it advances technique or methodology in some way. For example, a study could extend the validity and reliability of an instrument, develop new testing procedures, or advance a statistical or methodological technique. Usually this aspect of significance is coupled with other justifications as to why the study is important.

WHAT IS A THEORETICAL/ CONCEPTUAL FRAMEWORK?

A good bit of confusion exists even among some experienced researchers about the place of theory in the research process. Probably the most common reason given for manuscripts being rejected by research journals and conference steering committees is for lack of a conceptual or theoretical framework. Unfortunately, while it is relatively easy to spot the *lack* of a theoretical framework, it is considerably more difficult to explain what it is and how to go about incorporating it into your research study.

While some writers differentiate between theoretical and conceptual framework, we consider them to be referring to the same thing—and that "thing" is the underlying structure, orientation, and viewpoint of your research study. The topic you are interested in, the specific problem you have identified, the purpose of your study, all reflect a particular orientation to the world. That orientation may reflect a particular discipline, such as sociology or political science, or a particular theory or philosophy, such as psychoanalysis, behaviorism, phenomenology, and so on. The "trick" is to make that orientation explicit, to show how your study is situated within that particular orientation. How are the variables of interest derived from this orientation (that is, what does the previous literature say?), and how do these variables relate logically to each other? Think of the development of the problem as putting steel beams together to form the structure of a building. Each beam has to "fit" in with others in some logical way. So too, the components of your study—the concepts you are using, the literature and previous research you refer to, the instruments you select to assess the phenomenon—must coherently fit together. Once you have the structure, the theoretical framework of your study, you can fill it out with more in-depth information (often the literature review), with "raw" data that you've collected, with findings, and with your discussion of those findings in which you tell the reader how your study adds to the framework with which you started.

The same topic area can be approached from different theoretical perspectives. In so doing, the problem will be shaped to reflect a particular perspective. This in turn determines what the purpose of the study will be, what questions or hypotheses will be fashioned, and how data will be collected, analyzed, and interpreted. A recent publication on adult learning provides a good example of how the same topic can be approached from many perspectives (Merriam, 1993). Boucouvalas's chapter presents adult learning from a psychological perspective, in particular focusing on consciousness and learning. In this paradigm, levels, state, and structures of consciousness are important. Wilson, on the other hand, sees promise in the study of adult learning from a situated cognition perspective. This view holds that learning is situated in the everyday world of human activity and cannot be adequately understood apart from the world in which it takes place. In another chapter, Tisdell frames adult learning from a feminist pedagogy perspective where the focus is on understanding the nature of structured power relationships and facilitating women's personal empowerment. A research study from any one of these perspectives would be drawing from a different literature base, would be using concepts and terms unique to that orientation, and would shape the problem and study purpose to reflect the particular assumptions and concerns of the theoretical base. This is what is meant by a theoretical or conceptual framework of a study.

How do you know what the theoretical framework of your study is so that you can make it explicit? The way to identify your theoretical framework is to examine the assumptions you are making about the phenomenon of study as well as attending to the literature you are using to inform your study (see Chapter 3). Finally, how are you shaping your problem? What are the questions you are asking? An anthropologist is interested in culture, a sociologist in social structure, an educator in teaching and learning. The questions being asked will reflect particular interests which in turn reflect the "lenses" through which you view the world. Schultz (1988) in an article discussing how one develops a conceptual framework in vocational education research makes the point that

> any research problem may be approached from more than one theoretical perspective . . . The choice of a theoretical model/conceptual framework . . . will guide the research process in terms of the identification of relevant concepts/constructs, definition of key variables, specific questions to be investigated, selection of a research design, choice of a sample and sampling procedures, data collection strategies including instrumentation, data analysis techniques, and interpretation of findings. (p. 34)

Schultz goes on to include criteria for assessing the relationship between one's theoretical framework and each step of the research process listed above.

THEORY AND THE RESEARCH PROCESS

A theoretical or conceptual framework generally draws from some theoretical formulations, models, or philosophical assumptions. Research is not conducted in a vacuum; it is attached or anchored to a particular orientation or perspective. The conceptual framework makes that orientation explicit. The place of *a theory* in the research process is a consideration in addition to the establishment of a theoretical framework.

The place of theory in the research process depends to a large extent upon what is known in the particular area of investigation. In some areas of social science research, a considerable amount of data has already been gathered and interpreted by theory. Much is known, for example, about people's behavior in groups, and several theories have been advanced to explain and predict how people will act in various group settings. In other areas of human behavior, less is known and there are few theories. Thus, depending on the state of knowledge, the research process might be one of *testing* a well-developed theory, *clarifying* or *refocusing* tentative theories, or *developing* a new theory.

Much of scientific research tests what is called hypothetical-deductive or a priori theory. That is, a theory is proposed from which deductions are made about corresponding behavior or events in the real world. These deductions or hypotheses are tested and, to the extent that they can be verified, the theory becomes more credible. In this mode of inquiry one decides in advance what general principles will be applied to understanding specific phenomena. The theory provides a framework or guide for what is to be observed and which facts are to be collected. In a hypothetical-deductive mode, the particular theory you are working from defines the conceptual/theoretical framework of your study. Empirical evidence then confirms or refutes the theory. When a theory is being tested, control of extraneous variables is an important consideration; equal concern must also be given to the number and representativeness of the cases used to test the theory. Hence, research in this mode is often labeled "scientific" or "quantitive." Selltiz, Jahoda, Deutch, and Cook (1959) have delineated several advantages to theory-guided research:

- Theory provides a means of structuring the inquiry.
- Phenomena other than the theory's referent may be explained by the theory.
- Theory increases "the meaningfulness of the findings of a given study by making it possible to perceive them not as isolated bits of empirical information but as a special case of the working out of a set of more abstract propositions".
- Theory "provides a more secure ground for prediction than do the findings themselves." (pp. 490–491)

In some research, the role of theory is not as directive as the above discussion would suggest. There are not as many longstanding, well-established theories in the social sciences as there are in the natural sciences where phenomena are easier to observe and manipulate. Theories about human behavior thus tend to be more tentative than those dealing with physical and biological phenomena. Education and psychology, for example, are relatively new areas of investigation. Much of the research in the social sciences results in the extension or refinement of theory.

Theory may be tested or modified in the research process. In either case, it serves to guide the collection of information and the interpretation of results. Theory may also be the end result of research. It is necessary to develop theory when (1) there is none available or (2) when existing theory fails to provide an adequate or appropriate explanation. The process by which research leads to theory is an inductive one. Theories that evolve from a phenomenon are labeled "inductive" in contrast to the hypothetical-deductive mode mentioned earlier. Those studies that have as their goal the discovery of theory rather than verification are often called "qualitative" studies. Based in phenomenology, rather than in logical positivism, this type of inquiry differs from theory-testing approaches in that there is no manipulation of variables and no predicted outcomes. The phenomenon is observed, and an explanatory framework or theory is allowed to emerge from the data themselves. It is important to note that even if the purpose of a study is to generate theory, the researcher still sees the world through some sort of discipline- or value-based lens. This orientation or perspective constitutes the conceptual/theoretical framework of the study. Once a theory has emerged, it has the status of an a priori or hypothetical-deductive theory and might itself be tested. The role of theory in the research process can be seen in Figure 2.1. The process begins with a problem from which questions rise. A review of previous research will reveal the extent of knowledge and theorizing pertinent to the topic. A researcher must then decide whether existing theory can be used as a guide in the investigation, or whether the investigation will focus upon developing a theory.

If there is theory to guide the research, the hypotheses can be deduced from that theory. Hypotheses are tentative explanations that direct our search for order among facts. Once hypotheses are formed, the study can be designed; data are then collected and analyzed, and conclusions and implications are drawn with regard to the theory that originally informed the study.

If a literature review reveals that no theory fits the phenomenon under investigation, then one study goal might be to formulate a theory and/or hypotheses to explain observed events or behavior. In this case the researcher designs a study, collects data, and analyzes data just as in deductive inquiry. However, rather than using the results to modify or adjust a theory, the researcher looks for underlying order in the phenomenon and suggests hypotheses that encompass and explain the phenomenon.

Exactly how a researcher makes sense of data, "sees" relationships among facts, or, in short, "discovers" theory cannot be explained as a logical process. Theory building comes from the insights of a sen-

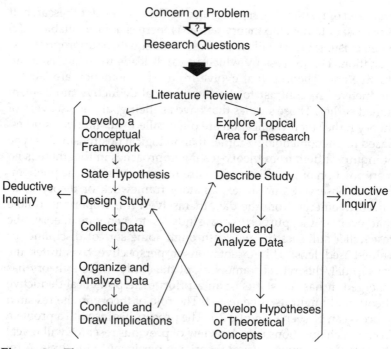

Figure 2.1 The process of systematic inquiry.

sitive observer (Glaser & Struass, 1967, p. 281). The insights that form the basis of new theory can come from several sources: personal experiences, experiences of others, and existing theory. The "trick" in using existing theory as a source for new theory "is to line up what one takes as theoretically possible or probable with what one is finding in the field" (Glaser & Strauss, 1967, p. 253). Theory, according to Strauss (1987, p. 6), emerges through an "intimate relationship with data, with researchers fully aware of themselves as instruments for developing grounded theory."

In summary, a research study can test, refine, or build theory. A theory is a shorthand account of how some aspect of our world works. If the account is a good one, it will be internally consistent, easy to understand, and applicable to similar situations. The more situations a theory can explain, predict, or control, the more powerful it is (Kerlinger, 1986). Further, even if one is not testing or building theory, one's theoretical framework, the "lenses" through which one sees the world and thus shapes the problem to be investigated, will most likely draw from a knowledge base containing, at the very least, theoretical formulations and models. It is to this knowledge base and its accompanying theories that one returns, showing how the findings of a study contribute to the knowledge base.

REFERENCES

Ary, D., Jacobs, L. C., & Ragavich, A. (1985). *Introduction to research in education* (3rd ed.). New York: Holt, Rinehart & Winston.

Boshier, R. (1992). Popular discourse concerning AIDS: Its implications for adult education. *Adult Education Quarterly, 42*, 125–135.

Dewey, J. (1933). *How we think.* Boston: D. C. Heath.

Glaser, B. C., & Strauss, A. (1967). *The discovery of grounded theory.* Chicago: Aldine.

Guba, E. G. (1978). *Toward a methodology of naturalistic inquiry in educational evaluation.* CSE Monograph Series in Evaluation, No. 8. Los Angeles: University of California.

Kerlinger, F. N. (1986). *Foundations of behavioral research* (3rd ed.). New York: Holt, Rinehart & Winston.

Merriam, S. B. (Ed.). (1993). *An update on adult learning theory.* New Directions for Adult and Continuing Education, No. 57 (Spring). San Francisco: Jossey-Bass.

Rowden, R. (1993, April). The role of human resource development in successful, small to mid-sized manufacturing businesses: A comparative case study. *Proceedings of Quest for Quality National Research Conference on Human Resource Development* (pp. 159–165). College Station, TX: Department of Educational Human Resource Development, Texas A & M University.

Scanlan, C. S., & Darkenwald, G. G. (1984). Identifying deterrents to participation in continuing education. *Adult Education Quarterly. 34,* 155–166.

Schultz, J. G. (1988). Developing theoretical models/conceptual frameworks in vocational education research. *Journal of Vocational Education Research. 13*(3), 29–43.

Selltiz, C. E., Jahoda, M. E., Deutsch, M. E., & Cook, S. W. (1959). *Research methods in social relations.* New York: Holt, Rinehart & Winston.

Selltiz, C., Wrightsman, L. S., & Cook, S. W. (1976). *Research methods in social relations.* New York: Holt, Rinehart & Winston.

Stein, P. (1991). How judges become expert about contemporary issues (Doctoral dissertation, University of Georgia, 1990). *Dissertation Abstracts International, 51,* 1087A.

Strauss, A. L. (1987). *Qualitative analysis for social scientists*. Cambridge: Cambridge University Press.

Tisdell, E. J. (1993). Interlocking systems of power, privilege, and oppression in adult higher education classes. *Adult Education Quarterly, 43*, 203–226.

CHAPTER 3

REVIEWING THE LITERATURE

An important step in the research process is to review the thinking and research relevant to the topic at hand. Only by becoming thoroughly familiar with prior research and theory can you hope to contribute something that others will build upon, thereby extending a discipline's knowledge base. A review of the literature thus safeguards against undertaking a study that may have already been done, that may not be feasible to conduct, or that may be trivial or insignificant when set against the research needs in a particular field.

Essentially, a literature review integrates and synthesizes what has been thought and researched in the area of interest. A review of the literature may be "freestanding"; this type of review presents the state of the art with regard to a particular interest or concern and is not a part of a research study. Such self-contained reviews offer readers a general overview of the problem area and, perhaps, suggestions for future research investigations. Most literature reviews, however, are part of a study. The task of locating, reading, synthesizing, and writing a review of the literature provides the researcher with a foundation from which to explore further.

In social science research, the literature review serves a variety of functions that precede the collecting and analyzing of data. These functions are discussed in detail in the next section. Certain types of research such as historical research, policy studies, literary analyses, and philosophical inquiries use "literature" or documents as the source of data. Nevertheless, these approaches still review what others have written about the topic and how others have interpreted the documents or literature to be used in the study at hand.

FUNCTIONS OF A LITERATURE REVIEW

The purpose of a literature review is to summarize and integrate previous work and to offer suggestions for future inquiries. Freestanding reviews often present interesting insights about a problem area and almost always provide a starting point for researchers who must acquaint themselves with work that was done prior to the setting up of their own study. A freestanding review will rarely focus upon the questions relevant to a particular study, however, and, for this reason, researchers must pull together their own. The following are functions of a literature review conducted prior to a research study:

1. To provide a foundation for building knowledge. No research problem in the social sciences exists alone as an area of human endeavor. There is *always* some related literature, and it is this literature that is reviewed to form the "pedigree" of the problem. In order to add to knowledge in a field, you must have a thorough understanding of the major theoretical points of view and the major research investigations relevant to the topic. A literature review should reveal what has been done or what is being done in a particular problem area. In a sense, the literature review sets the stage on which the study will be presented.

2. To show how a study advances, refines, or revises what is already known. All investigators are concerned that someone, somewhere, might have done or might be doing the very study being proposed. A thorough literature review should alleviate this concern. The review should state, rather precisely, just how the study being proposed deviates from previously conducted studies. A literature review is also necessary when a researcher intends to replicate an earlier study. In this case the review highlights the theoretical or methodological strengths and deficiencies present in earlier, significant studies and in so doing, supports the need for replication.

3. To help conceptualize the study. Knowing what hypotheses have been generated or tested previously, how terms have been defined, and what assumptions and limitations have been dealt with by other investigators can facilitate the task involved in the proposed study. Previous work can, in fact, be cited in a supportive manner as you establish the rationale for limiting a study in a certain way, for defining terms, for developing hypotheses to guide the study, and so on.

4. To provide clues to methodology and instrumentation. Knowing what approaches have been used before, and with what success, can save an investigator from wasting effort and expense. Depending upon the nature of a particular problem, an experimental design, for example, may or may not be ethically or logistically feasible, and even if it is feasible, using this de-

sign may not lead to answering the questions of interest. Similarly, a review of the literature may uncover survey instruments, tests, and other measures that have already been validated and thus save the researcher the trouble of designing a valid and reliable instrument.

5. To offer a collective point of reference for interpreting the researcher's own findings. Prior to collecting data, the literature review is used to show how the proposed study intends to extend, revise, or refine knowledge in an area. After the data have been collected and analyzed, previous work can become a point of reference for discussing the significance that the study has to the field. One's findings can then be assessed against the previous state of knowledge to see whether the intention has been realized. By making such a comparison, the researcher gives other investigators and consumers of the research a sense of what contribution the present study has made to advancing the knowledge base of the discipline.

A literature review, then, functions as a means of conceptualizing, justifying, implementing, and interpreting a research investigation. Without it you court the possibility of duplicating earlier work or investigating an insignificant problem. Without a literature review it is also impossible to ascertain the significance of the proposed study for contributing to the knowledge base of a field.

THE SEARCH PROCESS

The search for related literature is characterized, to a large extent, by how precisely a problem is formulated. If the investigator has a particular study in mind, the search is narrower in scope. The purposes of the search in this case are (1) to make certain no one else has done the same study and (2) to use previous writing in support of the need for the present study. The danger in being too focused is, of course, that the study may have been done previously, or that it may be an insignificant issue, or that the investigator may not be able to find literature on the particular topic. On the other hand, having only a vague sense of a problem area may result in a search so broad as to be unmanageable. The ideal topic lies somewhere in between—the literature both confirms that a previous study is not being duplicated (unless by intent), and also serves as a guide to actually formulating the study. Nearly all previous studies or literature reviews have suggestions for further research. Recurrent suggestions would indicate a significant research need in the field. How you delineate a manageable research topic has been discussed in a previous chapter. However, assuming that you have developed a reasonable topic, you are now ready to do a literature review.

FINDING THE LITERATURE

For most topics there are two kinds of literature: the theoretical or conceptual writing in the area and data-based research studies. The theoretical literature consists of writings that reflect an author's experiences or opinions. Research studies are based on the collection and analysis of data gathered from sources such as people, institutions, and documents that are extraneous to the author. The amount of each type of literature on any particular topic varies. At different points in a search, both types are helpful and important to the reviewer.

The place to begin your search is the library reference room. Here there are a multitude of resources that you can consult in identifying both the theoretical and data-based literature on your topic. Two of the most complete and helpful guides to publications in education are reference books by Berry (1990) and Buttlar (1989). Berry's book, *A Bibliographic Guide to Educational Research,* is an annotated bibliography of sources "useful or essential for research in the field of education" (p. 1). The sources are organized into chapters on books, periodicals, research studies (including ERIC documents, theses and dissertations), government publications, special types of materials (e.g., print and nonprint instructional materials, tests and measurements), other types of reference materials (e.g. yearbooks, handbooks), and the research paper (books on methodology and style guides). Buttlar's *Education: A Guide to Reference and Information Sources* (1989) is organized differently, but covers many of the same sources. She has chapters on general references in education and social science (e.g., bibliographies, indexes, dictionaries, online databases), and then breaks out resources by topic, including educational foundations, curriculum and instruction, educational administration, and evaluation.

How you begin your search will depend on how much you already know about the topic. If you are interested in a topic, but not very familiar with either the conceptual/theoretical literature or research studies, you will want to begin with an overview of the topic. If you are already knowledgeable in the area, or as you become more familiar with a topic, you can consult more specific resources such as indexes or abstracts of recent publications. There are numerous resources available to you for each stage of the search.

For an Overview of the Topic

An overview of the problem area can be gotten from a general text on the topic, from subject encyclopedias, dictionaries, or handbooks. Subject encyclopedias identify major trends and thinking in an area and contain bibliographies for further reading.

The *Encyclopedia of Education* contains short articles in various areas of education. It is becoming dated (1971), but so far has not been replaced by other sources. More recent encyclopedias are the *American Educator's Encyclopedia* (1991) and the *Encyclopedia of Higher Education* (1992).

There are also a number of international encyclopedias that provide overviews of various aspects of education from a global perspective. Some of these are multivolume, such as the 10-volume *International Encyclopedia of Higher Education* (1977). Other sources are the *Encyclopedia of Comparative Education and National Systems of Education* (1988), *World Education Encyclopedia* (1988), *International Higher Education* (1991), and the *International Handbook of Education Systems* (1983).

Dictionaries can be helpful for coming up with not only definitions of some aspect of your topic, but for finding related terms with which to conduct more focused searches in various data bases (see the section on computer searching). For approximately 3,700 terms in adult education, see Jarvis's *An International Dictionary of Adult and Continuing Education* (1990). The *International Dictionary of Education* (1977) includes definitions of more than 10,000 terms used in all levels of education. The *Dictionary of Education* (1959) is a standard work with definitions of approximately 40,000 professional terms and concepts.

Handbooks and yearbooks typically contain chapters on various aspects of a particular area of education. The *Handbook of Adult and Continuing Education* (1989), for example, has sections on foundations of the field, adult learners and the educational process, major providers of education for adults, program areas, and clienteles. A handbook in adult education has been published approximately every 10 years since the 1930s. The field of human resource development has several resources of this nature also. For an overview of training-related topics, you might want to consult *Training and Development Handbook: A Guide to Human Resource Development* (1987),

Human Resources Yearbook (1989), *The Human Resource Management Yearbook* (1993), and *The Resources Yearbook* (1989).

Reviews of Research

The above sources are helpful for gaining a general overview and understanding of a topic, including major issues, trends, points of view, people, and landmark studies. Once you feel comfortable with a topic, the next step involves moving on to reviews of research. Such reviews are narrower in scope than articles or chapters in encyclopedias and handbooks. They usually provide an extensive list of studies and articles for further reading.

The *Encyclopedia of Educational Research* is the standard reference source in educational research featuring critical syntheses and interpretations of all subject areas in education. The latest edition is the sixth, published in 1992. Areas covered that might be of interest to adult educators and trainers include development, distance education, older students, computer and vocational education, and human resources organization. The *Review of Educational Research* is published quarterly by the American Education Research Association (AERA), with each issue covering different topics. The *Review of Research in Education* is an annual volume published by AERA, summarizing research on specific topics. Finally, the *Handbook of Research on Teaching* (1986) includes topics such as research on teaching in higher education, research on professional education, moral and values education, media in teaching, cultures of teaching, and philosophy and teaching. The volume also has eight chapters on theories and methods of research. All of these publications have periodically reviewed research on topics that might be of interest to educators and trainers of adults. For example, the Spring 1991, issue of *Review of Educational Research* contains a review of research on adult undergraduates in higher education (Kasworm, 1990). In another issue, research on the topic of mentoring is reviewed (Jacobi, 1991).

Another research-specific publication is the *Bibliographic Guide to Educational Research* (1990) which includes descriptive annotations of more than 700 books, periodicals, collections of research studies, government publications, and reference works in education.

Bibliographies, Indexes, Abstracts

Up to this point the literature search will have given the reviewer a "feel" for the topic, some familiarity with basic theories, key sources, and a sense of the research base. This general reading should also have contributed to a better conceptualization of the problem, perhaps even a specific research focus. At this stage, bibliographies, indexes, and abstracts will be most helpful.

Bibliographies are published on nearly every topic. Finding a bibliography can be done by consulting the card catalogue or through the *Bibliographic Index*, an annual volume listing bibliographies by subject area in approximately 2,600 periodicals. Another source is *Bibliographic Guide to Education* (1992). In adult education, bibliographies exist on adult basic education, teaching methods, media and adult learning, staff development, and dissertations in adult education and training. From bibliographies you can develop a list of references that are particularly relevant to the research topic.

This pool of references expands through using indexes and abstracts. For every discipline, there are indexes that list by topic (and in some cases by author) pertinent articles to be found in various journals. *Education Index*, for example, lists articles by topic from over 200 education journals. In addition, *Master's Theses in Education, Social Science Index, Social Science Citation Index*, and ERIC's *Current Index to Journals in Education* (CIJE) and *Resources in Education* (RIE) (documents other than journal articles) are essential tools in locating sources. ERIC is an acronym for Education Resources Information Center. Funded by the National Institute of Education, ERIC is a national information network that collects, organizes, and disseminates educational research information and material. The ERIC system indexes and abstracts research projects, theses, conference proceedings, project reports, speeches, bibliographies, curriculum-related materials, books, and more than 750 educational journals.

A data base similar to ERIC, but for those in human resource development, is the Human Resource Information Network (HRIN). HRIN has more than 100 data bases divided into eight networks such as affirmative action, employment and recruiting, labor/legal, and safety/health. Of most interest to those in training would be the training and development network which provides research and information abstracts about training and development.

Once you have generated a list of sources, you can save many hours in the literature search by going to abstracts *before* locating the entire article or document. Abstracts can also be used for developing a bibliographic pool. Abstract resources present a full citation of the source, as well as a paragraph summary of the study or document. One of the most useful sources for abstracts that deal with education is *Dissertation Abstracts International* which lists most doctoral dissertations written at American universities and some foreign universities. Abstracts summarize objectives, procedures, and conclusions of each study. *Psychological Abstracts* has summaries and abstracts of American and foreign books and periodicals in psychology and related disciplines. *Sociological Abstracts* covers American and foreign periodicals in sociology and political science. *Higher Education Abstracts* and *Sociology of Education Abstracts* are two other education-specific sources. A search in ERIC or HRIN will also produce abstracts.

Computer Searching

There are three ways to search for pertinent references in the above sources—manual, online, and CD-ROM. Manual searching means handling the actual volumes in which the information is printed. While this approach is more time-consuming than using the computer, it may be preferable if cost is a consideration in the computer search, or if one's research question is not well defined; manually browsing through abstracts may result in identifying terms, issues, authors, and so on relevant to the topic.

Online computer searching involves accessing information stored in a mainframe computer. A phone line, modem, microcomputer, monitor, and printer are needed for this type of search. "The process explains the term *online*, which means that the librarian is, via the online wires, directly in communication with the computer's database which can be as little as a few miles or as far as a continent away" (Katz, 1992, p. 39). Bibliographic Retrieval Services (BRS) and Dialog are two common search services, each containing numerous data bases such as Dissertation Abstracts International, ERIC, Psychological and Sociological Abstracts. Both BRS and Dialog have lower evening and weekend rates for access through one's personal microcomputer. Online searching has several advantages over manual and CD-ROM. First, storage capacity for information is virtually unlimited, it is extremely fast, and data bases are updated at least on a weekly basis. The major disadvantage is that there is a charge for time spent online.

The most recent development in computer searching is the use of CD-ROM (Compact Disc-Read Only Memory). Entire data bases such as ERIC or Dissertation Abstracts International are placed on a compact disc. Users can search through data bases at leisure without incurring online costs. While initial and ongoing costs for this system are prohibitive to individuals, more and more libraries and media centers are investing in CD-ROM. Another disadvantage is that CD-ROMs are typically not as up-to-date as data bases available in online searching. On the other hand, CD-ROM searching allows for the leisurely browsing of a manual search.

As a side note, readers might be interested to know that depending on the type of search conducted, the same data base may have a different name. For example, one would look in Psychological Abstracts when doing a manual search. In an online search Psychological Abstracts exists as PsycINFO; the CD-ROM product name is PsycLIT. Likewise, the CD-ROM product name for Sociological Abstracts is Sociofile.

SELECTING THE SOURCES FOR REVIEW

The thoroughness of a literature search, whether done manually or by computer, depends upon several factors: the specificity of the topic, the resources of the library where the search is being conducted, the researcher's mastery of library techniques, the time available for the search, and the ingenuity or creativeness of the researcher in uncovering relevant sources. At the end of the first stage of finding the sources, you should have accumulated a reasonable list of references that appear to be directly relevant to the problem area. Now you halt the search and begin reading some of these articles or research studies. The bibliographies at the end of an article should be checked against your own list. Seemingly pertinent references should be located and read, and the bibliography should be checked again. The process at this stage involves shifting between indexes, abstracts, actual articles and their bibliographies, and your own list of sources. You will soon notice recurrent references and major articles of either a conceptual or data-based nature. At this point you are a detective, following the trail of a research problem. During the process of moving between references and original sources, decisions must be continually made with regard to the relevance of the material and whether or not certain pieces will be included in the final literature review. A reviewer can ask the following questions to assist in making decisions for relevance:

1. Is the author of the source an authority on the topic, one who has done much of the empirical work in the area, or one who has offered seminal theory upon which subsequent research and writing has been based? If so, that author's work will be quoted by others and listed in bibliographies on the topic.
2. When was the article or book or report written? As a rule, the more recent work in an area should be included in a review.

3. What exactly was written about or tested? If a particular resource or research study is highly relevant to your present research interest, it should be included even if the "who" and "when" criteria are not met.
4. What is the quality of the source? A thoughtful analysis, a well-designed study, or an original way of viewing the topic is probably a more significant piece of literature. In historical or documentary analysis, the quality of primary and secondary sources is a major criterion for inclusion into the data base.

As you decide which particular sources are important for inclusion in the review, how the material should be handled becomes an important consideration. If possible, a copy of the complete article, or the pertinent sections of it, should be made for reference when writing the review. If it is not possible or feasible to copy the article, notes should be taken in some systematic way. Direct quotations that state main ideas and supporting points should be extracted from conceptual/theoretical articles. At this point you cannot be certain whether the final review will include a summary of an idea or direct quotation. You can always summarize from a direct quotation, but it is impossible to resurrect a direct quotation from general notes. For data-based research articles, the abstract (if there is one) can be copied and/or notes taken on sample, methodology, and findings. Taking care in obtaining all pertinent information from a source cannot be overemphasized. Getting what seems to be too much information will save many hours searching back through the sources for a certain perfect quotation, the number in the sample, and so on.

Occasionally, there is a paucity of literature on a particular topic. This is a sign that the researcher is embarking onto a new area and that the study will form some contribution to the literature. On the other hand, the researcher cannot profit from previous work and may encounter insurmountable methodological problems or may be investigating an area of little interest to others. As stated earlier, however, there will always be some related literature. From what literature is available, it will be important to extract statements regarding the need for research or theory building in the area, the gaps or problems in what has been done, the reasons that the area has been neglected, and so on. Such statements, especially if made by authorities in related areas, can be effectively used to build support for the present research study.

The time, the energy, the resourcefulness of the researcher, and the resources of the library where the search is being conducted are among the factors that may artificially limit the search for, and the gathering of, sources. An authentic end to a literature search is one in which the investigator is satisfied that all relevant material has been uncovered and dealt with. There are two guidelines that can be used to determine when to end a search: (1) encountering lists of material already covered, and (2) a feeling of expertise in the subject area:

1. In the process of moving back and forth between indexes or abstracts and actual articles or books, the researcher becomes quite familiar with certain studies, certain names, certain publications. At some point in the process, the researcher turns to a reference list at the end of an article and discovers that *all* the listings are familiar and may, in fact, have been read. When this occurs two or three times, the reviewer can be reasonably certain that the relevant literature in an area has been uncovered. The search has, in a sense, become saturated, and no new material is likely to be found. How long it will take to reach this point and how many sources one will have to go through will depend upon prior familiarity with the topic, the amount of literature available, and the nature of the research problem or topic.

2. The second guideline is less objective. At some point in the search, a sense of expertise about the subject is acquired. This is reflected in the ability to recall and discuss major ideas, historical developments, important research topics, authors, and so on, that are relevant to the topic.

WRITING THE LITERATURE REVIEW

The process of doing a literature review is not unlike the process of doing research. In both cases, collecting the material or data constitutes half the task; writing the review or report requires an equal amount of effort. A literature review is a narrative essay that integrates, synthesizes, and critiques the important thinking and research on a particular topic. Whether freestanding or part of a study, the review should present a systematic overview of the topic.

Several strategies can be used to transform a stack of sources on a topic into a well-written analytical essay. Two that have worked especially well for the authors can be loosely labeled the "chart" method and the "conversation" approach. In the chart method, one lists down the left side of a large sheet of paper the authors and/or titles of each source to be reviewed. This listing might be done alphabetically, chronologically, or by type of literature (e.g., conceptual versus data-based). Categories appropriate to the literature, such as the major theme of the article, date of the study, sample, intervention or treatment, findings, or needed research, are then listed across the top of the chart.

After each source has been entered on the chart, the reviewer stands back and asks what generalizations can be made about all of the sources. These generalizations should be written down, for it is likely that these points will form the skeletal structure of the literature.

It is not uncommon for the "chart" method to result in the inclusion of the chart in the actual literature review. This visual display of the sources used and pertinent information about them enables readers to get a sense of the data base from which the review has been written. Table 3.1 presents a portion of one of the charts found in a recent review of the literature on the psychosocial development of women (Caffarella & Olson, 1993, pp. 130–131). This chart presents data-based studies of women's development that test women's development against traditional theories or models derived primarily from studies of men. Note the categories they have selected to organize information from each of the studies: author(s), cross validation of (name of theory), subjects, data collection techniques, and selected salient results.

Caffarella and Olson (1993) make several points in their discussion of these studies—points that can be derived from a careful examination of the information in the table. They point out, for example, that the majority of studies use Levinson's theory as the conceptual framework, that certain aspects of his theory were confirmed by some studies while others were not, and so on. Finally, from an assessment of these studies as well as studies based on alternative models of female development (for which they present a comparable chart), they are able to draw several conclusions overall regarding women's development.

While the chart in Table 3.1 is limited to data-based research studies, the same approach can be used for a literature review consisting of all conceptual/theoretical material, or one that has a mixture of opinion and data-based articles. In a review of the literature on mentoring conducted by one of the authors (Merriam, 1983), for example, a chart of all the sources revealed the following: there is no single, accepted definition of the phenomenon; there are a few studies from adult psychology, but most of the empirical studies are from business settings and relate to career advancement; the majority of literature is in the popular "how-to" vein and is almost always from the perspective of benefits to the protégé; there is a subgroup of literature consisting of both conceptual and data-based articles dealing exclusively with women. These generalizations formed the major points of organization for the literature review.

A second strategy for transforming sources into a narrative essay is the conversation approach. Imagine that someone who has no knowledge about a topic is having a conversation with the reviewer who is becoming an expert in this subject area. The novice would obviously have to ask many questions before there would be an understanding at all. The reviewer might be asked the following:

1. Who are the major authorities on the topic, and why are they considered experts?
2. What are the major theories or points of view about the topic?
3. What is the single most important source of information on the topic?
4. When was most of the work done?
5. What were the major breakthroughs?
6. What research is currently being conducted in this subject area?
7. What research still needs to be done?
8. What is unique and worthy of note from this literature?

Written answers to these questions should provide an overview and synthesis of the material.

Both methods also help the reviewer adopt a critical stance toward the literature. Being critical does not mean being negative, but rather being able to assess the strengths and weaknesses of a body of material. In a critical approach one praises *and* finds fault. Readers of a review should gain some sense of the relative importance of particular sources as well as an overall sense of the state of the art. Brief, evaluative, critical assessments of the individual sources in the literature review are both appropriate and expected. More lengthy assessments might also be woven into summary and conclusion sections. In any case, a literature review demands more than merely presenting the content of numerous sources.

There are probably as many systems for organizing material as there are reviewers. Whatever the structure, the reviewer must make an effort to stand apart from the individual sources in order to extract generalities, major themes, and salient issues from across the entire body of literature. It is only through withdrawing from the specifics that a researcher can create an overview that integrates, synthesizes and critiques.

Table 3.1 Sample of Chart Method (Caffarella & Olson, 1993): Empirical Studies: Testing of Traditional Models. *Used with permission.*

Author(s)	Cross-Validation of	Subjects	Data Collection Techniques	Selected Salient Results
Jeffries, D. L. (1985)	Levinson	N = 40; Age 20–40 SES = Appears middle and lower class; EI =Black	Biographical Interviewing using author designed structured inter-view (Jeffries-Winbush Black Lifespan Assess-ment Question-naire)	No correlation was found between age and the prescribed developmental tasks. Unique stages and characteristics exist that are culture-specific in nature and typically relate to Black female development
Josselson, R. (1987)	Erikson	Sample I N = 48; Age not given SES = All social strata represented EI = not specified College seniors Sample II N = 12; Same descrip-tion as above	First Data Collec-tion (Samples I & II) Marcia's identity— Status Interview Open-ended semi-structured interview protocol Follow-up Study Written question-naires with choice for individuals to tape record their responses	Confirmed the impor-tance of the structural component of identity development. Developmental issue of separation/ individualism is different in women and men. Separation involves becom-ing different and yet maintaining connections/rela-tionships at the same time.
		Sample III N = 34 (of the original 60 Subjects) Age not specified SES = not specified, implied across all strata EI = not specified	Telephone inter-views where necessary	The web of rela-tionships is crucial to women, both within family and friendship networks as well as work related endeavors Career does not provide a primary sense of identity for most women. Iden-tity construction comes primarily through connec-tions, relational embeddedness, spirituality, and affiliation.

Table 3.1 (continued)

Kahnweiler, J. (1980)	Levinson	N = 40; Age 30–50 SES = middle class EI = Caucasian Enrolled in college	Author-designed questionnaire	Respondents were focused on their own personal goals for the future. They felt a real time limitation as they were just getting to the point of forming a "dream" for their lives
Murrell, H. & Donahue, W. (1982)	Levinson	N = 44; Age 34–65 SES = upper middle class EI = not specified Senior level college administrators	Modification of Levinson (1977) interview guide	These women reported age-related transitional periods in their lives (e.g., in the 30's, if career oriented shift to family orientation and vice versa; in 40's an identity crisis.)
Roberts, P. & Newton, P.M.	Levinson	*N=39; Age 28-53 SES= Unknown EI=Predominantly Caucasian, with 8 Black subjects	Biographical interview based on modifications of the Levinson instrument	Suggest underlying pattern of women's development with age linked stable and transitional periods.
				The age 30 transition was especially consistent for these respondents.
				As women's dreams of their adult life were more complex than most men's (involving marriage, motherhood and career), their life structures seem less stable and more conflicted.
				The relational aspect was seen as key in shaping the lives of these women.

*Combination of 4 earlier studies.

Note: SES=Socio-Economic Status   EI=Ethnic Identity

PARTS OF THE LITERATURE REVIEW

There is no single formula for structuring a literature review. How a review takes shape depends in part upon whether the reviewer intends to make it a state-of-the art, freestanding review, or one that leads to a study with a particular focus. In most cases, the structure emerges from the literature being evaluated; this will be explained more fully in a discussion of the body of a literature review. However, there are usually several other parts of the review that precede and follow the body.

Like every other narrative essay, a literature review begins with an *introduction*. Here the reviewer lays out for the reader the topic to be reviewed, the nature of this topic, its scope, and its significance. The writer should assume that the reader knows nothing about the topic: therefore, the writer must be careful to introduce the subject in as clear and simple a manner as possible. Special terminology should be explained or defined. In most cases the introduction will begin very generally, explaining the nature of the subject and then gradually narrowing the focus to the specific topic to be reviewed. A review of the literature on women's reentry programs, for example, might begin with several paragraphs about the phenomenon of women returning to school. A review of the research on the dropout problem in Adult Basic Education programs should first introduce the reader to ABE in general and to the existing programs for adults who need assistance in mastering basic skills.

Once the specific topic has been identified, the author may want to discuss the *criteria* used in selecting the literature for review. Why were certain sources included and others ignored? Perhaps only literature within the last 10 years was selected, or perhaps only major writers were chosen, or perhaps only certain dimensions of the topic were considered important for review. The limits of the review are set in this section. That is, the reviewer can discuss what is not to be reviewed as well as what is included. The limits depend upon how much literature is available. To review all the research studies on Piaget's theories, for example, would be unmanageable, but it would be reasonable to limit such a review to studies that applied Piaget's theories to adults. A review might also be limited to a specific type of literature such as journal articles. Stating selection criteria and reviewing limits early in the essay prevents readers from questioning why particular sources were or were not included. Where there is a dearth of relevant literature, this section of the review may include a recounting of the efforts made to find sources, the results of such efforts, and perhaps the rationale for turning to certain tangential literature.

Following the introduction and criteria for selection is the *body* of the review. This is the heart of the essay, the critical synthesis of material reviewed. The organization of this section flows logically from the nature of the literature on a particular topic. As stated earlier, developing the body of the review involves much more than merely annotating or summarizing sources. If either the chart method or the conversation approach is used, the body of the review will emerge from the generalizations extracted across all the sources. In most literature reviews, the body is organized thematically. Certain recurring themes or subtropics emerge from the literature, and these themes form the major subheadings. In the following three examples, each literature review topic is subdivided into several themes that were generated from the material itself:

Topic A.   Locus of Control: Studies with Adults
            1. Adults in higher education
Thematic   2. Disadvantaged adults
Subtopics   3. Older adults
            4. Changing the locus of control with adults

Topic B.   Middle Age
            1. When does middle age occur?
            2. What are the physical characteristics of middle
               age?
Thematic   3. What are the psychosocial characteristics
Subtopics   of middle age?
            4. What are the developmental tasks of middle age?
            5. Is there a midlife crisis?

Topic C.   Competency-Based Education (CBE)
            1. What does competency-based mean?
            2. How is CBE related to performance?
Thematic   3. What are the objectives of CBE?
Subtopics   4. In what settings is CBE most likely to be found?
            5. What are the political overtures of this emphasis?
            6. Does the Adult Performance Level test measure
               competence?

Under each thematic subtopic the reviewer discusses research studies or other writings appropriate to the theme. Depending upon the nature and importance of a source, some discussions may be quite detailed while other sources may be only alluded to. A particular source may contain material appropriate to several subtopics, in which case the reviewer must choose where to discuss it (perhaps several places) and how thoroughly. Within each subtopic critical comments are appropriate. For example, a review might point out the methodological weakness of a particular study, might comment on several pieces as a whole, or might enumerate reasons why a particular work is an important contribution.

The most logical organization may be chronological, particularly when reviewing historical works or public documents that are records of a particular event. As with a thematic organization, the decision to use a chronological organization should be dictated by the literature itself. Some reviews may evolve into a combined thematic and chronological organization. You might handle the early, though important, literature on the topic under a chronological heading (pre-1970, post-World War II, for example) and then move on to relevant themes characteristic of the most recent work. Conversely, the bulk of the literature might be organized thematically with the most recent work under a heading such as "recent developments."

The body of the literature review should be followed by a *concluding section*. There the writer can summarize the review, discuss overall weaknesses and strengths in the literature, point out gaps that exist in the topic's conceptual development or research efforts, or note aspects that have been well covered, even saturated.

An essential part of this concluding section is the identification of potentially fruitful avenues for future inquiry. The reviewer who has been immersed in the literature in a certain area has become an expert on that topic. It is entirely appropriate, then, to offer guidance for the future development of this body of knowledge. The concluding section is also an appropriate place to move into a discussion of the reviewer's particular research study, how it addresses the gaps or weaknesses in the field, and how it should prove to be a manageable and rewarding line of inquiry.

The parts of a review, then, include: (1) introductory material, in which the nature of the topic, the scope of the study, and the criteria or process of selecting materials for review are discussed; (2) the body of the review, which provides the critical synthesis and integration of all the important literature and is arranged by the themes that evolve naturally from the material itself; and (3) the concluding section, which summarizes, evaluates, and offers suggestions for future study.

We suggest that readers consult several published reviews to see how different authors structure the review overall, as well as how the *body* of the review is subdivided into themes or subtopics. Two examples can be found in the Summer 1987 issue of *Adult Education Quarterly*. Merriam (1987) reviewed theory building efforts in adult learning. Following a discussion of the need for theory, she organized adult learning theories into three categories: theories based on adult learner characteristics; theories based on adult's life situation; and theories based on changes in consciousness. The article closes with a summary evaluation of theory-building efforts in adult learning.

In the same issue, Caffarella and O'Donnell (1987) reviewed the research and writing on self-directed learning. This large and growing body of literature was organized into the following framework: verifications studies (in the Tough tradition); nature of the method of self-directed learning (how questions); nature of the individual learner (who and what questions); and policy questions (roles of educators, institutions, and society). They conclude their review with six suggestions for future research.

A third example can be found in an essay review of major, recent publications in human resource development (HRD) (Watkins, 1991). This review was limited to recent books or monographs in HRD. Watkins structured the review according to six different philosophical stances found in HRD in which the human resource developer is characterized as competent performer, developer of human capital, toolmaker, adult educator, researcher/evaluator, and leader/change agent.

GUIDELINES FOR DOING A LITERATURE REVIEW

The process of doing a literature review can be roughly divided into two parts: (1) the search process and (2) the writing of the review. The following suggestions will make both parts of the process easier:

1. Read generally for an overview of the problem area before defining the topic precisely.
2. Define the limits of the review. Too broad a search will overwhelm you with material; too narrow a topic might make you overlook related work or not find enough material.
3. Through indexes and abstracts, locate a reasonable number of sources and begin reading those sources. Then move back to bibliographies and abstracts. This will allow you to develop a pool of relevant sources.

4. Establish criteria for selecting materials that will be included in the review.
5. Continue the search until the sources are saturated and you feel you are in command of the topic.
6. Copy the material to be reviewed, being especially careful to cite full bibliographic data.
7. Arrange the material reviewed into categories that are suggested by the material itself.
8. Structure the review into three parts: introductory material, the body of the review, and a concluding section.

REFERENCES

Berry, D. M. (1990). *A bibliographic guide to educational research* (3rd ed.). Metuchen, NJ: The Scarecrow Press.

Buttlar, L. J. (1989). *Education: A guide to reference and information sources.* Englewood, CO: Libraries Unlimited.

Caffarella, R. S., & O'Donnell, J. (1987). Self-directed adult learning: A critical paradigm revisited. *Adult Education Quarterly, 37,* 199–211.

Caffarella, R. S., & Olson, S. K. (1993). Psychosocial development of women: A critical review of the literature. *Adult Education Quarterly, 43,* 125–151.

Jacobi, M. (1991). Mentoring and undergraduates' academic success: A literature review. *Review of Educational Research, 61*(4), 505–532.

Kasworm, C. E. (1990). Adult undergraduates in higher education: A review of past research perspectives. *Review of Educational Research, 60*(3), 345–372.

Katz, W. A. (1992). *Introduction to reference work* (Vol. 1). Basic Information Sources (6th ed.). New York: McGraw-Hill.

Merriam, S. (1983). Mentors and proteges: A critical review of the literature. *Adult Education Quarterly, 33,* 161–173.

Merriam, S. (1987). Adult learning and theory building: A review. *Adult Education Quarterly, 37,* 187–198.

Watkins, K. E. (1991). Many voices: Defining human resource development from different disciplines. *Adult Education Quarterly, 41,* 241–255.

CHAPTER 4

EXPERIMENTAL AND DESCRIPTIVE DESIGNS

Various definitions exist to describe research designs, methods, approaches, or strategies. Some texts differentiate three major research categories—descriptive, historical, and experimental. Others label the categories by technique, such as "survey" research; still others make finer distinctions such as "experimental" versus "ex post facto" or "quasi-experimental" designs. We have organized various research designs into four chapters in which we examine differences in methodological purpose and procedure. This chapter focuses on experimental and descriptive designs. The next chapter examines historical and philosophical forms of inquiry. Chapter 6 reviews case study, grounded theory, and ethnographic approaches. Finally, Chapter 7 presents action, participatory, critical, and feminist research.

EXPERIMENTAL AND QUASI-EXPERIMENTAL DESIGNS

Experimental and quasi-experimental research designs are based on the positivist paradigm, first introduced by the French philosopher Comte, who used *positivism* to describe a particular view of knowledge in the natural sciences (Bredo & Feinberg, 1982). Following Comte's theory, scientific knowledge is made up of facts that may be organized under general laws. Through our senses and observation, combined with logic, we gain scientific knowledge. This approach to seeking knowledge results in logical postivism becoming "the paradigm for true knowledge of the world" (p. 14). Merriam (1991) explains that the primary assumption supporting logical positivism is the "single-world" concept; one world reality that can be seen, understood, and reduced to measurable laws. The logical postivist worldview has dominated educational and training research design

51

during much of the 19th and 20th centuries. Perhaps the research method most directly representative of positivist thought in the 20th century is the experimental design. Its purpose is to determine the cause of events and to be able to predict similar events in the future. Because of their purpose and basic science origins, some experimental methods are detailed and technical. However, rather than focusing on the complex nature of various experimental designs, the emphasis here will be upon providing an overview of the purposes and procedures of experimental inquiry.

Experimental research originally was based upon a set of laws introduced by John Stuart Mill in a work titled "A System of Logic," first published in 1873 (1990). In his treatise Mill proposed a number of principles in the form of canons or rules that he contended were requirements to establishing order among controlled events. One of those laws, the method of difference, stated,

> If an instance in which the phenomenon under investigation occurs, and an instance in which it does not occur have every circumstance in common save one, that one occurring only in the former, the circumstance in which alone the two instances differ is the effect, or the cause, or an indispensable part of the cause of the phenomenon. (p. 222)

Mill is saying that if two sets of events are alike and something is either added to or taken from one event, causing a difference between those two events, the difference is attributed to what was added or withdrawn. The law of the single variable was useful in designing research for the disciplines of basic science. However, when applied to the emerging behavioral sciences, it proved less than adequate because the multivariant nature of human events made application of the law difficult. Seldom could differences in complex human events be traced to a single cause. Also, interaction of variables made isolation and observation of single variables impossible to achieve in many cases. Thus, a method of analyzing effects of more than one variable was needed in order to conduct behavioral science studies effectively.

A method that provided the capability of assessing several variables simultaneously was introduced through the science of agriculture. R. A. Fisher (1960) presented the concept of factorial design as an outgrowth of his agricultural experimentation. The method was soon adopted to serve the research needs of behavioral researchers. By standardizing conditions before the experiment, using random selection of subjects and random assignment of experimental treatment, Fisher's factorial concept permitted researchers to study effects of more than one independent variable on more than a single dependent variable.

A type of factorial design can be illustrated through an example that is similar to the earliest factorial research—an agricultural experiment. Assuming that the study is to determine crop yield (dependent variable) in various field plots, factorial methods can be helpful in identifying the factors that contribute to yield. First, the independent variables that are expected to be related to crop yield are identified. These might include type of seed used (Brand X/Y), type of fertilizer used (fast grow/slow grow), and amount of irrigation (heavy/medium/light). Assignments of plots to these various conditions are done on a random basis. Each of the many combinations is the product of the number of levels of each independent variable. In this example, seed has two variations (Brand X/Y), fertilizer has two, and irrigation has three. The different comparisons (factor combinations) are $2 \times 2 \times 3$ or 12 combinations. At least 12 different plots are to be studied in carrying out the research.

A second example, this time from adult education, relates to participation. Our research question asks what type of learning setting produces the greatest achievement or satisfaction among participants in an evening math refresher program. Related factors might include location of the class (school/church/YMCA) and method of instruction (lecture/discussion).

Each class offered should represent a different combination of factors—instructors using the lecture method and teaching in a school environment; instructors using the discussion method, teaching in a YMCA, etc.—until all six combinations are represented. Participants are assigned randomly to a classroom setting. Assuming equal enrollment in each class, the number of participants exposed to the different conditions (independent variables) will be the same. Some measure of achievement or satisfaction is then administered at the conclusion of the course to determine effects. As Edwards (1985) stresses, factorial methodology

> means that the outcomes of the experiment provide a sounder basis for generalizing about the effectiveness of the experimental variables, since they are tested not only in isolation, but in conjunction with the effects of other variables. (p. 223)

Primary components of experimental design are a control group and an experimental group. After each group is equated through the process of random selection and assignment, the experimental group is either exposed to, or deprived of, some particular treatment (manipulation), while the control group does not receive the treatment. Changes in events associated with the experimental group are then compared with events of the control group. Because control is difficult to ensure in many natural settings of human interaction, even the best planned factorial designs do not always meet the needs of social science researchers in applied fields such as adult education and training.

Methods used with this form of inquiry necessarily must be modified in order to address research problems in education. Designs that do vary from the classical model are referred to as quasi-experimental methods. If research groups are unequal in number of participants, or in dimensions one wishes to study when an experiment is being planned, quasi-experimental designs are used to provide as much control as possible. For example, in the sample study of the best learning setting for math, preference of class location by participants makes random assignment difficult. If individual participants in the study self-select to attend a particular class, it is not possible to establish that individuals who chose to go to the church, as opposed to the YMCA, are equal regarding extraneous influences. The fact that some participants chose to attend the class at their church with friends could be an extraneous influential factor.

DESIGNING QUASI-EXPERIMENTAL RESEARCH

Obtaining a sample through randomization provides the experimental researcher the control necessary to study the effects of the independent variable. In planning quasi-experimental research, however, randomization is not always possible. At least four other ways bring about experimental control. First, the researcher can match participants having as many like characteristics as the researcher can identify. For example, each participant in a computer training program experiment might be matched with an individual in another group according to such characteristics as equal years of computer experience, equal math training, and equal level of education. This procedure gives greater assurance that differences at the conclusion of the experiment are attributable to the experimental treatment.

Experimental control is also attained by a second method—homogeneous selection. Participants in the computer training experiment might be selected only on the basis of age (e.g., 20 to 35 years old) and amount of past computer experience (e.g., over 2 years). A more homogeneous group of research participants controls for extraneous variables. The disadvantage of homogeneous selection is that results are not easily generalized to other situations, such as other computer programs.

A third way of achieving experimental control is by a statistical procedure called analysis of covariance. In this procedure, control is attained through a statistical analysis of differences between research groups found in the dependent variable at the beginning and end of the experiment. Also, differences in independent variables that are relevant are controlled through covariant analysis. Differences in performance of participants in the computer program at the conclusion of the experiment, for example, are statistically compared with pre-program achievement of the participants to determine actual change in performance. Also pertinent factors that may influence performance, such as past computer experience, are statistically compared with other independent variables to determine the degree of influence on participant performance.

A fourth means of gaining experimental control in addition to randomization is through the individual research participant. By subjecting the same individual to two or more experimental treatments intended to reach similar ends, the researcher has some assurance that extraneous variables have been limited. The individual, in this case, is the controlling agent. If participants in the computer training experiment, for example, were given three different experiences directed at teaching the same computer skills, an assessment at the end of each phase or experience might reveal how rapidly the individual's learning took place or how thoroughly the skill was learned as a result of the different approaches. Though using the individual research participant as a controlling agent is efficient, an obvious disadvantage is the confounding influence of sequential training experiences. One training experience may influence participant performance in a subsequent episode, therefore the researcher cannot always be certain of the actual effects of individual experiences.

The experimental controls explained in the previous discussion are used by the researcher in designing quasi-experimental studies. Attention to control is necessary to study effects of the independent variable. This is the essence of experimental methodology. The researcher should consult authoritative sources for a more detailed explanation of quasi-experimental designs (Kerlinger, 1986; Edwards, 1985).

Because controlled conditions are essential to experimental research, studies that employ experimental designs in adult education and training are rare. Those that are experimental usually use some form of pretest and posttest design. Research reported by Rosentreter (1979) is an example. The study examined the effectiveness of a training program for managers supervising production of work groups in a large corporation. Rosentreter studied effects of communication skills training upon the dependent variables of employee turnover, tardiness to work, appraisal of performance by managers, and number of formal grievances to the local union. The population for study was 68 department managers from a large corporation, who supervised small work groups of 16 to 30 subordinates. The managers were assigned randomly to experimental and control groups after being matched according to their relative employee turnover rate prior to the training. Employee turnover, employee tardiness, managerial performance ratings, and number of formal grievances were recorded for each manager prior to and following the training period. Conclusions of the study indicated that the training program significantly affected employee turnover, but did not result in significant change with regard to other dependent variables.

Two other examples of quasi-experimental research that explored adult learning processes are studies by Williams (1985) and Young (1986). Williams examined the degree to which perspective transformation, as a theory of adult learning, explained the process through which abusive behavior developed toward a spouse and how that behavior was changed through treatment. Five self-report instruments were used to measure anticipated changes in perspective, such as changes in self-esteem, locus of control, and role preference. Testing was done before and after a 12-week treatment program that included 25 self-selected male abuser participants. A followup of participants was conducted 12 weeks after the treatment was concluded. Williams concluded that the process of perspective transformation only partially explained abuser adaptation that led to changes in their self-esteem, locus of control, and role preference.

In the study conducted by Young (1986), cognitive restructing about world perspectives among adults who participated in a Conceptual Learning workshop was explored. Here, 42 teachers, evenly divided into two groups, one of which participated in the workshop, responded to a 28-item likert instrument, the Future World Perspective Values Scale. Young found a significant change in world values held by participants immediately following and 6 months after the workshop. Demographic variables, such as age, gender, subject taught, or years of teaching experience were found not to be significantly related to these changes.

Some terms and basic processes of the experimental design need definition. Descriptions of some key terms are provided in the following section.

Key Terms

Sample. A sample is a strategically and systematically identified group of people or events that meets the criterion of representativeness for a particular study. In order to detect causal relationships and project into the future, experimental design demands selection of research participants or events that accurately represent the total population of persons or the universe of events being studied. In research, to sample means to identify subjects or events for study in a systematic way.

Randomization. One common strategy used in selecting and assigning participants to groups for study is randomization. It "is the assignment of objects (subjects, treatments, groups) of a universe to subsets of the universe in such a way . . . that every member of the universe has an equal probability to be chosen for assignment" (Kerlinger, 1986, p. 114). Randomization is usually carried out by using a table of random numbers. Each subject or event is assigned a number and selection to groups is done by following the list of random numbers in the table.

Variables. In identifying interrelationships between variables in a phenomenon, functional terms are used to explain relatedness—i.e., independent, dependent, extraneous, and intervening variables. An independent variable is one that is independent from the phenomenon being studied. Conversely, a dependent variable "may change depending on the presence or absence of the independent variable" (Johnston & Pennypacker, 1993, p. 365).

In the crop production study mentioned earlier, the amount of irrigation and type of fertilizer both are independent of any property of the crop being grown and are, therefore, referred to as independent variables. In contrast, crop growth is dependent upon cultivation and moisture; therefore, crop growth is functionally described as the dependent variable.

Extraneous variables are variables that may influence the dependent variable but are not or cannot be identified by the researcher.

For example, undetected detrimental chemical elements in the soil could constitute an extraneous variable in crop production. An intervening variable is one that is observed to have an influence during the experiment, but cannot be controlled, such as, an outbreak of leaf blight.

Treatment and Control. Part of experimental design is observing or introducing different independent variables in the research procedure to see their effects upon the dependent variable. The process of introducing different variables is referred to as manipulation, or treatment. To ensure that any influence of independent variables on the dependent variable is accurately assessed, rigid controls are used in the research design of an experimental study. Control of experimental conditions reduces the possibility of influence from extraneous variables. In the factorial design study previously discussed, method and location of the refresher course were independent factors that were observed to see their influence upon achievement and satisfaction in math. In this case, the control to minimize effects of possible extraneous variables, such as teacher personality or type of participants attending the program, was a 2×3 design which combined each independent variable with all other variables. By including two different combinations of site and instruction, extraneous factors of teacher personality and type of participant are at least partially equated.

Observation. The word *observation* is frequently used in experimental methodology. Although the term does include "viewing" behavior or events, it is generally thought of as any form of assessment, in addition to visual observation. For example, an assessment of events represented by performance on pretests and posttests is a form of observation. It simply is documentation of events associated with the phenomenon being studied.

Internal and External Threats to Validity. Basic to conducting experimental research are steps to ensure the validity of research results. The degree to which a study is valid is important in that it indicates to the research consumer how accurately cause was established and future events can be predicted. The degree to which a study may be judged valid is determined in two ways—internally and externally. Steps to ensure both types of validity are carefully considered in planning experimental research studies.

Validity is of concern to any researcher in carrying out research, but threats to validity are of particular concern in the design of an experimental study because the researcher hopes to make predictions from the research results. Internal threats to validity may be interpreted as those factors which affect the degree to which the research procedure measures what it purports to measure, such as:

1. History of events in the experiment
2. Maturation of subjects through time
3. Effects of testing upon subjects
4. Errors of measurement or observation
5. Biased selection of subjects
6. Statistical regression

External threats pertain to the extent results of a study are generalizable to other situations. Such threats relate to:

1. Extent of randomization in subject selection
2. Effects of pretesting on subjects
3. Effects of the experimental setting (Hawthorne/placebo effects)
4. Effects of multiple treatments in the experiment

The effects of life experience (history) or physical and emotional development (maturation) of research participants during the course of a study, for example, are internal threats that may affect the validity of results generated. Participants change through experience and develop over time and, therefore, may naturally respond differently at the end of a study from how they responded at the outset of the experiment. Also, the way research subjects are selected is sometimes biased: one type or group of persons may have a better chance of being selected, for example, or may learn through the experimental process, beyond what is intended by the treatment. Additionally, simple errors in observation and measurement by the researcher, along with statistical regression (the tendency for participant scores to move closer to the mean upon retesting) all may contribute to invalid research results.

Generalizability of findings is influenced by the degree a study is controlled through the research design. Lack of representativeness within the sample group is an example of a potential external threat. Changes brought about because of the aura of experimental conditions or the secondary influences of experimental treatment also are external threats that affect the researcher's ability to generalize research beyond the present study.

Hypothesis. A hypothesis is a tentative explanation of phenomena that may be empirically tested and gives direction to the research (Ary et al., 1985). Each hypothesis developed to guide the experimental study is usually related to an important variable or set of relationships that make up the phenomenon under study. Research hypotheses are converted to quantitative, negative statements, or null hypotheses, for use in statistical testing. The null hypothesis states that no significant difference exists between the experimental and control groups pertaining to the specific variables mentioned in the hypothesis. Inferential statistics are used as tools to test hypotheses, as well as to estimate parameters—the type of distribution of the population being used in the study. The inferential test is to prove the null hypothesis incorrect and, therefore, permit the researcher to reject the null hypothesis. Rejection of the null and acceptance of the original or alternative hypothesis indicate that a difference does indeed exist. Acceptance or rejection of the null hypothesis is done using standard levels of probability. The level of probability indicates the extent to which observed differences could have resulted by chance.

Summary

An obvious advantage of experimental research designs includes the predictive nature of results. Theoretically, experimental approaches make it possible to accurately predict events in similar settings without actually observing those events. Another advantage is the careful delineation of research phenomena that takes place through the experimental process; meticulous care is taken to sort out and examine factors that may influence outcomes of the study.

A disadvantage is the difficulty of implementing the method in the study of human events. True experimental conditions are difficult to arrange in natural settings. Consequently, researchers are forced to use quasi-experimental methods in the educational enterprise, and the use of quasi-experimental methods reduces the predictive power that the researcher has available. Another disadvantage of experimental approaches is the narrow scope of investigation induced by the empirical/deductive mode of inquiry. Use of intuitive sources of knowledge, for example, are minimized, and reality is reduced to minuscule, stop-action snapshots. The power of experimental design lies in precision; its major limitation is narrowness of scope as related to the ongoing milieu of human events.

In summary, the assumption upon which experimental methodology rests is that use of tightly controlled conditions and application of statistical probability lead to determination of causal relationships. Adherence to the experimental method allows the researcher to generalize results of one study to other similar situations.

As stressed in the discussion of advantages and disadvantages, not all research problems or concerns can or should be pursued using experimental methods. Actually, with some research problems, the researcher merely wants to describe or to interpret relationships surrounding a phenomenon. Descriptive research methodology, which describes rather than predicts, is discussed in the following section.

DESCRIPTIVE DESIGNS

One of the most commonly used methodologies in the study of adult education and training is descriptive research. The central focus of descriptive research is to examine facts about people, their opinions and attitudes (Kerlinger, 1986). Its purpose is not to give value to sets of relationships between events, but simply to draw attention to the degree two events or phenomena are related. Because social science researchers find arranging subjects into experiments for manipulation or treatment to be artificial, and often not possible, descriptive research is a common choice of method. In descriptive research, the researcher does not manipulate variables or control the environment in which the study takes place. Its purpose is to systematically describe the facts and characteristics of a given phenomenon, population, or area of interest. Description may include (1) collection of facts that describe existing phenomena; (2) identification of problems or justification of current conditions and practice; (3) project or product evaluation; or (4) comparison of experience between groups with similar problems to assist in future planning and decision making.

Causal/Comparative Research

A form of descriptive research that has many of the design characteristics of the experimental method is causal/comparative (or ex post facto) research. Here the investigator attempts to explain phenomena that already have taken place. Such studies do not predict events in the future; rather, they seek results indicating the relationships that may point to cause.

Research done on the effect of using seatbelts in automobiles is an example of causal/comparative research that influenced development of safety equipment. Reports of research indicated individuals who used seatbelts experienced fewer injuries and fatalities. This research led to legislation dictating that all new cars purchased after January 1, 1968, must have lap and shoulder belts installed. Reports that followed indicated drastic reduction of skull and facial injuries among accident victims who used shoulder/lap belts. In the 1990s causal/comparative studies are being conducted regarding vehicle ergonomics. For example, passive restraints (airbags) for car passengers and the type and location of fuel tanks on trucks are being investigated. Results of these studies will influence the decisions of vehicle manufacturers about the introduction of additional safety features in the future.

Another example of causal/comparative research is the study reported in *Americans in Transition: Life Changes as Reasons for Adult Learning* (Aslanian & Brickell, 1980). A representative sample of approximately 2,000 adults in the United States over 25 years of age was surveyed using face-to-face and telephone interviews. Research questions included "Why do adults choose certain learning activities?" and "Why are more adults choosing to take part in learning activities?" The researchers found that of those engaged in learning, over 80 percent described some change in their lives as the reason for learning. More than half of the transitions were career related; a smaller but substantial number were family or leisure transitions. The findings therefore suggest that transitions in adult life are linked to learning. Results also confirmed findings of earlier participation studies—adult learners tend to be younger, more highly educated, and from higher income levels.

A precaution researchers should take in using the causal/comparative method is not to assume independent variables either do or do not cause outcomes reflected in the dependent variable. Arriving at conclusions of cause based on relational data in causal/comparative research is referred to as "post hoc fallacy." In the *Americans in Transition* study, for example, the researchers did not say that transitions cause learning, only that transitions and learning are related, which suggests cause.

An example of coming to unsupported conclusions using the causal/comparative method is found in the following example. A researcher is interested in attrition of adults in evening classes at a particular community college. In pursuing the study, the researcher gathers various descriptive data related to participants in the evening program and discovers that females between the ages of 18 and 25 who attend the community college are more persistent in attending classes than are females in the 26 to 40 age range. A conclusion that the researcher might incorrectly draw is that being younger causes participants to be more persistent in attending classes. In fact, if variables were manipulated under experimental conditions, we may find the cause to be the responsibilities of child care, stronger commitment to career, or numerous other factors. Data gathered after the event has taken place can only indicate relationship and give clues to probable cause.

The researcher who engages in descriptive research finds the way data are selected or sampled to be of great importance. Generally, three different procedures are used to gather descriptive research data when large populations are being studied—cross-sectional, longitudinal, and sequential sampling. These three approaches have two main distinguishing characteristics: (1) the time at which the data are collected and (2) the type or nature of the sample (Wiersma, 1986). A discussion of descriptive data gathering follows.

APPROACHES TO DESCRIPTIVE DATA GATHERING

In a cross-sectional approach, data are gathered at a single point in time, whereas a longitudinal approach collects data from the same sample on several occasions. The combination of these two—cross-sectional and longitudinal—is referred to as cross-sequential. Each approach has a special use that may be valuable to the researcher, depending upon the purpose of a study. The following examples of sampling designs are taken from adult development and learning research, an area of study that has impacted upon both education and training. The examples are selected to illustrate how the three approaches are distinct and to discuss strengths and limitations of each one.

In cross-sectional developmental study, the performances of people from different age groups are measured at the same point in time. For example, a group of 20-year-olds, 40-year-olds, and 60-year-olds are tested, and their mean scores compared. The major reason for using this methodology would be to identify differences in people of various age groups.

The major problem in cross-sectional research is the construing of age differences in performance or attitudes as age-related changes. With cross-sectional studies, one can say that people of a given age or stage are characterized a certain way. One cannot say that people will change in a certain way as they grow older.

In longitudinal research, the performance of a group of subjects is compared with their own performance at another period in time. A group of 20-year-olds, for example, may be observed at age 20, again at age 25, 30, 35, and so on. This design allows for age-related conclusions to be drawn. However, because only one cohort is being studied, generalizations can safely be made only to people born at the time that group was born. Other limitations with this design are: the long-term commitment of money, time, and personnel needed for such a study; survivor bias, that is, those who survive for successive rounds of study are most likely healthier and more intelligent than those who do not survive; the practice effects of successive testing; and changing interest of the researcher in topics for study.

Besides the basic problems of internal and external validity common to all research, studies in adult development and aging are particularly sensitive to the following methodological problems:

1. Selective Sampling. Cross-sectional studies have the problem of achieving representative samples for each age group tested. In addition, those who volunteer tend to be above average in intelligence and of a higher socioeconomic status than those who do not.

2. Survivor Bias. A given population at birth changes its composition as the members age. The survival rate of cohort members is correlated with intelligence, socioeconomic factors, and psycho-pathology. Successively older groups in a cross-sectional study and survivors in longitudinal studies represent samples unrepresentative of their birth cohorts.

3. Selective Dropout. A longitudinal sample measured later may not be comparable to the earlier sample because the dropout from the sample may not follow the random pattern that would be equivalent to attrition of the larger population. Consequently, results will be biased.

4. Testing Effects and Instruments. A longitudinal design assumes that repeated measurements with the same sample have no effect on the dependent variable. Practice effects and increased sophistication at test taking do, however, become sources of error. Measurement or test instruments themselves pose an additional problem. The difficulty of finding or designing instruments that measure the same attribute, such as intelligence in young adults and older adults, is no small task. Age differences in performance of an instrument may indicate that different attributes are being measured rather than age-related changes of the same attribute.

5. Generation Effects. Generation effects hamper the internal validity of cross-sectional designs and the external validity of longitudinal designs. In cross-sectional designs, samples vary by age and by generation cohort, and measurement differences

thus reflect age and cultural changes. In longitudinal designs, the same cohort is measured, and thus differences are not confounded by generation differences. On the other hand, changes are specific to that generation only.

To control for testing and generation effects, several sequential design strategies have evolved in the study of development and aging. Sequential or "mixed" designs are characterized by the simultaneous application of cross-sectional and longitudinal factors. Age changes are assessed at the same time for several groups over a period of time. For example, a group of 20-, 40-, 60-year-olds are measured, and then either the same subjects or different subjects from the same cohort are tested again in 10 years, at the same time adding a new group of 20-year-olds. The original 20-year-olds are now 30, the 40-year-olds are now 50, and the 60-year-olds are now 70. With this method, age changes occurring within generations can be contrasted with age differences between generations at a given point in time. Also, environmental impact is constant for all age groups, thus allowing the differences that emerge to be attributed to maturation.

Some descriptive approaches are intended to give adult educators, planners, policy analysts, or human resource developers a sense of what to expect in the future. The following section describes a form of descriptive research called futures research.

FUTURES RESEARCH

Trend analysis, Delphi technique, scenario writing, and simulation gaming are terms used to describe a group of approaches collectively called *futures* research methods. Futures researchers emphasize the importance of using the past to illuminate the future, referring to these approaches as "applied history" (Cornish, 1977).

Futurologists commonly allude to two principles in their studies; the Principle of Continuity and the Principle of Analogy. The Principle of Continuity suggests that what is observed in the present will continue in the future (Cornish, 1977, p. 103). This principle assumes that the future will be very much like the present. The Principle of Continuity allows us to predict that what we observe today will not change, or will change in the same way it has changed in the past. By accepting the Principle of Continuity, for example, we can count on the rivers to flow tomorrow, the air to be present next year, and the sun to shine in the year 2000. An example of applying this concept in the field of adult education might be that the gradual, but inevitable increase in the median age of adults combined with a larger work-force within the United States means more training will be required for adults in the future.

The Principle of Analogy involves observing recurring patterns or cycles of events as means of studying the future. For example, a study of the decreasing temperatures in the late fall may be used to predict snow, or the southward flight of geese may be a predictor of winter weather.

McHale (1978) points out three current approaches to futures research in which these principles are applied:

1. Descriptive Approach (the "imagined future")—including con-jectures, speculations, and imagined situations as in many clas-sical utopian futures (*20,000 Leagues Under the Sea* by Jules Verne and *War of the Worlds* by H. G. Wells).
2. Exploratory Approach (the "logical future")—forecasting based on methodical and relatively linear extrapolation of past and present developments into the future (RAND Corporation Report, 1964).
3. Prescriptive Approach (the "willed future")—normatively ori-ented projections of the future in which explicit value insertions and choices are made about how a specific future may be viewed or attained, e.g., *The Year 2000* by Kahn and Wiener (1968) and Plan Europe 2000 group's publication *The Future Is Tomorrow* (1973).

McHale also suggests that these categories overlap a great deal in actual practice. Research activities may be grouped according to type and range of activity. Some activities focus on forecasting causal re-lationships, while others concentrate upon long-range planning. Fu-tures research tends to be oriented toward a time frame of "the next two to three decades and beyond" (McHale, 1978, p. 10).

Contributions such as those of Sir Thomas More's *Utopia* and Fran-cis Bacon's *New Atlantis* in the 16th century opened the era of mod-ern futurism. A number of methods for studying the future have developed since the beginning of this modern era. The methods dis-cussed here—trend extrapolation, Delphi technique, scenario writ-ing, and simulation gaming—are commonly used in applied fields of social science.

Trend Extrapolation

A method that has application in the fields of adult education policy analysis and human resource development is trend extrapolation. As defined by Hill (1978), a trend is "a tendency for the values in a time series to increase or decrease with some steady regularity" (p. 249). Based on the Principle of Continuity, this form of futures research also uses graphic displays of significant statistical information, such as the average number of work-related injuries in the company over a number of years, or employee attrition on a monthly basis over several months. Other statistical procedures used in futures research include use of correlation analysis that quantitatively describes the relationship of events over time and regression analysis, observing the degree to which events adhere or depart from statistically predicted patterns of events.

Trend extrapolation can also be conducted through a review of literature. Hoare (1982), for example, did a comprehensive review of adult education and related literature for the decade of the 1970s to determine issues that might impact the future of adult education. Various sources were used in the trend study, such as conference proceedings, surveys, action-inquiry forums, and informed opinion of experts. Future issues that were identified from Hoare's research were related to various forms of education—work and leisure education, education for aging, health education, continuing professional education, social and civic responsibility, personal adaptation, functional competency and adult teacher education.

Still other phenomenona that may be analyzed using this technique that have relevance for adult education and training are population trends, work patterns, migration patterns, and housing patterns.

Delphi Technique

In a report by the RAND Corporation, "Report on Long-Range Forecasting Study" (Helmer-Hirschberg & Gordon, 1964), a second method of studying the future called the Delphi technique was introduced. The aim of the RAND study was to determine "the direction of long-range trends, with special emphasis on science and technology, and their probable effects on our society and our world" (Linstone, 1978, p. 273). Since its introduction, the method has gained acceptance for forecasting the future in areas other than the business world. The process involves a series of questionnaires, each one being more structured and requiring more focus by the respondent than the preceding one. The Delphi process includes the following steps:

1. Formation of a team to undertake and monitor a Delphi study on a given subject

2. Selection of one or more panels to participate in the exercise—normally experts in the subject or area
3. Development of the first round Delphi questionnaire
4. Testing of the questionnaire for proper wording (e.g., ambiguities, vagueness)
5. Transmission of the first questionnaire to the panelists
6. Analysis of the first round responses
7. Preparation of the second round questionnaires (and possible testing)
8. Transmission of the second round questionnaire to the panelists
9. Analysis of second round responses (Steps 7 to 9 repeated until desired or necessary data are gathered)
10. Preparation of a report by the analysis team to present conclusions of the exercise (Linstone, 1978, pp. 274–275)

The original process used in the Delphi technique incorporated three important elements; (1) structuring of information flow, (2) feedback to the participants, and (3) anonymity for the participants.

An example of the Delphi method applied to adult education research is the study conducted by Long (1991) with the Commission of Professors of Adult Education. In the study, 22 members of the commission were invited to participate in the study of continuing higher education research futures. Ten professors completed Delphi rounds two and three. The Delphi technique was used to investigate (1) future prospects for continuing higher education research and (2) the degree of consensus among selected professors on the identified futures. The research was specifically designed to identify trends, topics, important findings to be reported, valuable research procedures, and sources of funding to support continuing higher education research during the 1990s.

Results of the study indicated a strong consensus among professors about the significance of contemporary social and technological developments as important areas for research. Also, professors strongly agreed upon the need for field-based qualitative research methods. Some areas in the study that reflected lack of consensus pertained to evaluations of continuing higher education effectiveness, learning and technology. Differences in anticipated futures for professors of the commission seem to be related to their original field of adult education practice. Adult basic education professors were not in agreement with continuing higher education professors as to what the future holds.

As Linstone (1978) points out, the Delphi method can be used in discovering priorities of personal values and social aims, examining the pros and cons of an issue, evaluating budget allocations, assessing the importance of a historical event, and even sorting out perceived and real human motivations.

Two particularly useful situations in which the Delphi method may be applied are (1) when the problem does not lend itself to precise analytical techniques, but can benefit from subjective judgments on a collective basis, and (2) when the individuals who need to interact cannot be brought together in a face-to-face exchange because of time or cost constraints (Linstone, 1978, p. 275). Also, the technique minimizes the influence of strong personalities. An obvious weakness of the Delphi technique is the amount of time required to conduct a thorough study.

Scenarios

Most dictionary definitions of *scenario* apply when it is used as a method of studying the future. The scenario is "dramatic, fictional and sketchy" (Wilson, 1978). These descriptions are all essential in futures research, according to Wilson, because the purpose is to raise consciousness. A more specific definition of scenario used for futures studies is "an explanation of an alternative future" (p. 225).

Scenarios can be described as being hypothetical, that is, a suggested alternative; sketchy, where only an outline that seeks to map the branching points of the future is used; and multifaceted or holistic, which involves an attempt to paint a broad picture of future possibilities.

One of the earliest futures scenarios was Plato's description of the ideal state in *The Republic*. From this source Sir Thomas More developed his treatise, *Utopia*. A well-known scenario is *The Limits of Growth* (Meadows et al., 1972) which deals with population explosion and ecological change. *The Future of Adult Education: An Inductively Derived Scenario* (Boshier, 1979) is an example of a scenario which used the Delphi method to gather information from a group of conference participants in projecting the future of a field of study. A more recent application of scenarios of the future is the work by Naisbitt and Aburdene (1990), *Megatrends 2000*. In this second in a series of two books (Naisbitt 1982), the authors develop 10 predictions of the 1990s that were the result of using content analysis of newspapers with a number of experts around the world called the Naisbitt Group.

Scenarios help individuals and organizations to plan environments by sorting out priorities and options. The method can also free planners from the conventional environment and allow them to see the future holistically, rather than in pieces. A limitation of the method is that scenarios, no matter how creative, are developed from and perceived through the data of the present.

Simulation Gaming

A method for futures study that has particular application to adult education and training is simulation gaming. Simulation games are developed to assist people in conveying views and explaining alternative situations. Simulation gaming is not a device for projecting, but for explaining and helping us prepare for the future.

There are four basic functions of simulation games:

1. To transmit information
2. To extract information
3. To establish discussion between players
4. To motivate players and prepare them for future experience (McLean, 1978, p. 345)

Some examples of simulation games that have application in adult education and training are the HEX Game developed to study the human settlement planning in Third World nations for UNESCO, the Metro-Apex Game used by the U.S. government as an air pollution control training method, and the SNUS (Simulated Nutrition System) Game developed to implement nutrition planning in Third World nations. Ultimately the individual employing simulation gaming as a method of studying the future is trying to acquaint research participants with the future. The researcher also attempts to provoke participants in the game to think expansively —to enlarge their perceptions and to reach logical conclusions only after exploring a problem or situation from multiple angles. Each of the four research approaches, collectively referred to as futures research approaches, are part of descriptive research design.

DESCRIPTIVE DATA-GATHERING TECHNIQUES

The most common technique used for gathering data in descriptive research is the survey. Participants are asked to respond to a written or orally administered schedule of questions. Written forms of surveys are questionnaires; orally administered surveys are interviews.

Typically, surveys are carefully planned to elicit whatever information is needed.

An advantage of using questionnaires to conduct research is the opportunity for careful construction and validation of questions in advance of conducting the study. Also, written instruments are usually easier to administer. In some cases, the researcher's presence is unnecessary, thus reducing time and expense. Many surveys are administered through the mail, permitting access to a potentially larger group of subjects.

An advantage of the interview technique is its effectiveness in surveying special populations and gaining in-depth information. Interviewing is particularly useful in gathering data from "hard-to-reach" populations, such as persons who are handicapped, illiterate, or culturally different. Also, when it is not possible to anticipate all that the researcher may need to know in preparing the schedule of questions before meeting the research participants, an unstructured interview may yield more reliable data than a written questionnaire. A personal, face-to-face interview is recommended to develop rapport and gain the widest range of data. However, the telephone interview may be used in gathering data if face-to-face interviews are not feasible. Each of these techniques is more thoroughly discussed in Chapter 7 of this book.

Descriptive research is the most common form of research used in adult education. Because of immediate need to define and describe the fields of practice, this methodology will continue to be important in advancing knowledge. The researcher should be aware, however, that descriptive research also has certain strengths and limitations.

STRENGTHS AND LIMITATIONS OF DESCRIPTIVE RESEARCH

One obvious advantage or strength of the descriptive method is its ease of use. It produces data that are accurate and representative. It describes "what is." The rigor of research design in descriptive research is not typically as demanding as in experimental studies.

A second advantage is that it allows the researcher to study relationships or events as they happen in human life situations. None of the contrived or manipulative techniques that are common in experimental designs is used.

A third advantage is the exploratory nature of the descriptive methods. Not only can variables be studied that indicate probable cause, but additional variables may be discovered that shed new light upon the phenomenon.

One prominent disadvantage or limitation is the lack of predictive power. The researcher discovers and describes "what is," but is unable to generalize or predict with certainty "what will be."

An aspect of research methodology that seems to be both a positive and a negative influence in conducting research is the application of statistics. Statistical explanation and analysis can give the researcher the advantage of greater power of expression in the case of descriptive research, and increased power of prediction when experimental methods are used. However, substitution of statistical terms for narrative discourse in the analysis and reporting of research often perplexes, frustrates, and discourages researchers and research consumers.

In experimental and descriptive research, as well as in many other methods of research, statistics are commonly used for comparison of data, analysis of data, and interpretation of research findings. It is important to be aware of the ways in which statistics assist or hinder the researcher.

Numerous statistical techniques are available. A full treatment of type and methods of conducting various statistical procedures is found in sources devoted to the topic of statistical design (Edwards, 1985; Kerlinger, 1986).

Use of terms such as statistic, control, treatment, and sample in a discussion of research methods raises some ethical questions. What is the moral or ethical responsibility of the researcher to participants in a study? What are the boundaries of intervention in the lives of research subjects in the name of science? Persons conducting experimental and descriptive research are particularly sensitive to the concerns these questions represent. Although definitive answers are difficult to provide, a discussion of factors that are related to the researcher's ethical responsibility is important to understand planning and conducting research. These issues are discussed in more detail in Chapter 10.

CONCLUSION

In summary, both experimental and descriptive designs are used in social science research. Descriptive research, however, is more commonly found in the study of adult education and training. Each provides a unique approach to inquiry. Experimental research attempts to establish cause by isolating the independent variable(s) that influence change observed in the dependent variable. Descriptive research, on the other hand, describes the variables, describes the phenomenon of which the variables are part, and may indicate degrees of relationship existing between them. Results of causal/comparative descriptive research may even point to potential cause.

Experimental research provides the power of prediction through carefully designed studies utilizing treatment, control, and statistical probability. The multivariant nature of the educational enterprise and the natural, human settings in which research related to education and training of adults is conducted, however, make experimental research of limited use. Ethical considerations regarding rights and propriety of research participants also limit the researcher's application of experimental methods.

Descriptive research utilizes various forms of survey, cross-sectional, longitudinal, and cross-sequential approaches to gathering data. The strength of the descriptive research design is in the exploratory capability it provides. This feature has resulted in significant contributions to developing fields, such as the education and training of adults.

REFERENCES

Ary, D., Jacobs, L. C., & Ragevich, A. (1985). *Introduction to research in education* (3rd ed.). New York: Holt, Rinehart & Winston.

Aslanian, C. B., & Brickell, H. M. (1980). *Americans in transition: Life changes as reasons for adult learning.* New York: College Entrance Examination Board.

Boshier, R. (1979). The future of adult education: An inductively derived scenario. *Adult Eduction Research Conference Proceedings.* Ann Arbor, MI.

Bredo, E., & Feinberg, W. (Eds.). (1982). *Knowledge and values in social and educational research.* Philadelphia: Temple University Press.

Cornish, E. (1977). *The study of the future.* Washington, DC: World Future Society.

Dickinson, G., & Blunt, D. (1971). A content analysis of adult education, *Adult Education, 21,* 177–185.

Drew, C. J. (1985). *Introduction to designing and conducting research.* St. Louis: The C. V. Mosby Company.

Edwards, A. L. (1985). *Experimental design in psychological research* (5th ed.). New York: Holt, Rinehart & Winston.

Fisher, R. A. (1960). *The design of experiments.* Edinburgh: Oliver and Boyd.

Helmer-Hirschberg, O., & Gordon, T. J. (1964). *Report on long-range forecasting study.* Santa Monica, CA: RAND Corporation.

Hill, K. Q. (Ed.). (1978). Trend Extrapolation. In J. Fowles (Ed.), *Handbook of futures research* (pp. 249–272). Westport, CT: Greenwood Press.

Hoare, C. H. (1982). Future issues in adult education: A review of the literature of the seventies. *Adult Education, 33,* 55–59.

Johnston, J. M., & Pennypacker, H. S. (1993). *Strategies and tactics of human behavioral research sciences.* Hillsdale, NJ: Lawrence Erlbaum Associates.

Kerlinger, F. N. (1986). *Foundations of behavioral research* (3rd ed.) New York: Holt, Rinehart & Winston.

Linstone, H. A. (1978). The delphi technique. In J. Fowles (Ed.), *Handbook of futures research* (pp. 273–300). Westport, CT: Greenwood Press.

Long, H. B. (1991, Spring). Continuing higher education research futures: A delphi study of professors of adult education. *The Journal of Continuing Higher Education.*

McHale, J. (1978). The emergence of futures research. In J. Fowles (Ed.), *Handbook of futures research* (pp. 5–16). Westport, CT: Greenwood Press.

McLean, J. M. (1978). Simulation modeling. In J. Fowles (Ed.), *Handbook of futures research* (pp. 329–352). Westport, CT: Greenwood Press.

Meadows, D., & Meadows, D. (Eds.) (1972). *The limits to growth.* New York: Universe Books.

Merriam, S. B. (1991). How research produces knowledge, in J. M. Peters, and P. Jarvis (Eds.), *Adult education: Evolution and achievements in a developing field of study.* San Francisco: Jossey-Bass.

Mill, J. S. (1990). *A system of logic.* New York: Harper & Row.

Naisbitt, J. (1982). *Megatrends.* New York: William Morrow & Company.

Naisbitt, J., & Aburdene, P. (1990). *Megatrends 2000.* New York: William Morrow & Company.

Rosentreter, G. (1979). Evaluating training by four economic indices. *Adult Education, 24,* 234–241.

Wiersma, W. (1986). *Research methods in education* (4th Ed.) Boston: Allyn & Bacon.

Williams, G. B. (1985). Perspective transformation as an adult learning theory to explain and facilitate change in male spouse abusers. Unpublished doctoral dissertation, Northern Illinois University.

Wilson, I. H. (1978). Scenarios. In J. Fowles (Ed.), *Handbook for Futures Research* (pp. 225–248). Westport, CT: Greenwood Press.

Young, J.D. (1986). An examination of cognitive restructuring in an adult continuing education workshop. Unpublished doctoral dissertation, Northern Illinois University.

CHAPTER 5

HISTORICAL INQUIRY AND PHILOSOPHICAL INQUIRY

Research can be thought of as systematic inquiry. Some approaches have already been discussed in Chapter 4. The particular system or method followed depends upon the nature of the problem and the type of question being asked. Historical inquiry and philosophical inquiry each have a "system" for answering questions about the past or about underlying assumptions and beliefs. The purposes of this chapter are to discuss how history and philosophy can be used in the understanding of a field of social practice, and second, to discuss how to engage systematically in historical or philosophical study.

HISTORICAL INQUIRY

Like other areas of research, historical inquiry is motivated by curiosity: it begins with wondering about some event, institution, idea, or person. In applied fields like allied health, vocational education, or human resource development, there are many historical questions to be asked. One might be curious about the inception, purpose, or evolution of a particular institution or practice or ideal. For example, how has the current emphasis on career counseling come about in the field of counseling? What has been the black person's experience in vocational education? Why is the federal government willing to finance adult basic education but not liberal education programs?

A meaningful research topic not only arises out of curiosity, but also relates in some way to a larger problem or broader question. In focusing upon a particular segment of a problem, the researcher hopes to contribute to understanding the larger problem area. It is not enough, for example, to chronicle the history of an institution such as an adult evening school or a community health clinic. One must also ask questions about the role of that particular institution in society, and the sociohistorical context in which it evolved. This anchors the specific question in a larger context, the understanding of which may lead to a better appreciation of present practice. Carlson (1981) writes that historical research and philosophical research are in fact the *most* effective methodologies for understanding practice. They "provide the sort of perspective that lets us determine where we have come from, what we are doing and why, where we appear to be going, and how we might influence events in a human direction" (p. 3). Whether articulated or not, all the planning and decision making that practitioners do in their work (and in their personal lives as well) are based on former experiences, knowledge, and values. The more knowledge one has, the more informed one's decisions in practice can be.

Thus, significant historical questions in applied fields are those that relate to the practice of that field. Using the Chautauqua movement of the 19th century as an example, Rose (1982, p. 15) distinguishes between the "traditional historian" and an adult educator involved in historical research. The traditional historian would be "primarily interested in questions which were derived from the period" such as Chautauqua's relationship to reform and social gospel movements, or its intellectual origins. While not ignoring these questions, adult educators would focus on issues of "participation and actual impact" such as

> Where did participants come from; how did they hear about Chautauqua; did they buy homes on the lake or were they visitors; how long did the average person stay; what was the educational background of participants; is there a connection between the growth of a summer community such as this and large resorts which were also being developed during the same period; what were the differences? Finally, what does participation tell us about how adults viewed learning during this time? (p. 15)

Many historical research problems in applied fields deal with events, institutions, or persons. Historical research may also deal with ideas, concepts, or theories that have had an effect upon practice. Stubblefield (1988) discusses the ways in which the first generation of American adult education thinkers began to theorize about the field. He traces the development of notions of the diffusion of knowledge and culture, liberal education, and social education. Other concepts that might be the subject of a historical investigation are human resource development, patient education, distance learning, and community development.

Perhaps because they are young, fields such as adult education, human resource development, gerontology, social work, and such have sought to establish their own bodies of knowledge through more "scientific" methodologies. Historical research has tended to be descriptive of institutions and programs (Knowles, 1962). While chronicling has its place, historical inquiry is of greater service to a field when it is used to examine:

1. The origin of assumptions held to be "true" in the field
2. A field's failures as well as its "great feats" (Rockhill, 1976, p. 196)
3. The impact a practice has had on people's lives (Rose, 1982, p. 19)
4. The total context of an event, not just the event itself (Rose, 1982, p. 18)

Readers might want to refer to the following studies as examples of how historical research in an applied field might address a field's assumptions, failures and feats, impact on people's lives, and/or the total context of an event. Stubblefield and Rachal (1992) trace the origins and changing meanings of the term *adult education* in the United States, challenging the commonly-held assumption that it originated in the 1920s with the founding of the first professional association. Rose (1989) traces the founding of the American Association for Adult Education (AAAE). Rather than merely chronicling the history of this event, Rose sets it within the context of the times with particular attention to the Carnegie Corporation's involvement in its founding.

Other examples are Rohfeld's (1990) study of James Harvey Robinson, an early leader in adult education; Rose's (1991) research into efforts to accredit the learning of World War II servicemen and women, the precedent set by these reforms and the impact they have had on present-day adult education; and Rohfeld's (1989) study of the Army's efforts to establish a university to prepare World War I soldiers for a peacetime world.

Thus, engaging historical research with an applied field involves more than detailing the chronological history of some aspect of that field. It is looking at the context of an event, examining assumptions related to the topic, and being cognizant of its impact on the lives of participants. This approach holds the potential for adding to the knowledge and understanding of present practice. It may even offer some guidelines for future practice, although prediction per se is not a goal of historical research. Instead, historical studies offer "clues to *possible* rather than *probable* behavior" and allow one to "*anticipate* rather than to *predict*, to take *precautions* rather than to *control*" (Gottschalk, 1963, p. 269).

DOING HISTORICAL RESEARCH

Doing historical research necessitates having a historical topic. As noted earlier, problems arise out of a curiosity about the past of an event, institution, concept, or person. Studies have already been conducted of such diverse topics related to the education and training of adults as university extension, settlement houses, and adult basic education. Occasionally one begins with a question about present practice and finds that it leads to a historical problem. A question about the effectiveness of using programmed instruction materials with adults might lead to wondering how long programmed instruction has been used, how it was originally developed, how it found its way into present practice, why it was adopted as an instructional technique, and what the impact of its use has been on adults.

Having a general topic and posing some questions about the topic are sufficient to begin a historical study. Working through material on the topic will eventually lead to a thesis or proposition to be argued. At the outset, however, a researcher "should judiciously refrain from stating hypotheses, locking into a social science theory, or articulating the study in the form of a problem . . . Historical research is not the discipline with which to 'solve problems' but a means of exploring the mystery that is man" (Carlson, 1980, p. 44).

After becoming acquainted with the general topic, the task becomes one of focusing upon a particular segment of the problem area. As with other types of research, knowing what is a manageable topic in historical research is a trial-and-error process. If the topic is too broad or too narrow, it can be reduced or expanded by manipulating the extent of the geographical area covered, the number of persons involved, the span of time covered, or the scope of human activity included (Gottschalk, 1963). For example, the history of adult illiteracy in the United States may be too broad a topic for an individual to handle. Using Gottschalk's suggestions, the topic could be narrowed by (1) studying the history of illiteracy in one section of the country or in one state; (2) limiting the investigation to a segment of the population such as women, immigrants, Jewish Americans; (3) focusing on a prominent person who fought illiteracy; or (4) limiting the study to a particular time frame such as adult illiteracy during colonial times.

In delineating a manageable topic or focusing a study, one is probably already "doing" historical research. Furthermore, there is no standardized format that all historians subscribe to. L. P. Curtis (1970) discovered this when he attempted to pull together an anthology revealing "just how historians went about choosing their subjects, doing their research, shaping their interpretations and writing up the results" (p. xi). Several prominent historians who were invited to contribute declined with comments with "I am a bad person to write about methods—I have none," or "If all the contributors complied really honestly with your request, the history profession would be shattered fore and aft. What we now merely suspect would be proved without question—that nobody proceeds as the research manuals say we should" (Curtis, 1970, p. xv).

However elusive the techniques of historical research might be, all who do historical research are concerned with obtaining the best information available on the topic. The handling of historical material is very systematic and involves distinguishing between primary and secondary sources.

Primary sources are the basic material used in historical studies. Under the leadership of the Syracuse University Kellogg Project, efforts are now underway by North American adult educators, historians, and archivists to identify and preserve primary source material and collections of historical interest to adult education. Oral or written primary sources are those where the author was a direct observer, or eyewitness, of the event. Barzun and Graff (1957) differentiate between "intentional" and "unpremeditated" transmitters of facts. Intentional primary sources are (1) written records including chronicles, annuals, memoirs, inscriptions; (2) oral recordings; and (3) works of art such as portraits, paintings, and films. Unpremeditated sources are relics such as human remains, public documents, language and customs, tools, or other artifacts (pp. 132–134).

Secondary sources report the observations of those who did not witness the actual event. These secondary or secondhand sources can be useful in familiarizing the researcher with the topic and in suggesting new areas for further study. While the best primary sources are those recorded closest in time and place to the phenomenon, the farther removed a secondary source is from the phenomenon, the better, for such sources draw from the accumulated wisdom of earlier scholars.

It is not always possible to separate sources into primary and secondary categories. An eyewitness account may also include the observations or opinions of others, and, interestingly, a particular source may be classified primary or secondary depending upon the research problem. For example, a director's report of how a program has interpreted adult vocational education legislation would be a primary source if the study were investigating how federal legislation is translated into practice. The same report would be a secondary source in a study of the history of adult vocational legislation.

Locating primary sources is followed by the researcher's assessing the value or worth of the sources. In general, the best sources will meet the following criteria:

1. Proximity. The account closest in time to the event is preferable to others.
2. Competence of the author. The better record is one written by a person trained to observe the matter at hand. An instructor is not expected to be an expert on the institution's public policy, for example, yet a police officer is expected to record events accurately.
3. Purpose. The document that has as its purpose an impartial recording of events is likely to be more accurate than a spontaneous impression. Public records such as sports events, election returns, census data, and so on attempt to be accurate. At the same time, documents such as personal correspondence that are intended to be read by a few people are likely to be more revealing than those written with a large audience in mind.

In determining the genuineness of a document, the researcher attempts to establish authorship, time and place of writing, and whether it is an original copy. Internal criticism ascertains the trustworthiness of the information *within* the document. A researcher looks internally for the biases and motives of the author, as well as for incongruities in the account which may indicate exaggeration, misinterpretation, distortion, or outright fabrication. While full discussion of the principles of criticism is beyond the scope of this chapter, a person who undertakes a historical study should become acquainted with the procedures and problems inherent in assessing the value of the sources used.

Being careful about the material used for a historical study and being systematic in the handling of those sources help ensure that what is said about a phenomenon is as close an approximation of the truth as possible. But because the past can never be replicated, and we can never have complete faith in the facts found in primary sources,

> truth absolute is not at hand; the original with which to match the copy does not exist . . . the historian finds truth by the unremitting exercise of his and his peers' judgement upon the material. Judgement is a comparative act that takes in the evidence and the report . . . and eliminates the untenable. The resulting truths are built, not reached . . . (Barzun, 1974, pp. 147–148)

In the end, Felt (1976, p. 6) writes, "all of us have to settle for the highest probabilities we can get, based on whatever observations, documents, and confirmations of deductive and inductive reasoning we can muster." As Barzun and Graff (1957) point out, we can trust history to the extent that we have documents that are critically tested, that our judgments are governed by probability, and that the notion of replicating the past as it actually was is a "delusion" (p. 144).

In recent years historical research has experimented with new methods in an attempt, one historian feels, to become more "scientific" (Barraclough, 1978), more certain, more precise. The use of measurement and quantification has "affected practically every branch of historical research during the last one or two decades" (Barraclough, 1978, p. 84). Any phenomenon that can be counted or measured (such as voting behavior, settlement patterns, and so on) may be the subject of a quantitative history employing sophisticated statistical techniques and computer analysis. Among the applications of quantitative analysis to history are:

1. Collective biography—delineating biographical characteristics of a particular group of individuals such as Swedish immigrants, Civil War congressmen, prohibition-era police officers.
2. Content analysis—establishing the frequency of certain ideas, attitudes, or words within a particular body of material. For example, the employment opportunities for women during the 1950s might be ascertained by doing a content analysis of period newspapers.
3. Historical demography—studying the composition of the population, such as birthrate or age of marrying. This can be determined by aggregating public records. These and other quantitative history methods are discussed at length in Beringer's *Historical Analysis: Contemporary Approaches to Clio's Craft* (1978).

In addition to quantitative history, psychosocial history has become an accepted historical method. Broadly defined, this approach uses modern psychological and sociological theories and concepts to interpret personalities, events, groups, or movements of the past. Examples of this approach are Erikson's psychobiography of Luther (1958) and Donald's interpretation of abolitionist behavior in terms of status and reference group theory (1956).

Both approaches to historical research have their supporters and their critics. While it is not within the scope of this chapter to enter the debate over these methods, it can be pointed out that each is an attempt to deal more precisely with the problems of an increasingly complex world through historical analysis. Barzun, a critic of these approaches, nevertheless recognizes the reason for their popularity:

> The joint popularity of psycho- and quanto-history is not an accident or a contradiction; for although nothing is more impalpable than the Id and more dense than town-hall records, they stand respectively for the individual and society, and the past of one or the other or both may well contain the influential secret about present and future. The two branches of the new history give an equal hold to the strong desire mentioned in an earlier connection: to solve pressing problems. (Barzun, 1974, p. 78)

Like history itself, the methods of historical inquiry are changing, but each new method represents an attempt to find the best way to uncover the truths of the past. Researchers in applied fields—especially those dealing with the training and education of adults—more often than not have been trained in other disciplines and so may be quite familiar with other theories and methods of doing research. Creative applications of these methods to historical questions may lead to a better illumination of the past.

INTERPRETATION

Doing historical research is more than collecting information by various means from primary data sources, "History," Halle (1982, p. 2) writes, "is not simply a heap of details, any more than the cathedral of Chartres is a pile of stones. Just as the individual stones are not what count in Chartres, so the details are not what count in history." The collection of facts must be arranged into some order and given some interpretation. It is this task of interpreting the data, of bringing insight and coherence to a set of facts, that requires skill and imagination on the part of the researcher. "The greatest historians," Commager writes, "have been the interpreters . . . that is they tried to extract some meaning out of the inchoate raw materials of history, or to impose some philosophy upon it" (1965, p. 6).

Explaining how a person actually interprets a set of facts is as difficult as explaining how to have insight or how to make a discovery. Interpretation is dependent upon the individual researcher. The facts can be organized and interpreted in many ways. Such multiplicity of histories "mirrors the character of mankind, which is no more at one in its view of the present or recently endured past than it is about any other subject, including the past" (Barzun, 1974, p. 101).

While the process for arriving at interpretation cannot be delineated, some of the characteristics of the interpretive step can be pointed out. As noted above, the narrative is more than a listing of facts. It also involves ideas. An idea is "an image or a suggestion that goes beyond the bare facts ... The statement of a fact gives the impression of ending with itself, whereas an idea leads us on" (Barzun & Graff, 1957, p. 117). Ideas link facts together and infuse the narrative with meaning.

A historical account is a personal interpretation of the best, most relevant evidence available to the researcher. The researcher exercises judgment at two points in this process—first, in deciding what is "relevant" evidence, and then in choosing how to present the evidence in narrative form. Carlson (1980) captures the subjective dimension of historical research in the following passage:

> Historians present a reasoned argument regarding the past, based on evidence and their own values ... Historians interpret the past by sifting through the available relevant evidence and by mixing this information with their own values and philosophy. Through this sometimes agonizing process, they create or discover patterns in the thinking, action, motivation, and relationships that occurred in the past. Disciplined only by reality and their own common sense, historians tease out, dream up, and spin out their interpretation of why the events they are describing have occurred. (p. 42)

Just as the brilliance of a historical interpretation is dependent upon the imagination and intellect of the researcher, the perspective of the interpretation is shaped by the investigator's biases and values. One limitation of the historian that is particularly difficult to overcome is what Commager calls " 'present mindedness'—our instinctive habit of looking at the past through our own eyes, judging it by our own standards, recreating it in our own words or reading back into the language of the past our own meanings, assuming that whatever happened, happened in some 'past' and forgetting that every past was once a present" (1965, p. 46). While researchers cannot divest themselves of the present, an effort can be made to understand events from the point of view of those participating in them. For example, Lemisch (1969) recounts how merchant seamen in early America have been portrayed by historians as irresponsible, boisterous, and manipulated, because little attempt was made to understand their behavior from the perspective of the seamen themselves. Lemisch (1969) argues that historical research from the point of view of the "inarticulate" may well dispel some erroneous assumptions and preconceptions about the history of a field. In a parallel example from adult education, Seller (1978) uncovered a whole new facet of immigrant education by examining records of educational opportunities—opportunities offered by the immigrants themselves.

In summary, historical research in applied fields can bring some clarity to the practice of that field. Training in history or historical methods, although desirable, is not necessary to engage in a historical study. The researcher does need to be curious about the past of an institution, event, person, or practice; about its relationship to the times in which it occurred; and about the people involved. Then the researcher can acquire the knowledge needed to examine sources for their authenticity and value in answering the questions posed by the study. Finally, the information must be skillfully organized into a narrative that both explains and interprets the past. In so doing, the present becomes enlightened.

PHILOSOPHICAL INQUIRY

The many methods of doing research presented in this text have in common the systematic handling of data and the interpreting of that data for others. Philosophical research or, as it is more commonly referred to, philosophical inquiry is no exception. Like historical inquiry, philosophical inquiry begins with a question or problem, proceeds to the selection and examination of data according to certain rules, and ends with an insightful interpretation of the question. Philosophical inquiry has been grouped with historical inquiry in this chapter because both forms of inquiry are concerned with the foundations of a discipline or field of practice. Historical inquiry goes back to the past events and people—the early building blocks of a field—in order to illuminate present practice. Philosophical inquiry examines the underlying opinions, beliefs, values, and assumptions to bring clarity to a field of practice. What distinguishes philosophical research from historical inquiry is the nature of the questions raised and the methods philosophers employ in addressing those questions.

To some extent all human beings wonder about their lives, the things they experience, and where they fit into the world as a whole. Wanting to know, to understand, to satisfy curiosity are urges characteristic of us all:

> Even the least educated or the most simple-minded, are of necessity engaged in a ceaseless effort to find meaning behind apparent mean-

inglessness, to discover unity beneath surface diversity, and (above all) to impose some degree of order on the seeming chaos of our personal experience. Much of this effort may be unconscious or unarticulated, but we cannot escape making it. (Mead, 1962, pp. 23–34)

In contrast to most other people, philosophers are those who "do" philosophy consciously and systematically. How one "systematically" approaches answering philosophical questions is at the heart of philosophical inquiry as a research methodology.

Like other forms of inquiry, philosophy attempts to uncover truth and to add to our knowledge. The subject matter of philosophical inquiry is the ultimate nature of things. Of course no one person could manage an investigation of "all things." Rather, we wonder about a selected segment of the world and our existence in it. To bring some order to such an undertaking, problems of a philosophical nature traditionally have been divided into categories. There are *epistemological questions* dealing with the origins and nature of knowledge and how we know something is true, *metaphysical questions* dealing with what is ultimately real, *axiological questions* about value—the nature of good, the beautiful and so on—and *questions of logic* which focus on rules of correct reasoning.

These basic classifications are useful in thinking about problems in applied fields. A simple statement such as: "All adults should have access to learning opportunities," for example, can be analyzed philosophically from several perspectives. What constitutes the classification of a person as "adult"? Why "should" adults have access to learning opportunities? Who are "all" adults? What does "access" mean? What are "learning opportunities"? How can such an ideal become a reality? Answering any of these questions would bring some clarity to the practice of adult education. Philosophers strive for clarity, for perspective, for a sense of order and wholeness. Thus, philosophical questions or problems in an applied field arise out of curiosity or uncertainty about the assumptions underlying practice. In education, a philosophical problem often centers on the aims of the endeavor, education's relationship to society, the teaching-learning process, and curriculum.

METHODS OF PHILOSOPHICAL INQUIRY

Philosophical inquiry is as systematic and rigorous as any other form of inquiry. Its method depends upon the philosophical school with which the investigator is aligned. "The endorsement of a method," Johnstone notes, "amounts to the same thing as acceptance of a view of the nature of philosophy" (1965, p. 19). If, for example, one believes that the ultimate nature of things lies in human consciousness, one would investigate consciousness according to certain procedures, and those procedures would be different from those of the person who believes answers to philosophical questions can be found in language or in rational thinking or in experience.

While methods of philosophical inquiry are usually considered within the framework of a particular school of philosophy, at least "three fundamental methods" of inquiry have been delineated by grouping several schools of thought together (McKeon, 1965). Each of the three methods reflects a different conceptualization of the nature and purpose of philosophy itself.

1. Dialectic. This method aims to reconcile disputes and unify experience. It seeks a whole within which seemingly disparate assertations can coexist. McKeon points to Plato, Hegel, and Marx as major philosophers employing this method. The various forms of dialectic have a common purpose: "to transcend or remove contradictions as they are eliminated in the processes of nature, in the sequence of history, or in the insights of art, the stages of scientific thought, or the interplay of group inquiry in conversation" (McKeon, 1965, p. 94).

2. Logistic. This method does not concern itself with resolving contradictions but instead seeks to "trace knowledge back to the elements of which it is composed and the processes by which they are related" (McKeon, 1965, p. 94). For example, certain philosophers have proposed that axioms and postulates are the simple elements of mathematics, rules of logical syntax are the basic elements of language, and simple ideas are the basis of formal knowledge.

3. Problematic. This method is "aimed at solving particular problems one at a time and without reference to an all-inclusive whole or to a simplest part. A solution is regarded as acceptable just so long as it 'works' " (Johnstone, 1965, p. 22). William James and John Dewey made extensive use of this method.

Dialectic, logistic, and problematic methods are general approaches to doing philosophical research. Being more specific about the steps involved in a philosophical investigation or the "rules" one might employ to ensure that an inquiry is systematic necessitates becoming familiar with a particular philosophical system. The process of inquiry as exemplified in its application to phenomenology and linguistic analysis will be discussed later. For now, however, two additional observations about philosophical inquiry in general are worth noting.

First, the "data" one gathers and examines in a philosophical investigation can be anything the researcher feels will reveal the truth. In the past, philosophers have used faith, reason, material objects, observation, intuition, and language as the data in their search. Once the source of data has been selected, philosophical inquiry becomes a disciplined mental activity. Most philosophers would agree that the only equipment necessary for this activity is language. Language is the medium through which philosophers reflect upon their data and by which they record their observations.

Second, there is no standard format for reporting the findings of philosophical research, other than that they be "presented *systematically*, in the form of an orderly, consistent development of the thinker's views" (Matczak, 1975, p. 27). Matczak discusses several different formats that have been used by philosophers from various schools of thought:

1. Dialectic or conversational approach—used by Socrates, Plato, Hume, Hegel, Engels, and Marx
2. Commentaries—works that comment on original philosophic work, such as modern interpretations of St. Thomas Aquinas
3. Literary forms—expressing one's views in dramas and novels, used by modern existentialists, such as Camus and Sartre
4. Confessions or journals—especially common among philosophers concerned with questions of faith, such as Kierkegaard and St. Augustine
5. Mathematical form—expressing one's views with mathematical precision using numbers and equations, such as in the writings of Spinoza and Wittgenstein

To summarize, philosophical research cannot point to a single source of data, a preferred format for disseminating findings, or a standardized method for investigating a problem. These aspects of the research process are defined by particular schools of thought. Thus, in order to give the reader a better sense of what it means to *do* philosophical research, it is necessary to become better acquainted with particular approaches. Following is a brief discussion of two contemporary schools of philosophy and their methods of inquiry. Linguistic analysis and phenomenology have been selected for discussion because of their prominent position in modern Western philosophy. More importantly, each has a well-defined method for doing research that is easily applied to a field of practice.

LINGUISTIC ANALYSIS

Linguistic analysis, also called conceptual analysis or analytic philosophy, uses human language as its data base. Unlike traditional philosophy, linguistic analysis is not concerned with developing a system of thought that encompasses human nature, knowledge, the universe, and so on. Rather, philosophical analysis is interested

> fundamentally in the clarification of basic notions and modes of argument rather than in synthesizing available beliefs into some total outlook, in thoroughly appraising root ideas rather than in painting suggestive but vague portraits of the universe. (Scheffler, 1960, p. 7)

Just as all people, to some extent, attempt to make sense out of their lives, everyone at one time or another has felt the need to clarify a concept or the meaning of a statement or the definition of a word. For linguistic analysts, language is the key to understanding "the many puzzles and paradoxes of traditional philosophy" (Elias & Merriam, 1980, p. 180). While there are several variations in emphasis within the school itself, all linguistic analysts believe "that by studying the ways in which words are used we can shed a great deal of light on philosophical problems and in many instances avoid becoming the victims of 'pseudoproblems' " (Kurtz, 1966, p. 36).

Two general types of analyses are undertaken by proponents of this school. One type strives for precision in explaining what language means for those who use it. Korner (1969, p. 26) labels this "exhibition-analysis" because its aim is "to exhibit the meanings of expressions used by a group of speakers and thinkers." The second type—"replacement-analysis"—goes beyond making meanings and rules of language explicit. The aim of replacement-analysis

> is to replace a concept or set of concepts, which is in some ways defective, by another concept or set of concepts, which is free from these defects, but nevertheless preserves those features which are useful and desirable. (Korner, 1969, p. 29)

Actual steps involved in analyzing language usage employ standard tools of logic such as pointing out fallacies, establishing criteria for truth and falsehood, and defining terms. In addition, linguistic analysts have developed conventions or procedures of their own. Specifically, the type of question being asked is determined, cases that exemplify the concept are sought, and a definition that best reflects the concept's usage is given.

Analysts first determine what type of question is being raised. There are questions of fact—How many millions of dollars are spent on training adults each year? —and questions of value—Is training the same as education? Philosophical analysis concerns itself with questions of concept. Once these have been answered, questions of fact and value become easier to answer. If, for example, we can distinguish training from education, then the extent of training becomes easier to assess. Likewise, if we know exactly what training is, we might more readily determine who should participate.

In analyzing concepts, researchers turn to model cases, contrary cases, and borderline cases. Model cases are those instances "in which the concept is used in such a way that everyone would agree that this is a good use of the concept" (Elias & Merriam, 1980, p. 184). Everyone would agree, for example, that General Motors, Bell Telephone, and the Army "train" their employees. Contrary cases are those instances where the term cannot be used. We do not think of a church as "training" its adult members. Borderline cases are situations in which a concept is stretched or applied beyond its common usage. We might say that faculty members at a particular college are being trained to use computers, but it has an odd ring to it. One would be more likely to say that faculty are *learning* to use computers.

Concepts can also be ambiguous—that is, have several meanings—or they can be vague—that is, have varying degrees of a quality. For example, "program" has several meanings and is therefore classified as ambiguous, whereas "age" is a vague concept because it refers to a quality that exists in degrees. By exposing ambiguity and vagueness in language, linguistic analysts bring clarity to thinking and to everyday activity.

Conceptual clarity is the presumed end product of language analysis. As noted above, some thinkers prefer to "exhibit" the essential meaning or definition or criteria of a concept. Others may find it necessary to go a step further and "replace" a defective concept with a better one. Definitions of concepts can be stipulative, descriptive, or programmatic. A stipulative definition specifies the ways in which a term or concept is to be used. Descriptive definitions explain the common usage of a term. Programmatic definitions "overtly or implicitly" reveal "what should be done rather than what is done" (Elias & Merriam, 1980, p. 186).

In discussing questions, models, and definitions, we have attempted to introduce the reader to some of the techniques linguistic analysts employ in doing research. The techniques of this particular school of philosophy can be applied to any area of human endeavor. Several writers have, in fact, extensively analyzed the field of adult education from this perspective. Two British analysts, Lawson (1975) and Paterson (1977), have done pioneering work in analyzing such fundamental concepts in adult education as adult training, the teaching-learning process, and adult education. One American philosopher, Monette (1979), has published articles analyzing the concept of need in adult education and training. His philosophical analysis of the literature of need reveals that the field has had an overly technical preoccupation with meeting needs to the exclusion of political and ethical considerations.

There are many concepts yet to be analyzed—"lifelong learning," "accountability," "community education," and "adult development" are but a few examples. The value of this type of research is tested by the extent to which it can bring clarity to conceptual confusion and the extent to which such clarity affects the practice of a field.

PHENOMENOLOGY

Phenomenologists also deal with language and, on occasion, engage in an analysis of concepts or linguistic expressions as part of their inquiry. Stanage (1987, p. 53) points out that linguistic phenomenology "is a way of articulating as precisely as possible the distinctions within what adults say in direct investigation and descriptions of phenomena which we feel, experience, and conscious (know-with)." Rather than an end in itself, however, linguistic analysis for a phenomenologist is "merely preparatory to the study of the referents, i.e., of the phenomena meant by the expressions. Phenomenological analysis, then, is analysis of the phenomena themselves, not of the expressions that refer to them" (Spiegelberg, 1965, p. 669). Language is thus an insufficient basis for studying phenomena: too many dimensions of life and experience cannot be captured by language.

Phenomenologists are also dissatisfied with modern science's efforts to categorize, simplify, and reduce phenomena to abstract laws for theories. Rather, phenomenology is expansive as it seeks to deepen our level of consciousness and broaden our range of experiences. Phenomenology requires us to go directly " 'to the things themselves' . . . to turn toward phenomena which had been blocked from sight by the theoretical patterns in front of them" (Speigelberg, 1965, p. 658). Phenomenologists are interested in showing how complex meanings are built out of simple units of direct experience. This form of inquiry is an attempt to deal with inner experiences unprobed in everyday life. Such an arena, phenomenologists feel, has been abandoned by science as too subjective. Common in phenomenology are descriptive studies concerned with the themes of perception, intention, time-consciousness, and the origin of experiences and the relationship among experiences.

That phenomenological research lends itself to applied fields of study is evidenced by several investigations. In one study, adult learning was explored from the perspective of the inner experiences of adults and their reflections upon experiences with learning (Bates, 1979). In another study, the theoretical basis for the practice of competency-based education was investigated phenomenologically (Collins, 1987). In a third example, "throwing like a girl" and other "feminine" body movements were analyzed (Young, 1980). Finally, Stanage's book on *Adult Education and Phenomenological Research* (1987) deals with "the four fundamental questions, Who Am I?, What Can I Know?, What Ought I To Do?, What May I Hope?, as vital questions in the lives of adults" (p. 3). These questions are addressed in his book by considering definitions of adult education, by reflecting upon the meaning of being an adult, by clarifying what phenomenology is and what scientific methods are, and how all of this relates to problems of curriculum and methods in adult education practice.

The "data" of a phenomenological investigation are phenomena, or more precisely, the conscious experience of phenomena. "Phenomena" includes both the acts—such as thinking, believing, perceiving—and the things to which these acts are related—such as ideas or material objects. Experience is thus "intentional," that is, directed upon some object. One does not, for example, merely experience fear or love, but rather one experiences fear or love *of* something, such as fear of heights or love of beauty. Beliefs about the reality of objects are held in abeyance; no preconceived theories or presuppositions are allowed to determine the analysis of the experience itself. The basic method for this type of research is "seeing" or "intuiting" or "reflecting" upon one's experiences. Its objective is "to trace the elements and structure of the phenomena obtained by intuiting" (Spiegelberg, 1965, p. 669).

Essential to the method of phenomenology are the pure description of inner experiences and something Edmund Husserl, founder of phenomenology, calls "phenomenological reduction." This involves the suspension of one's natural attitude or beliefs toward the world and everyday activities (Korner, 1969). The reality of our world "is not denied but temporarily 'put into brackets' " (Collins, 1981, p. 5). In suspending our beliefs, consciousness *itself* becomes heightened, and can then be examined rather than examining the object of consciousness. While the description of inner experience and the suspension of our attitude toward that experience are essential characteristics of phenomenology, the process of phenomenological inquiry involves several specific steps. Spiegelberg describes how phenomenology arrives at "systematic and intersubjective knowledge":

> it does so by (a) describing first what is subjectively experienced ('intuited') insofar as it is experienced, whether real or not (the 'pure phenomenon') in its typical structure and relations ('essences' and 'essential relations'), and by (b) paying special attention to its modes of appearance and the ways in which it constitutes itself in consciousness. (1975, p. 112)

If, for example, we were to try to phenomenologically analyze our own learning, we would first describe what is "subjectively experienced," such as the setting, the feelings, and reactions to the content involved. In attending to its "modes of appearing," we might see that learning involves a sensory experience, a mental activity, and/or an emotional dimension. Finally, the ways in which learning "constitutes itself in consciousness" involve tracing the sequence of steps through which learning establishes itself or takes shape in our consciousness. Perhaps there is first an interest in the nature of the thing being learned, then there might be the gathering of information about the thing to be learned, then an organization of the information in the mind, and so on.

Spiegelberg (1965, pp. 659–700) presents seven steps in the phenomenological method, which include the above activities. While all phenomenologists would not agree with all seven or the order in which they are listed, the steps do offer us some glimpse into the rigor of a phenomenological inquiry.

- Step 1. Investigating Particular Phenomena. This step includes "the intuitive grasp of the phenomena, their analytic examination, and their description" (p. 659).
- Step 2. Investigating General Essences. Here we intuit the general essence of the phenomena being investigated. We can look at particular examples before or simultaneously with intuiting the general essences (several instances of learning can lead to a sense of its general essence, for example).
- Step 3. Apprehending Essential Relationships Among Essences. Here we assess whether the components of the internal relations within an essence are essential and in what way there are relationships between several essences.
- Step 4. Watching Modes of Appearing. This is the "systematic exploration of the phenomena not only in the sense of *what* appears, whether particulars or general essences, but also of the way

in which things appear" (p. 684).
- Step 5. Exploring the Constitution of Phenomena in Consciousness. At this stage we analyze how a phenomenon has come into our consciousness.
- Step 6. Suspending Belief in Existence of the Phenomena. This is the same as "bracketing" the phenomena, of suspending judgment as to its existence or qualities.
- Step 7. Interpreting the Meaning of Phenomena. Once the experience has been brought into consciousness and analyzed, an attempt is made to grasp the meaning of the experience.

In summarizing phenomenological inquiry, Spiegelberg highlights some of its characteristic features that set it apart from other forms of philosophical inquiry. In the words of Spiegelberg:

> One might describe the underlying unity of the phenomenological procedures as the unusually obstinate attempt to look at the phenomena and to remain faithful to them before even thinking about them . . . What distinguishes phenomenology from other methods is not so much any particular step it develops or adds to them but the spirit of philosophical reverence as the first and foremost notion of the philosophical enterprise. (1965, pp. 700–701)

CONCLUSION

This chapter has discussed the nature and techniques of two research methodologies—historical inquiry and philosophical inquiry. Both are foundational methods in the sense that each is concerned with fundamental questions of human existence. History turns to the past for an explanation of how things have come to be as they are. Philosophy applies the mind to itself or to some other phenomenon in grappling with the nature of human existence. Both forms of inquiry are foundational in a second sense: they provide a means for exploring the foundations of a discipline or field of study. Historical inquiry asks what happened and what meaning the past has for the present. Philosophical inquiry asks what assumptions, values, or ideas constitute the framework by which human behavior can be understood. In applied fields of study, historical and philosophical research can have very practical ramifications. Knowing how something was done in the past, why it was done the way it was, can clarify present practice and shape future practice. Likewise, understanding the assumptions and values upon which everyday activity rests can permeate even the most mundane daily activities with a sense of purpose and vision.

REFERENCES

Adams, J. T. (1944). *Frontiers of American culture: A study of adult education in a democracy.* New York: Charles Scribner's Sons.
Barraclough, G. (1978). *Main trends in history.* New York: Holmes & Meier.
Barzun, J., (1974). *Clio and the doctors.* Chicago: University of Chicago Press.
Barzun, J. & Graff, H. F. (1957). *The modern researcher.* New York: Harcourt, Brace & World.
Bates, H. (1979). A phenomenological approach to the study of experience. *Proceedings of the Adult Education Research Conference.* Ann Arbor, MI.
Beringer, R. E. (1978). *Historical analysis: Contemporary approaches to Clio's craft.* New York: John Wiley & Sons. Reprint (1986). Malabar, FL: Krieger Publishing Co.
Carlson, R. (1980). Humanistic historical research. In H. B. Long, R. Hiemstra, & Associates (Eds.), *Changing approaches to studying of adult education* (pp. 41–49). San Francisco: Jossey-Bass.
Carlson, R. A. (1981, November). *Philosophical and historical research: The importance of a humanistic orientation in adult education.* Paper presented in Finland and available from the author, University of Saskatchewan, Saskatoon, Saskatchewan, Canada.
Collins, M. (1981, February). *Phenomenological perspectives in adult continuing education: Implications for research and practice.* Paper presented at the Lifelong Learning Conference, College Park, MD.
Collins, M. (1982). Competency in adult education: Applying a theory of relevance (Doctoral dissertation, Northern Illinois University, 1980). *Dissertation Abstracts International, 42,* 54A.
Collins, M. (1987). *Competence in adult education: A new perspective.* Lanham, MD: University Press of America.
Commager, H. S. (1965). *The nature and the study of history.* Columbus, OH: C. E. Merrill.
Curtis, L. P. (1970). *The historian's workshop: Original essays by sixteen historians.* New York: Alfred A. Knopf.
Donald, D. (1956). *Lincoln reconsidered: Essays on the Civil War era.* New York: Alfred A. Knopf.
Elias, J., & Merriam, S. (1980). *Philosophical foundations of adult education.* Malabar, FL: Krieger.
Erikson, E. (1958). *Young man Luther: A study in psychoanalysis and history.* New York: W. W. Norton.

Felt, T. E. (1976). *Researching, writing and publishing local history,* Nashville: American Association for State and Local History.

Gottschalk, L. (1963). *Understanding history.* New York: Alfred A. Knopf.

Halle, L. J. (1982). The historian's vocation. *Manas, 35,* 1–2,7.

Johnstone, H. W. (Ed.). (1965). *What is philosophy?.* New York: Macmillan.

Knowles, M. (1962). *The adult education movement in the United States.* New York: Holt, Rinehart & Winston.

Korner, S. (1969). *What is philosophy?.* London: Allen Lane.

Kurtz, P. (Ed.). (1966). *American philosophy in the twentieth century.* New York: Macmillan.

Lawson, K. G. (1975). *Philosophical concepts and values in adult education.* Nottingham, UK: Barnes & Humby.

Lemisch, J. (1969). Listening to the 'inarticulate.' *Journal of Social History, 3,* 1–29.

Matczak, S. (1975). *Philosophy: Its nature, methods and basic sources.* New York: Learned Publications.

McKeon, R. (1965). Philosophy and method. In H. W. Johnstone (Ed.). *What is philosophy?* (pp. 93–97). New York: Macmillan.

Mead, H. (1962). *Types and problems of philosophy* (3rd ed.). New York: Holt, Rinehart & Winston.

Monette, M. (1979). Need assessment: A critique of philosophical assumptions. *Adult Education, 29,* 83–95.

Paterson, R. W. K. (1977). *Values, education and the adult.* Boston: Routledge, Kegan, Paul.

Rockhill, K. (1976). The past as prologue: Toward an expanded view of adult education. *Adult Education, 26,* 196–208.

Rohfeld, R. W. (1989). Preparing World War I soldiers for peacetime: The Army's university in France. *Adult Education Quarterly, 39,* 187–198.

Rohfeld, R. W. (1990). James Harvey Robinson: Historian as adult educator. *Adult Education Quarterly, 40,* 219–228.

Rose, A. D. (1982, March). *The history of adult education: Questions of context and utility.* Paper presented at the Mini-Conference on Historical Research in Adult Education, Adult Education Research Conference, Lincoln, NE.

Rose, A. D. (1989). Beyond classroom walls: The Carnegie Corporation and the founding of the American Association for Adult Education. *Adult Education Quarterly, 39,* 140–151.

Rose, A. D. (1991). Preparing for veterans: Higher education and the efforts to accredit the learning of World War II servicemen and women. *Adult Education Quarterly, 42,* 30–45.

Scheffler, I. (1960). *The language of education.* Springfield, IL: Charles Thomas.

Seller, M. (1978). Success and failure in adult education: The immigrant experience. *Adult Education, 28,* 83–99.

Spiegelberg, H. A. (1965). *The phenomenological movement* (Vol. 2). The Hague, Netherlands: Martinus Nijhoff.

Spiegelberg, H. A. (1975). *Doing phenomenology.* The Hague, Netherlands: Martinus Nijhoff.

Stanage, S. (1987). *Adult education and phenomenological research.* Malabar, FL: Robert E. Krieger.

Stubblefield, H. W. (1988). *Toward a history of adult education in America.* New York: Routledge, Chapman & Hall.

Stubblefield, H. W., & Rachal, J. R. (1992). On the origins of the term and meanings of "adult education" in the United States. *Adult Education Quarterly 42,* 106–116.

Young, I. M. (1980). Throwing like a girl: A phenomenology of feminine body comportment, motility and spatiality. *Human Studies, 3*(2), 137–156.

CHAPTER 6

MEANING AND INTERPRETATION: QUALITATIVE METHODS

Rather than determining cause and effect, predicting, or describing the distribution of some attribute among a population, researchers may want to uncover the meaning of a phenomenon for those involved. Qualitative methods allow us to do just that. Qualitative methods are especially well suited for investigations in applied fields such as adult education and training because we want to improve practice. The improvement of practice comes from understanding the experiences of those involved. Further, applied fields often lack well-developed theories from which hypotheses can be deduced and tested; qualitative research is an inductive strategy which allows us develop theory. This chapter will first present an overview of qualitative research, including the philosophical assumptions upon which it is based. Second, three major types of qualitative research—ethnography, case study, and grounded theory—will be discussed.

COMMON CHARACTERISTICS

We use the term *qualitative research* to cover a number of research strategies that share some common characteristics. In addition to the three types noted above, qualitative research has also been termed naturalistic inquiry, interpretive research, field study, phenomenological research, participant observation, and inductive research. The key philosophical assumption upon which all types of qualitative research are based, is the view that reality is constructed by individuals in interaction with their social worlds. Thus, there are many "realities" rather than the one, observable, measurable reality which is key to research based in the positivist paradigm (see Chapter 4).

Drawing from phenomenology and symbolic interaction in particular, qualitative researchers are interested in how people interpret their experiences, how they construct their worlds, what meaning they attribute to their experiences. The overall purposes of qualitative research are to achieve an *understanding* of how people make sense out of their lives, to delineate the process (rather than the outcome or product) of meaning-making, and to describe how people interpret what they experience.

In all forms of qualitative research, the *researcher is the primary instrument* for data collection and analysis. Since understanding is a key goal of this research, the human instrument, which is able to be immediately responsive and adaptive, would seem to be the ideal instrument for collecting and analyzing data. Guba and Lincoln (1981) point out that in addition to responsiveness and adaptability, the researcher as primary instrument is also able to: consider the total context of the phenomenon, rather than a particular segment; immediately process data as it is being collected, leading, if necessary, to refining data collection procedures; clarify and summarize material, checking with respondents for accuracy of interpretation; explore atypical or idiosyncratic responses. Of this last ability they write,

> within the boundaries of standardized inquiry the atypical or idiosyncratic response would be lost, masked, or treated as a statistical deviation . . . The ability to encounter such responses and to utilize them for increased understanding is possible, in fact only with human . . . instruments. (p. 138)

Being the primary instrument for data collection and analysis carries with it a responsibility to identify one's shortcomings and biases that might impact the study. One does this not to make a qualitative study more "objective," but to understand how one's subjectivity shapes the investigation and its findings. Peshkin (1988, p. 55), in fact, points out that subjectivity "can be seen as virtuous, for it is the basis of researchers' making a distinctive contribution, one that results from the unique configuration of their personal qualities joined to the data they have collected."

Another characteristic of qualitative research is that it usually involves *field work*. The researcher physically goes to the site, the group of people, the institution, "the field" to collect data. This is, of course, always the case in anthropology where the intent is to learn about people of different cultures. Field work involves becoming intimately familiar with the phenomenon under study, whether it be a case study of a single individual or a grounded theory study of a complex social interaction. Occasionally, qualitative studies have been conducted using written documents alone, but these are the exceptions.

Finally, qualitative research is primarily an *inductive research strategy*. As mentioned above, qualitative research is a particularly appropriate strategy to use where there is little knowledge about the problem. If there is a lack of theory, or if existing theory does not adequately explain the phenomenon, hypotheses cannot be used to structure an investigation. Rather, the researcher goes into the field with the intent of discovering the meaning a phenomenon has for those involved. What is uncovered is mediated through the researcher's own perspective, resulting in an interpretation, description, or explanation of the phenomenon. Typically, the researcher presents the findings in the form of categories, typologies, concepts, working hypotheses, even theory, which have been inductively derived from the data.

THE DESIGN OF A QUALITATIVE STUDY

Your beliefs about the nature of reality and about how knowledge is constructed, in addition to the problem you have identified and the question(s) you seek to answer, determine the selection of your research design. If you want to understand a phenomenon, uncover the meaning a situation has for those involved, or delineate process—how things happen—then a qualitative design would be most appropriate. Most problem areas can be shaped to reflect these goals. For example, if you were interested in how to retain students in adult basic education programs, you could identify a program with a high retention rate and conduct a qualitative case study of that program, delineating those factors which seem to contribute to its success in retaining students. In another example, a researcher identified the problem area as how women executives have managed to be successful in a work setting (corporate America) that has not been particularly conducive to their advancement (Bierema, 1993). The researcher could have identified barriers and strategies from the literature and from her personal experience and surveyed women executives in Fortune 500 companies. However, she was more interested in how these women themselves perceived how they learned to succeed in a white male-dominated culture and undertook a qualitative study to address that purpose.

Once one has formulated a problem statement and research purpose (see Chapter 2) that is best addressed from a qualitative perspective, the next step is to select a sample and then collect data. Sample selection in qualitative research is purposeful. Since you are interested in the in-depth understanding of those who know the most (rather than the average opinion of the many), you select a purposeful sample. A purposeful sample, according to Patton (1990), is one from which you can learn the most; it is an "information-rich" case. In Bierema's study above, she selected high-level executive women in Fortune 500 companies to interview. She was not interested in the secondhand opinions of others about how woman in the organization had become successful. (For more on sample selection in qualitative research see LeCompte & Preissle, 1993; Merriam, 1988; Patton, 1990).

There are three basic ways to collect data in qualitative research. Interviewing is probably the most used in qualitative studies in adult education and training. Interviews range from highly structured, where specific questions and the order in which they are asked are determined ahead of time, to unstructured where one has topic areas to explore but neither the questions nor the order are predetermined. Most interviews fall somewhere in between in what is known as the semi-structured interview (Merriam, 1988). A second major means of collecting data is through observation. Like interviewing, there is a range here also from being a complete observer to being an active participant. A complete observer is unknown to those being observed, such as from behind a one-way mirror or in a public place. A very active participant observer might be someone who is a member of the group or organization who is thus participating while observing. A third major source of data is documents (written, oral, and visual) and artifacts. These are a natural source of information and usually already exist within the context of the study (interoffice memos, mission statements, press releases, student papers, photographs, to name a few). Documents can also be researcher-generated as when an investigator asks participants to keep logs or diaries regarding the phenomenon of interest.

In qualitative research, data are analyzed *simultaneously* during collection. That is, one analyzes data as they are being collected. This allows the researcher to make adjustments along the way, even to the point of redirecting data collection, and to "test" emerging concepts, themes, hypotheses. There are several strategies for data analysis, the most common being the constant comparative method discussed under grounded theory further in this chapter (see also Merriam, 1988; Miles & Huberman, 1994; Patton, 1990; Strauss, 1987; Wolcott, 1994).

The final step in a qualitative study is writing up the findings. While this is covered regarding research in general in Chapter 9, some points can be made about writing up qualitative research in particular. There is a standard format for writing up a research study that can be generally followed for qualitative research. However, since findings are usually in the form of words rather than numbers, it is sometimes difficult to know how much supporting data to include versus interpretation and analysis. Probably the best rule-of-thumb is to be sure to present as much data in the form of quotes from interviews, episodes from field observations, or documentary evidence to adequately and convincingly support your findings. In qualitative research it is the rich, thick descriptions, the words (not numbers) that persuade the reader of the trustworthiness of your findings. Nevertheless, in any report, there is tension between having the right amount of supporting data versus analysis and interpretation. A second problem is finding the right "voice" to present your findings. In qualitative research, writeups can vary from intimate, first-person accounts to more formal presentations (see Van Maanen, 1988; Wolcott, 1990). Reading a number of reports of qualitative research might be helpful in striking a balance between these two components.

VALIDITY AND RELIABILITY

Both producers and consumers of research want to be assured that the findings of an investigation are to be believed and trusted. In applied fields where practitioners intervene in people's lives, it is particularly important that new practices derived from research are solidly supported. Thus issues of validity and reliability are important considerations in any kind of research. But how one views validity and reliability in qualitative research differs somewhat from positivist research. Following is a brief discussion of internal validity, reliability, and external validity or generalizability and the strategies that can be employed to ensure for each (for fuller discussions see Firestone, 1993; Guba & Lincoln, 1981; Merriam, 1988).

Internal validity asks the question, How congruent are one's findings with reality? In quantitative research this question is usually construed as, Are we observing or measuring what we think we are observing or measuring? The question hinges on our understanding of reality and as was discussed earlier, qualitative inquiry assumes that there are multiple, changing realities. Reality is constructed by individuals. Thus in qualitative research the understanding of reality is really the researcher's interpretation of someone else's interpretation. Because qualitative researchers are the primary instruments for data collection and analysis, interpretations of reality are accessed directly through observations and interviews. We are "closer" to reality than if an instrument had been interjected between the researcher and the researched. For this reason, internal validity is considered a strength of qualitative research.

To ensure that we are getting as close to reality as possible, we can use several strategies: (1) triangulation - the use of multiple investigators, multiple sources of data, or multiple methods to confirm the emerging findings (Mathison, 1988); (2) member checks - taking data collected from study participants and your tentative interpretations of these data back to the people from whom they were derived, asking if the data "ring true"; (3) peer/colleague examination - asking colleagues to examine your data and to comment on the plausibility of the emerging findings; (4) statement of researcher's experiences, assumptions, biases; and (5) submersion/engagement in the research situation - collecting data over a long enough period of time to ensure an in-depth understanding of the phenomenon.

Reliability asks the question of the extent to which one's findings will be found again. That is, if the inquiry is replicated, would the findings be the same? In social science, the notion of reliability is problematic because human behavior is never static, nor is what many experience necessarily more reliable than what one person experiences. Consider the magician who can fool the audience of hundreds, but not the stagehand watching from the wings. Replication of a qualitative study will not yield the same results but this does not discredit the results of any particular study; there can be numerous interpretations of the same data. The more important question for qualitative researchers is *whether the results are consistent with the data collected*. Guba and Lincoln (1981), in fact, prefer to think of reliability as consistency or dependability.

There are at least three strategies one can use to ensure consistency. Triangulation and peer examination, defined above, can be used. The third, suggested by Guba and Lincoln (1981), is the audit trail. The audit trail operates on the same premise as when an auditor verifies the accounts of a business. "In order for an audit to take place, the investigator must describe in detail how data were collected, how categories were derived, and how decisions were made throughout the inquiry" (Merriam, 1988, p. 172).

External validity, or the extent to which findings can be generalized to other situations, has been the source of much debate in the qualitative research literature (Firestone, 1993). Findings cannot be generalized in the statistical sense, that is, from a sample to a population. However, generalizability can be viewed as something different than this. Some authors think empirical generalizations are too lofty a goal for social science; instead we should think in terms of *working hypotheses*. In qualitative research one might end up with working hypotheses—hypotheses that reflect situation-specific conditions in a particular context. While there are other ways to think of generalizability, the most common conception is *reader or user generalizability*. In this view, the extent to which findings from an investigation can be applied to other situations is determined by the people in those situations. It is not up to the researcher to speculate how findings can be applied to other settings; it is up to the consumer of the research.

As with internal validity and reliability, there are strategies one can employ to strengthen this aspect of rigor. Thick description is most often cited. This involves providing enough information/description so that readers will be able to determine how closely their situations match the research situation, and hence, whether findings can be transferred. Multisite designs is another strategy. The use of several sites, cases, situations, especially those representing some variation, will allow the results to be applied to a greater range of other situations. Modal comparison is a third strategy that involves describing how typical the program, event, or sample is compared with the majority of others in the same class. Finally, one could randomly sample within the phenomenon being studied since there may be numerous component parts (teachers, administrators, students in a school system, for example), each of which could be sampled for inclusion in the study.

In summary, the trustworthiness of the findings of a study with a small, nonrandom sample is dependent upon the internal validity, reliability, and external validity of the study. As discussed above, there are ways to view each of these concerns that are congruent with the underlying assumptions and worldview of qualitative research. Likewise, there are strategies that investigators can employ to ensure for each of these components of rigor.

THREE TYPES OF QUALITATIVE RESEARCH

As mentioned earlier in the chapter, qualitative research is an umbrella term that covers several distinct forms of qualitative research. Three of the most common are ethnography, case study, and grounded theory. A fourth common form, phenomenology, is discussed in Chapter 5 under philosophical inquiry. The three to be discussed here all draw upon the same assumptions and worldview and are characterized by (1) the goal of research being understanding, (2) the researcher being the primary instrument of data collection and analysis, (3) fieldwork (in most instances), and (4) the inductive building of concepts, themes, categories, hypotheses, or theories. Each approach is distinguishable from the other two, however. A more detailed discussion of each method's purposes and procedures follows.

ETHNOGRAPHY

Ethnography is the research methodology developed by anthropologists to study human society and culture. Recently the term *ethnography* has been used interchangeably with *field study, case study, naturalistic inquiry, qualitative research,* and *participant observation.* Anthropologists and others familiar with ethnography, however, do not find these terms interchangeable. The term *ethnography* has two distinct meanings. Ethnography is (1) a set of methods or techniques used to collect data and (2) the written record that is the *product* of using ethnographic techniques.

Ethnographic techniques are the methods researchers use to uncover the social order and meaning a setting or situation has for the people actually participating in it. The five procedures commonly used in this type of investigation are participant observation, in-depth interviewing, life history, documentary analysis, and investigator diaries (records of the researcher's experiences and impressions). Employing any one of these procedures involves going into the field, "immersing oneself in a collective way of life for the purpose of gaining firsthand knowledge about some facet of it" (Shaffir et al., 1980, p. 6). Fieldwork involves entering the chosen setting, establishing rapport with the residents of that setting, maintaining some type of relationship with the subjects, and, finally, leaving the setting. What comes to mind here is the archetypical anthropologist who travels to exotic places, lives with the people for a period of time, and returns home to write an account of their cultural norms and social practices. Not all ethnographic researchers travel to foreign places, however. Much fieldwork has been conducted with particular social groups within the ethnographer's own society. In the United States, ethnographic studies have been published on many segments of society including ghetto dwellers, coal miners, and suburban housewives.

Participant observation is the cornerstone technique of ethnography, and a researcher might assume any of several variations of this technique. Junker (1960, pp. 35–38) describes four variations:

1. Complete participant. The researcher becomes a member of the group being studied, concealing the fact that he or she is observing as well as participating.
2. Participant as observer. The observer's activities are not concealed but are secondary to activities as a participant.
3. Observer as participant. The role of observer is publicly known, and participation becomes a secondary activity.
4. Complete observer. The observer is invisible to the activity (as in the case of a one-way mirror or hidden camera) or tries to become unnoticed (camera crews that live with their subjects, classroom observers).

The role assumed depends upon the type of information being sought and the idiosyncracies of the group being investigated. The researcher's role can also shift during the process of the investigation. In an interesting account of her firsthand experiences in a home for the aged, Posner (1980) relates how she moved from being a participant observer as a volunteer worker, to complete participant as a programmer, to the stance of observer participant.

Participant observation is a time-consuming and demanding technique. One must establish rapport and trust with a group and become familiar enough to gain insights into the meaning of their lives. At the same time, one must be an observer, remaining as objective as possible while collecting information. This schizophrenic condition is exacerbated by medical problems, ethical issues, and the psychological stress inherent in employing a relatively unstructured research procedure in unfamiliar settings (Shaffir et al., 1980, p. 18). Indeed, several writers have commented upon the lack of description of fieldwork techniques and the lack of guidelines for conducting fieldwork (Berreman, 1968; Pelto, 1970; Shaffir et al., 1980). Pelto (1970) recommends that

> any extensive discussion of the art of fieldwork should include (among other things) sections on selection of informants, on gifts and payments, on when to take notes, on tactics with photographic equipment, on interactions with outsiders, on the giving of parties, on when to break taboos, and on many other subjects related to the central issue of 'impression management.' (p. 225)

Another ethnographic technique used in fieldwork—interviewing—has been described and refined in recent years. Prospective researchers can take courses in interviewing techniques, or they can read about the technique in the many books and articles on the topic. An interview is a "conversation with a purpose" (Dexter, 1970, p. 136). In ethnographic research, interviewing usually follows, or is integrated with, participant observation. Observations will often reveal which persons are important to interview as well as the type of information the researcher wants to extract in the interview. Interviewing is an indispensable tool in certain situations. "The ability to tap into the experience of others in their own natural language, while utilizing their value and belief frameworks, is virtually impossible without face-to-face and verbal interaction with them" (Guba & Lincoln, 1981, p. 155).

There are several types of interviews that can be employed in an investigation: team and panel interviewing, covert or overt interviewing, oral history interviewing, structured and unstructured interviewing (Guba & Lincoln, 1981). In most ethnographic studies, interviews are open ended or loosely structured so that the respondents' views of the topic can be obtained. By using an open-ended format, investigators hope to avoid predetermining the subjects' responses and, hence, their "views" of reality. Interviewing as a data collection technique is discussed more fully in Chapter 8.

Occasionally interviewing key informants (people who have a great amount of knowledge and can conceptualize their group's norms and beliefs) leads to the collection of life histories. Life histories are intensive autobiographical studies of selected members of the sociocultural group under study. "The richness and personalized nature of life histories afford a vividness and integration of cultural information that are of great value for understanding particular life ways" (Pelto, 1970, p. 99).

In addition to using participant observations, interviews, and life histories, an ethnographer may want to evaluate all available documents on the phenomenon being studied. As a resource, documents and records often (1) are easily accessible, low-cost, or free; (2) "constitute a legally unassailable base from which to defend oneself against allegations"; (3) represent the context of the research problem; (4) may be more objective sources of information than an interview; and (5) provide a base for further inquiry (Guba & Lincoln, 1981, pp. 232–234).

Fieldworkers are also encouraged to keep a diary (in addition to fieldnotes) of each day's happenings and record personal feelings, ideas, impressions, or insights with regard to those events. This diary becomes a source of data and allows researchers to trace their own development and biases throughout the course of the investigation.

From the foregoing description of ethnographic techniques, the role of investigator as instrument emerges as a paramount consideration. Several writers have elaborated on the personal qualities essential in a researcher who intends doing ethnographic research. Most suggest that the researcher needs to be empathetic, bright, flexible, energetic, imaginative, and adventuresome. Guba and Lincoln (1981), commenting on the many lists of desirable attributes, note that a person who possessed all of the suggested qualities

> not only could be a good inquirer but undoubtedly would make a good president, a fine doctor, another Margaret Mead, or could lead the United Nations to a peaceful resolution of world conflict . . . They are above all human beings who attend carefully to the social and behavioral signals of others and who find others intrinsically interesting. Many of these skills can be taught; others can be continuously cultivated and refined. (pp. 144–145)

The centrality of the investigator in ethnographic research has remained untouched even with the introduction of quantitative research methods. Statistical tools have become important aids in gathering demographic information, in assessing the magnitude and regularity of certain cultural behaviors and values, and in evaluating the strength of relationships among cultural phenomenon. But, as Mitchell (1967) points out,

> The fieldwork data, quantitative or qualitative, which social anthropologists use to base their conclusions on are all derived ultimately from observation. From this point of view there is no essential difference in the two types of data. Quantification has no magical property to confer accuracy on the data: if the basic observations are inaccurate or incomplete, statistics derived from them will assuredly also reflect those weaknesses. What quantification achieves is a condensation of facts so that the regularities and patterns in them are more easily discernible. (pp. 25–26)

The techniques of ethnography—participant observation and interviewing in particular—have been adopted by people in applied fields of study where research problems or questions have warranted an exploratory, rather than hypothesis-testing, approach. However, anthropologists take issue with educators and others who use ethnographic techniques and then think they are doing ethnography. For ethnography is more than techniques; it is also an account of the data, an account that interprets the data within a sociocultural framework. Ethnography has as its intent the interpretation of a situation that incorporates the participants' symbolic meanings and ongoing patterns of social interaction. Concern with the cultural context is what distinguishes ethnography from grounded theory—which builds theory—and case study—which describes and interprets a situation or social unit from the perspective of the researcher. Wolcott (1980) makes this distinction between technique and account:

> Specific ethnographic techniques are freely available to any researcher who wants to approach a problem or setting descriptively. It is the essential anthropological concern for cultural context that distinguishes ethnographic method from fieldwork techniques and makes genuine ethnography distinct from other 'on-site-observer' approaches. And when cultural interpretation is the goal, the ethnographer must be thinking like an anthropologist, not just looking like one. (p. 59)

Many of the same techniques of ethnography are used in case studies and grounded theory studies. Case study and grounded theory approaches do not have as a major focus sociocultural interpretation and so are even more useful to educators and trainers of adults who wish to conduct exploratory research within their field of practice.

CASE STUDY

The case study is an intensive description and analysis of a phenomenon or social unit such as an individual, group, institution, or community. In contrast to surveying a few variables across a large number of units, a case study tends to be concerned with investigating many, if not all, variables in a single unit. By concentrating upon a single phenomenon or entity ("the case"), this approach seeks to uncover the interplay of significant factors that is characteristic of the phenomenon. The case study seeks holistic description and interpretation. "The content of a case study is determined chiefly by its purpose, which typically is to reveal the properties of the class to which the instance being studied belongs" (Guba & Lincoln, 1981, p. 371). If conducted over a period of time, the case study may be longitudinal; thus, changes over time become one of the variables of interest. Other case studies are concerned with describing a phenomenon as it exists at a particular time.

Unlike ethnography, which has been associated with only one discipline in particular, the case study method can be appropriately used in many fields. There are legal case studies, medical case studies, psychological case studies, and social case studies; there are even anthropological case studies of primitive cultures. Perhaps because of its widespread use, case study is sometimes confused with the terms *case work, case method,* and *case history*. Case study, as defined above, refers to an intensive study of a particular social unit, whereas *case work* denotes "the developmental, adjustment, remedial, or corrective procedures that appropriately follow diagnosis of the causes of maladjustment" (Good & Scates, 1954, p. 729). *Case method* is an instructional technique whereby the major ingredients of a case study are presented to students for illustrative or problem-solving purposes. *Case history*—the tracing of a person, group, or institution's past—is sometimes part of a case study.

The case study is a basic design that can accommodate a variety of disciplinary perspectives (Merriam, 1988). In particular, case studies in education often draw upon concepts, theory, and research techniques from anthropology, history, sociology, and psychology. Thus a sociocultural analysis of a single social unit or phenomenon would produce an ethnographic case study, whereas a description of an institution, program or practice as it has evolved over time would be a historical case study.

One of the characteristics of the case study approach is its adaptability to different research problems in many fields of study. Merriam (1988, pp. 11–13) has delineated four essential properties of a qualitative case study. Case studies are:

1. Particularistic. Case studies focus on a particular situation, event, program, or phenomenon.
2. Descriptive. The end product of a case study is a rich description of the phenomenon under study.
3. Heuristic. Case studies illuminate the reader's understanding of the phenomenon under study. They can bring about the discovery of new meaning, extend the reader's experience, or confirm what is known.
4. Inductive. Qualitative case studies for the most part rely upon inductive reasoning for the formulation of concepts, generalizations, or tentative hypotheses.

The process of conducting a case study consists of several steps, the first of which is the selection of the "case" to be analyzed. The selection is done purposefully, not randomly; that is, a particular person, site, program, process, community, or any other social unit is selected because it exhibits characteristics of interest to the researcher. The next step is to collect raw data. A wide range of data-collection techniques can be used by the case study researcher; observation, interviewing, and document analysis are probably the most common, although surveys and other instruments are sometimes used, depending upon the unit under investigation.

As information from various sources is being collected, the researcher may begin aggregating, organizing, and classifying the data into manageable units. Data can be organized chronologically, categorically, or placed within a typology. Aggregation is a process of abstracting generalities from particulars, of looking for patterns characteristic of most of the pieces of data. Several publications give detailed instructions for organizing and analyzing data (Merriam, 1988; Miles & Huberman, 1994; Patton, 1990; Strauss, 1987; Wolcott, 1994). Following is the sequence of procedures described by Guba and Lincoln (1981): First, any item of information from interviews, observations, or documents should be abstracted onto index cards, the first card beginning the first pile; "the second card is then assessed to determine whether it is similar or different from the first. If it is similar, it is placed into the same pile, but if it is different, a new pile is formed" (p. 314). Each pile is then given a name that best reflects the content of the cards in that pile. This name becomes a category or concept central to the study. As new data are collected, these categories become refined and reinforced. New data may also necessitate the formation of a new pile, and thus a new category.

While the index card method detailed by Guba and Lincoln may sound cumbersome, it is a good representation of the process of inductive data analysis. Essentially, the researcher's task is to sort, analyze, and interpret the data collected in the study. This can be done with index cards as described, with zeroxed pages of data which can be sorted into labeled file folders, or with software programs. The use of computers in qualitative research has become quite common within the last decade or so (Fielding & Lee, 1991; Pfaffenberger, 1988; Tesch, 1990). Miles and Weitzman (in Miles & Huberman, 1994) in fact, review 22 different software programs designed for qualitative research. The vast majority of computer programs allow you to efficiently *manage* your data through coding, memoing, counting, searching, and retrieving; they do not analyze your data for you. The more sophisticated programs may allow you to link data through rule-based or logic-based formats, but the hard work of analysis, of figuring out how data might be linked and what it all means, still resides with the researcher.

The data organization procedure described above by Guba and Lincoln is essentially inductive and results in the uncovering of new categories and concepts. Maimon et al. (1981) make the suggestion that grouped observations might also be labeled according to theoretical concepts already present in the social sciences, for example, "in child development—sibling rivalry, attention-getting behavior, motor skills, language development; in sociology—alienation, conformity, deviance; in psychology—identity diffusion, depression; in political science—single-issue campaigning, fear mongering" (p. 225). Categories, concepts, and themes can thus be derived from the literature in an area, from an interpretation of the data by the researcher, or from exact words used by participants themselves (Constas, 1992).

Writing the case study narrative constitutes the final step in the process. The narrative is a highly readable, descriptive picture of a phenomenon or social entity. It should "take the reader into the case situation, a person's life, a group's life, or a program's life" (Patton, 1990, p. 386).

As with other research strategies, the case study has obvious strengths counterbalanced by limitations. The strengths of the case study approach are that it offers large amounts of rich, detailed information about a unity or phenomenon; it is useful as supporting information for planning major investigations in that it often reveals important variables or hypotheses that help structure further research; it allows researchers the flexibility to understand and even to answer questions about educational processes and problems. Some of the limitations of the case study are the following:

- Case studies can be expensive and time consuming.
- Training in observation and interviewing techniques and/or documentary analysis is necessary.
- Case study narratives tend to be lengthy documents, which policy makers and others have little time to read; also, writing the narrative to meet the needs of potential, though perhaps unknown, readers is a difficult task.
- Findings from case studies cannot be generalized in the same manner as findings from random samples; generalizability is related to what each user is trying to learn from the study.

In applied fields such as the education and training of adults, counseling, and vocational education, the case study has been used to describe and/or evaluate the efficacy of a new program or new approach to ongoing problems. For example, a multi-case study of in-service in innovative schools attempted to "determine the features of effective in-service and to establish the impact of these programs in terms of educational change at the school level" (van Tulder, van der Vegt, & Veenman, 1993, p. 129). Others have used the case study to explore aspects of practice not previously examined. Rowden's (1993) study of how human resource development functions in small to mid-size successful manufacturing businesses is an example as is Tisdell's (1993) study of power relations in adult higher education classes.

Finally, readers are referred to a case study by Zeph (1991) of a career enhancement award program for community-based adult educators. Data were collected through interviews with participants, through observations of three group seminars, and through reviewing documents related to the program including the participants' applications for the award. Zeph found that involvement in the program resulted in significant personal development, which she labeled "The Expanded Self," and significant career development, labeled "The Reflective Practitioner."

In summary, the case study is a particularly useful methodology for exploring an area of a field of practice not well researched or conceptualized. In-depth describing and understanding of a phenomenon are needed before generalizations can be made and tested. Case study, which has as its purpose the description and interpretation of a unit of interest, can result in abstractions and conceptualizations of the phenomenon that will guide subsequent studies.

GROUNDED THEORY

Grounded theory is a distinctive research methodology popularized in the late 1960s with the publication of Glaser and Strauss's book, *The Discovery of Grounded Theory* (1967). As with ethnography and case study, the investigator in a grounded theory study is the primary instrument of data collection and analysis, and the mode of investigation is characterized by inductive fieldwork rather than deductive hypothesis testing. The end result of a grounded theory study is the building of theory—theory that emerges from, or is "grounded" in, the data. Grounded theory research emphasizes discovery: description and verification are secondary concerns.

As a qualitative, exploratory methodology, grounded theory is particularly suited to investigating problems for which little theory has been developed. The explanation of an area of human interaction or a social process emerges from a grounded theory study as either substantive or formal theory. Substantive theory deals with phenomena limited to particular real-world situations such as nursing home care, the academic life of community college adult students, or the budgeting of community resources. Formal theory is more abstract and general (Weber's theory of bureaucracy, for example) and usually requires analysis of data from more than one substantive area.

In one scholar's opinion, generating substantive theory "is, or should be, a concern of researchers in applied professional fields such as adult education" (Darkenwald, 1980, p. 67). Darkenwald goes on to list several substantive areas well suited to grounded theory building: "literacy education in development countries, program development in university extension, rural community development, and continuing professional education" (p. 69). The major purpose of doing grounded theory research in an applied field "is to improve professional practice through gaining a better understanding of it" (p. 69).

Just how professional practice is enhanced is discussed at length by Glaser (1978) in a followup publication to the original book on grounded theory. Glaser recognizes that practitioners are knowledgeable, efficient, even expert in their particular fields of practice. "What the man [sic] in the know does not want is to be told what he already knows. What he wants to be told is how to handle what he knows with some increment in control and understanding of his area of action" (p. 13). A practitioner's knowledge is usually experiential and nontheoretical. The researcher can offer ideas, categories, and a theory that integrates the diverse elements of practice. Grounded theory—if it has truly been generated from the situation and is "grounded" in the data—will give the practitioner a conceptual tool with which to guide practice. As Glaser points out:

> With substantive theory the man [sic] in the know can start transcending his finite grasp of things. His knowledge which was heretofore not transferable, when used to generate theory, becomes transferable to other areas well known to him. His knowledge which was just known but not organized, is now ideationally organized. This allows him perceptible breakthroughs. (p. 13)

Grounded theory, whether substantive or formal, consists of categories, properties, and hypotheses. Categories, and the properties that define or illuminate the categories, are conceptual elements of the theory. Categories and properties need to be both analytic— "sufficiently generalized to designate the characteristics of concrete entities, not the entities themselves"—and sensitizing—"yield a 'meaningful' picture, abetted by apt illustrations that enable one to grasp the reference in terms of one's own experience" (Glaser & Strauss, 1967, p. 38). Hypotheses are relationships among categories and properties. Unlike hypotheses in experimental studies, grounded theory hypotheses are tentative and suggestive rather than tested. In a study of a college faculty's participation in in-service workshops, for example, the researcher identified "workshop credibility" as one of several categories explaining faculty participation (Rosenfeldt, 1981). A property that helped to define workshop credibility was called "identification with sponsoring agent." The author hypothesized that "workshop participation will depend on the extent to which faculty members identify with the workshop sponsors. Namely, the greater the identification of the potential participants with the sponsoring agent, the greater the likelihood that professors will participate in a given workshop" (p. 189). In another grounded theory investigation, a study of middle-aged men uncovered "career malaise" as a category reflective of the career situation of most of the men in the study. "Boredom," "inertia," and "feeling trapped" defined the category. It was hypothesized that the more acute one's "career malaise," the more burdensome the sense of responsibility to one's children and one's parents (Merriam, 1980). Numerous other examples of grounded theory studies in sociology can be found in a reader compiled by Glaser (1993). Several of the studies, such as "Cutting Back After a Heart Attack: An Overview," "New Identities and Family Life: A Study of Mothers Going to College," and "Doing Time: A Grounded Analysis of the Altered Perception of Time in the Prison Setting and Its Effects" are likely to be of interest to educators and trainers for both content and grounded theory methodology.

Two studies that investigated concepts related to continuing professional education were ones by Wagner (1990) and Ritt (1990). Wagner used grounded theory methodology to identify factors that influenced professional nurses who were recognized by their colleagues to be lifelong learners. Her study resulted in two major propositions—(1) lifelong learning for the professional nurse is a value developed early in life through family support as part of the socialization process that is strengthened through professional education; and (2) the result of lifelong learning is an expanded personal and professional understanding of self that is the source of empowerment.

In a contrasting grounded theory study, Ritt (1990) examined the evolution of a rather recent phenomenon in the nursing profession— the role of the nurse consultant. Through indepth interviews with nurse consultant practitioners, Ritt discovered how an individual becomes a nurse consultant and interventions that appropriately prepared the nurse to function in that role. The study resulted in a theoretical model that described the development of the role of the nurse consultant.

In most grounded theory studies, data come from interviews and participants' observations. Glaser and Strauss (1967) note that a wide variety of documentary materials, fiction, and previous research are also potential sources of valuable data. Procedures for collecting and handling data can best be understood through familiarity with the techniques of grounded theory research. Theoretical sampling, comparison groups, constant comparative analysis, and saturation are grounded theory techniques that determine what data to collect, how to handle the data, and when to stop gathering data.

Data collection is guided by *theoretical sampling* in which "the analyst jointly collects, codes, and analyzes his data and decides what data to collect next and where to find them, in order to develop his theory as it emerges" (Glaser & Strauss, 1967, p. 45). An initial sample is chosen by its logical relevance to the research problem. The reader uses insights gleaned from early analysis to determine where to go next for more data. In a grounded theory study of adult education growth in New Jersey community colleges (MacNeil, 1981), for example, data were originally gathered from divisions of continuing education and community service. Early fieldwork revealed that studying adult student participation could not be limited to a single administrative unit. Subsequently, data were collected from interviews with a wide range of personnel involved in adult education programming.

The discovery of grounded theory is facilitated through the use of *comparison groups.* Comparing several groups reveals quickly the similarities and differences that give rise to theoretical categories. The strength of these emerging categories is tested by collecting data from diverse groups. In Glaser and Strauss's study of the process of dying (1965a), premature babies who died were first studied, and the emergent concepts then tested with terminal cancer patients. Glaser and Strauss (1965b) describe the use of comparison groups as follows:

> Significant categories and hypotheses are first identified in the emerging analysis, during the preliminary fieldwork in one or a few groups and while scrutinizing substantive theories and data from other studies. Comparison groups are then located and chosen in accordance with the purposes of providing new data on categories or combinations of them, suggesting new hypotheses, and verifying initial hy-

potheses in diverse contexts . . . These groups can be studied one at a time or a number can be studied simultaneously. They can also be studied in quick succession in order to check out major hypotheses before too much theory is built around them. (pp. 292–293)

The basic procedure in grounded theory research is the *constant comparative analysis* of data, which consists of four stages (Glaser & Strauss, 1967; Strauss, 1987). In the first stage one compares incidents, generates tentative categories and/or properties to cover the incidents, and codes each incident into as many tentative categories as are appropriate. The researcher also records in memo form any insights that occurred during the comparison of incidents.

In the second stage the comparison of units changes from "incident with incident" to "incident with properties of the category" (Glaser & Strauss, 1967, p. 108). The researcher attempts to integrate categories and their properties.

The third stage is characterized by the delimitation of the theory. Here, similar categories are reduced to a smaller number of highly conceptual categories; hypotheses are generated; data are further checked for their "fit" into the overall framework. The simultaneous collection and analysis of data end when the categories become saturated. *Saturation* means that "no additional data are being found" whereby the researcher "can develop properties of a category" (Glaser & Strauss, 1967, p. 61). Further incidents of that category need not be coded since so doing "only adds bulk to the coded data and nothing to the theory" (p. 111).

The fourth stage—the actual writing of the theory from coded data and memos—occurs when "the researcher is convinced that his analytic framework forms a systematic substantive theory, that it is a reasonably accurate statement of the matters studied, and that it is couched in a form that others going into the field could use" (Glaser & Strauss, 1967, p. 113).

In order to assess the credibility of theory generated through constant comparative analysis of comparison groups, it is essential that readers be told how data were collected, how coding was done, and how the categories, properties, and hypotheses emerged from the data. The value of the theory itself can be determined by the following criteria suggested by Glaser and Strauss (1967):

1. Fitness. A theory must fit the substantive area to which it will be applied; a theory that is closely related to the reality of the substantive area of investigation is one that has been carefully inducted from the data.

2. Understanding. Laypersons working in the substantive area should be able to understand and use the theory.
3. Generality. Categories of the generated theory "should not be so abstract as to lose their sensitizing aspect, but yet must be abstract enough to make . . . theory a general guide to multiconditional, everchanging daily situations" (p. 242).
4. Control. A theory must provide understanding of enough concepts and their interrelations "to enable the person who uses it to have enough control in everyday situations to make its application worthwhile" (p. 245).

Grounded theory as a research methodology is not without its critics. Some consider the approach to be undisciplined and impressionistic. The constant comparative method, if used properly, however, allows for a very systematic and even rigorous handling of data. Admittedly, the success of a grounded theory investigation depends to some extent upon the sensitivity and analytical powers of the investigator. Discovery, or the process of arriving at an insight that may later form a category or property in the theory, is not a process that can be mapped out for other researchers to follow. Only the tools that may facilitate discovery can be given to the researcher. The investigator remains central to this type of research.

Finally, the charge has been made that other investigators would have evolved different theories from the same data. While this may be true, it does not mean that the theory that has been developed is invalid or inconsistent with the data. Rather, the validity of the theory is judged by its overall explanatory power, by how well assertions are supported, by how well integrated the elements are, and by whether there is an internal, logical consistency to all dimensions of the theory. These same canons are applied to *any* theory.

Most would agree that applied professional fields such as those related to the education and training of adults do not yet have theoretical bases sufficient to structure all of future research. These fields can be advanced by the addition of theoretical frameworks derived from practice. These frameworks, in turn, can be tested by professionals who are concerned with expanding the knowledge base of their field.

REFERENCES

Berreman, G. D. (1968). Ethnography: Method and product. In J. A. Clifton (Ed.), *Introduction to cultural anthropology* (pp. 336–373). Boston: Houghton Mifflin.

Bierema, L. (1993). *Executive businesswomen in the United States: A study of how they learn corporate culture.* Unpublished doctoral dissertation, The University of Georgia, Athens.

Constas, M. (1992). Qualitative analysis as a public event: The documentation of category development procedures. *American Educational Research Journal, 29*(2), 253–266.

Darkenwald, G. G. (1980). Field research and grounded theory. In H. B. Long, R. Hiemstra, & Associates (Eds.), *Changing approaches to studying of adult education* (pp. 63–77). San Francisco: Jossey-Bass.

Dexter, L. A. (1970). *Elite and specialized interviewing.* Evanston, IL: Northwestern University Press.

Fielding, N. G., & Lee, R. M. (1991). *Using computers in qualitative research.* London: Sage.

Firestone, W. A. (1993). Alternative arguments for generalizing from data as applied to qualitative research. *Educational Researcher, 22*(4), 16–23.

Glaser, B. G. (1978). *Theoretical sensitivity.* Mill Valley, CA: The Sociology Press.

Glaser, B. G. (1993). *Examples of grounded theory: A reader.* Mill Valley, CA: Sociology Press.

Glaser, B. G., & Strauss, A. L. (1965a). *Awareness of dying.* Chicago: Aldine.

Glaser, B. G., & Strauss, A. L. (1965b). The discovery of substantive theory: A basic strategy underlying qualitative research. *The American Behavioral Scientist, 8,* 5–12.

Glaser, B. G., & Strauss, A. L. (1967). *The discovery of grounded theory.* Chicago: Aldine.

Good, C. V., & Scates, D. E. (1954). *Methods of research.* San Francisco: Jossey-Bass.

Guba, E. G., & Lincoln, Y. S. (1981). *Effective evaluation.* San Francisco: Jossey-Bass.

Junker, B. H. (1960). *Field work.* Chicago: University of Chicago Press.

LeCompte, M. D., & Preissle, J. (1993). *Ethnography and qualitative design in educational research.* New York: Academic Press.

MacNeil, P. (1983). The dynamics of adult education growth in community colleges (Doctoral dissertation, Rutgers University, 1981). *Dissertation Abstracts International, 43,* 1795A.

Maimon, E. P., Belcher, G. L., Hearn, G. W., Nodine, B. F., & O'Connor, F. W. (1981). *Writing in the arts and sciences.* Cambridge, MA: Winthrop.

Mathison, S. (1988). Why triangulate? *Educational Researcher, 17*(7),13–17.

Merriam, S. (1980). *Coping with male mid-life: A systematic analysis using literature as a data source.* Washington, DC: University Press.

Merriam, S. (1988). *Case study research in education: A qualitative approach.* San Francisco: Jossey-Bass.

Miles, M. B., & Huberman, A. M. (1994). *Qualitative data analysis* (2nd ed.), Thousand Oaks, CA: Sage.

Mitchell, J. C. (1967). On quantification in social anthropology. In A. L. Epstein (Ed.), *The craft of social anthropology* (pp.17–45). New York: Tavistock.

Patton, M. A. (1990). *Qualitative evaluation methods.* Beverly Hills: Sage.

Pelto, P. J. (1970). *Anthropological research.* New York: Harper & Row.

Peshkin, A. (1988). In search of subjectivity—One's own. *Educational Researcher, 17*(7), 17–22.

Pfaffenberger, B. (1988). *Microcomputer applications in qualitative research.* Newbury Park, CA: Sage.

Posner, J. (1980). Urban anthropology: Fieldwork in semifamiliar settings. In W. B. Shaffir, R. A. Stebbins, & A. Turowetz (Eds.), *Fieldwork experience* (pp. 203–211). New York: St. Martin's.

Ritt, E. (1990). The evolving role of the nurse consultant (Doctoral dissertation, Northern Illinois University, 1989). *Dissertation Abstracts International, 50,* 2355A.

Rosenfeldt, A. B. (1981). Faculty commitment to the improvement of teaching via workshop participation (Doctoral dissertation, Virginia Polytechnic Institute and State University, 1981). *Dissertation Abstracts International, 42,* 2529A.

Rowden, R. (1993, April). The role of human resource development in successful, small to mid-sized manufacturing businesses: A comparative case study. *Proceedings of Quest for Quality National Research Conference on Human Resource Development* (pp. 159–165). College Station, TX: Department of Educational Human Resource Development, Texas A & M University.

Shaffir, W. B., Stebbins, R. A., & Turowetz, A. (Eds.). (1980). *Fieldwork experience.* New York: St. Martin's.

Strauss, A. L. (1987). *Qualitative analysis for social scientists.* Cambridge, UK: Cambridge University Press.

Tesch, R. (1990). *Qualitative research: Analysis types and software tools.* New York: Falmer.

Tisdell, E. J. (1993). Interlocking systems of power, privilege, and oppression in adult higher education classes. *Adult Education Quarterly, 43,* 203–226.

Van Maanen, J. (1988). *Tales of the field: On writing ethnography.* Chicago: University of Chicago Press.

van Tulder, M., van der Vegt, R., & Veenman, S. (1993). In-service education in innovating schools: A multi-case study. *International Journal of Qualitative Studies in Education, 6*(2), 129–142.

Wagner, P. A. (1990). Select factors influencing lifelong learning of professional nurses (Doctoral dissertation, Northern Illinois University, 1989). *Dissertation Abstracts International, 50,* 2357A.

Wolcott, H. F. (1980). How to look like an anthropologist without really being one. *Practicing Anthropology, 3,* 1.

Wolcott, H. F. (1990). *Writing up qualitative research* (Qualitative Research Methods Monographs, Vol. 20). Newbury Park: Sage.

Wolcott, H. F. (1994). *Transforming qualitative data: Description, analysis, and interpretation.* Thousand Oaks, CA: Sage.

Zeph, C. (1991). Career development for community adult educators: Interrelating personal and professional development. *Adult Education Quarterly. 41,* 217–232.

CHAPTER 7

ACTION, PARTICIPATORY, CRITICAL, AND FEMINIST RESEARCH DESIGNS

Researchers in applied fields of study, such as those involved with the education and training of adults, are constantly searching for more appropriate means to acquire knowledge. This search often leads to entirely new conceptualizations, not only of the role research is to play in the pursuit of knowledge, but also in the purpose of knowledge itself. The four research methodologies discussed in this chapter—action, participatory, critical, and feminist—represent conceptualizations of knowledge and techniques for acquiring knowledge that depart from the more conventional methods discussed in previous chapters.

These less conventional paradigms differ primarily in their definition of what is considered valid knowledge. In the traditional research paradigm, validity rests with the methods used in seeking knowledge and the extent to which those methods achieve internal and external control. For the newer paradigms discussed in this chapter, valid knowledge is defined in terms of those "doing" the knowing. As Reason and Rowan (1981, p. 241) point out, validity in this context "must concern itself both with the knower and what is to be known; valid knowledge is a matter of relationship."

We have chosen to discuss action, participatory, critical, and feminist research from among several possibilities because of the contribution each has made to the study of education, social and developmental psychology, community development, and human resource development.

ACTION RESEARCH

Several characteristics distinguish action research from other forms of social science research:

1. The researcher serves as a facilitator for problem solving and, in some cases, as a catalyst between the research findings and those individuals most likely to benefit or take action from the findings.
2. Results of research are intended for immediate application by those engaged in the research or by those for whom the research was initiated.
3. The design of action research is formulated while the research is in progress, rather than being totally predetermined at the onset of the study.

Action research can be used to solve specific practical, social, or individual problems that may be found in a community, a social agency, a school, a classroom, or even within an individual researcher. According to Isaac and Michael (1981, p. 42), action research is designed "to develop new skills or new approaches and to solve problems with direct application to the classroom or other applied settings." In a broader interpretation, Bogdan and Biklen (1992) describe action research as a systematic collection of information that is designed to bring about social change.

Action research methods may be traced to a study by Kurt Lewin (1947) that reported on change in people's food habits. Lewin studied the effects of lecture and discussion on the food habits of adult women from various income levels. The problem focused on getting women to use less popular, but more accessible and nutritious foods during World War II. Half the women in each income group were given a thirty-minute lecture by a nutritionist, followed by a fifteen-minute question and answer session. The other half participated in a discussion, with the nutritionist acting as a resource person. Lewin found that ten times more women who participated in the discussion groups tried the recommended food, as compared with women who experienced the lecture and question session. According to Marrow (in Sanford, 1981, p. 174), Lewin's greatest contribution to research may have been "the idea of studying things through changing them and seeing the effect." The theme or principle around which Lewin patterned action research was that in order to gain insight into a process, the researcher must create a change and then observe the effects and new dynamics of the change.

Action research departs from more conventional methods in the following ways:

1. Its purpose is to obtain knowledge that can be applied directly to a particular situation, (e.g., class, school, social agency, community).

2. The research problem emerges from events that are disturbing the researcher, such as efficiency of a teaching method or a local pollution problem in the community.
3. The problem is stated generally; hypotheses are seldom used.
4. Secondary sources of literature, rather than primary sources, are used extensively; the researcher simply wants an idea about the phenomenon being studied.
5. The participants are not systematically sampled or selected; they are part of a natural "flow" of human activity.
6. Procedures for conducting research are only planned generally at the beginning of a study and are altered as needed throughout the course of investigation.
7. Little attention is given to control and experimental conditions in conducting the study.

Bogdan and Biklen (1992) point out that action researchers sometimes collect data to change practices of social injustice, such as discrimination or creation of a harmful environment. Action research is used to effect social change by: (1) collecting information that identifies people and institutions that have a negative affect upon lives of other people; (2) helping people to become more aware of problems, to understand themselves, and to develop more commitment to addressing problems; and (3) serving as a catalyst to get people involved, organized, and active concerning particular issues within the community.

An example of action research at a practical, local level would be a study conducted by a teacher that focuses upon effective methods for teaching English as a second language. In this instance, the teacher becomes the researcher. During the progress of a class, the teacher recognizes that participants are having difficulty with the curriculum material. In search of a more effective method, the teacher tries a different set of materials with some individuals in the class. Over a period of time, the teacher carefully observes the progress of participants using the new material. By using each set of materials for approximately the same amount of time and by giving the same proportion of instructional attention to each group, the teacher attempts to follow procedures that will allow confidence in the study results. After a period of time, an assessment of participant achievement and satisfaction is conducted by the teacher. Since no attempt is made to strategically select a sample from the class for the study, no application of results to other second language classes is made. Through this action research activity, the teacher arrives at results that will assist in choosing second language curriculum material for the entire class later in the term.

A more assertive stance with regard to the meaning of action research is espoused by researchers at Deakin University in Australia (Kemmis & McTaggart, 1990). The Deakin version of action research focuses primarily upon the mileau of formal educational systems. Briefly, it is a form of collective self-reflective inquiry undertaken by participants in social situations. The purpose of the inquiry is to improve the rationality and justice of the group's own social and educational practices and to better understand these practices and situations. Participants can be parents, teachers, principals or students—anyone with a concern. As Kemmis and McTaggart point out, it is action research only "when it is collaborative activity that is achieved through critically examined actions of individual group members" (p. 5).

The method is further explained through the interrelationships of three domains of individual and cultural action: language, activity, and social relationships. Reform requires both individual and cultural action. Therefore, educational reform requires examination and modification of the institutional forms of language, activity, and social relationships that constitute education, the authors maintain.

An example of this form of action research was carried out in a series of projects that addressed aboriginal education and teacher education in Australia. The projects conducted by Deakin University personnel were intended to guide the preparation of aboriginal teachers. Beginning with a self-examination by the faculty, followed by a review of problems that existed within the curriculum, placing emphasis upon non-aboriginal and aboriginal participant involvement, the projects led to a teaching education concept of "both ways" education, eventually offered by aboriginal teachers. This concept development promoted and encouraged communities to remain bicultural by retaining and strengthening two alternative modes of life—the new way of living along with the traditional (McTaggart, 1991).

In addition to the more community-based, participatory mode of action research promoted by Deakin University researchers, action research and its variations have been adopted in organizations, most notably business and industry. In a recent book by Cunningham (1993), action research is linked with organizational development; here change is the overall goal. These models of action research emphasize assessment of factors blocking change.

Within action research and organizational change, Cunningham (1993) and others distinguish between action learning and action science. Action learning is defined as "a process for the reform of organizations and the liberation of human vision within organizations" (Garratt, 1991). There are four key elements in the process: "(1) a crucial organizational problem; (2) people willing to take risks to develop themselves and their organizations; (3) authority to take action on the problem; and (4) a system for learning reflectively" (Garratt, 1991, p. 54). In a recent issue of *Training*, Froiland (1994) explores some of the successes and some of the problems of organizations attempting change through action learning.

Action science varies from action learning in its emphasis on interpersonal contexts. Meanings, even in organizations, are socially constructed, so it is important to focus on the actor in the social context, "unfreezing" individuals' perspectives. Unfreezing involves disturbing a person's equilibrium, creating mild anxiety and dissonance, so that a context can be created for learning and constructing new meaning systems wherein change *can* take place. Argyris, the founder of this approach, argues for the creation of "actionable knowledge" that facilitates "human competence, confidence, and efficacy and, at the same time leads to innovative, flexible, and effective organizations" (1993, p. xi).

There is much debate in the action research literature as to the desirable balance between action and research within any one of these forms. There is also a difference in where the emphasis should be— on diagnosis, problem identification, individuals or groups, learning, or implementation. In each form, however, the action research process is one of analyzing, getting facts, identifying the problem, planning and taking action on the problem, then repeating the cycle as new concepts and information result from the process. The benefits of this method are that it is relevant to an actual situation in the field of practice, it focuses on a systematic process for problem solving and project development, and it is responsive to experimentation and innovation (Isaac & Michael, 1981). As with the case of the Deakin teacher-training projects in Australia, the method may lead to social change on a large scale. However, action research also has limitations. Because it lacks external and internal controls, generalizability of results are limited to the specific circumstances and conditions in which the research was done.

PARTICIPATORY RESEARCH

Another form of inquiry described as participatory research is intended to address human inequality. Participatory research focuses upon the political empowerment of people through group participation in the search for and acquisition of knowledge.

Participatory research methodology is supported by a social philosophy of human equality (Hall, 1984). As with action research, one of the strengths of this method is its immediate application. Although participatory research is closely associated with processes of community development, one distinction between them is the role played by the researcher and research participants. In participatory research, the one conducting research activities plays an active part and is not just an objective observer of data. The researcher is a catalyst in achieving research results to solve social problems. Participants take on the role of colleagues in collecting and analyzing data. Through the participatory process, the researcher is integrated into the community and, with community members, seeks solutions to social problems.

Participatory methodology is a reaction against the highly empirical, deductive methods commonly found in the social sciences. Its proponents argue that it is less oppressive than these more traditional methods. Hall (1984) makes three major distinctions between social science methods and participatory approaches to research. Social science research methods imply value, whereas participatory methods attempt to be free of values. Second, techniques used in social science research have a "hidden process" to manipulate the subjects of research, whereas the people engaged in participatory research control the research. Third, most social science research is conducted and reported for other researchers; therefore, the monopoly of knowledge is with intellectuals. Research results should be useable, Hall suggests, by those individuals in the world recognized as subjects of inequality.

Participatory research is a tool for individuals working in groups to address problems of social inequality and to curb exploitation of those persons with less economic and political power. The participatory movement, along with other research paradigms discussed in this chapter, represents a counter position to the logical/posivitist way of thinking about conducting research which has dominated the methodology repertoire of researchers in the past.

A key assumption of participatory research is that it will lead to change by the people who do the research (Couto, 1987). A number of characteristics seen in action research also distinguish participatory research. As Couto points out, what makes participatory methodology different is:

(a) The problem under study and the decision to study it have origins in the community affected by the problem;

(b) The goal of the research is political or social change derived from the information gathered;

(c) Local people control the process of problem definition, information gathering and decisions about action following from the information; and

(d) Local people and professional researchers are equals in the research process. They are both researchers and learners. (p. 84)

Participatory research permits individuals to study and better understand the influences that social institutions have upon them. Better understanding leads to more economic and political control of their lives by consolidation of information and effort within the group. Participatory research focuses upon the subtle and overt psychological and social dimensions of oppression, such as messages transmitted through public media, religious institutions, government, and educational institutions. The method challenges the way knowledge is produced and disseminated through traditional channels of social institutions.

Three interrelated processes are carried out in conducting participatory research:

1. Collective investigation of problems and issues with the active participation of the constituency (community) in the entire process.

2. Collective analysis, in which the constituency develops a better understanding not only of the problems at hand but also of the underlying structural causes (socioeconomic, political, cultural) of the problem.

3. Collective action by the constituency aimed at long-term as well as short-term solutions to these problems. (Couto, 1987, p. 2)

Beginning with a "problem posing" session, participants work together to identify and solve a problem of mutual concern, such as inadequate housing, unemployment, or poor health conditions. The process leads the group to better understand the problem and to question its underlying causes. Paulo Freire (1974) made a significant contribution to the concepts and methods of participatory research by introducing the terms *conscientization* and *thematic investigation* in his work in South America. The concept involved in conscientization is explained as "learning to perceive social, political, and economic contradictions and to take action against the oppressive elements of reality" (p. 3). The method that grows from conscientization, called thematic investigation, involves participants in the analysis of words and experiences common to their reality, and in

128 / A Guide to Research for Educators and Trainers of Adults

the identification of inconsistencies that lead to increased understanding of their reality. Participatory research has been conducted primarily in Third World countries. Some examples of participatory research in nonformal adult education around the world include evaluation of a cooperative weaving project in Botswana, evaluation of literacy programs in Tanzania, development in Canada of a curriculum for teaching English in the workplace, and development of women's clubs in Aadias, India.

According to Kassam and Mustafa (1982), features that distinguish participatory research from the so-called "objective" social sciences are (1) a subjective commitment on the part of the researcher to the people under study; (2) close involvement of the researcher with the researched community; (3) a problem-centered approach that utilizes data gathering, from which action may be taken; (4) an educational process for both the researchers and the people for whom the research is conducted; and (5) respect for the capability and potential of people to produce knowledge and analyze it (pp. 70–71).

Antecedents of participatory research, as explained by Hall (1981), can be traced to the early field work of Engels and his association with working classes of Manchester, England, as well as to the "unstructured interview" with French factory workers by Karl Marx. Parts of the work of Dewey, George Herbert Mead, and the Tavistock Institute in London have provided guidelines for this type of social investigation, which departs from empirical positivism, the research approach that dominated the scene in the 1950s and 1960s, according to Hall.

Participatory research received its major thrust from the International Council of Adult Education in the mid-1970s, within which the Participatory Research Project grew under the direction of Budd Hall. The general objective of the project was to "investigate methods of research in adult education and related social transformation programs which focus on the involvement of the poorest groups or classes in the analysis of their own needs" (Status Report on the Participatory Research Project International Meeting, 1977, p. 1). Hall (1984) stresses that the purpose of participatory research is to democratize research, to let more participate in carrying out the research and benefit from the results of research. Evidence that democratization of research is beginning to take place, according to Hall, includes (1) the shift of research being conducted in metropolitan countries to countries in the Third World, (2) shift of responsibility for conducting research from "outside" persons to people within the country, (3) increased involvement of untrained persons in professional research roles, (4) increased interest in making research accessible to local decision makers, and (5) the increased involvement of the poor and exploited in the research process.

An example of participatory research conducted within a local community setting is the study done by Wright (1988) that compared two nontraditional adult education programs (participatory research and technical assistance programs) used with residents of two Chicago public housing developments. Although Wright could not conclude that one program was superior to the other, the study did provide evidence of the compatibility of participatory research methodology when low-income family concerns are being addressed. The study also detected major obstacles, such as how to help people to move toward empowerment when residents within the groups have had limited experience with being in power.

An example of participatory research conducted in a larger setting is the Citizen's Research Project in Appalachia (Gaventa & Horton, 1981). In this project, an Appalachian Alliance was formed to study land ownership. The problem identified was that land ownership patterns were resulting in conditions detrimental to residents along the Appalachian range—destruction of land due to strip mining, lack of land for housing, low tax bases and poor services, flooding, loss of agricultural land, and irregular deeding and leasing of land.

Approximately 100 citizens from some 80 counties in Alabama, Kentucky, North Carolina, Tennessee, Virginia, and West Virginia were brought together to study who actually owned the land on the Appalachian range. Reported findings of the study confirmed (1) all the land and minerals in Appalachia are owned by relatively few people, (2) Appalachian land and mineral resources are absentee-owned, (3) large corporations dominate the ownership picture in much of Appalachia (40% of land and 70% of mineral rights), and (4) mineral rights are greatly underassessed for property tax purposes (p. 34). In keeping with the participatory concept, findings of the study were disseminated through pamphlets, local papers, community meetings, workshops, and regional meetings. Three months after research results were reported, activities that indicated action being taken by local groups included efforts to organize a tax reform coalition in Kentucky, tax challenges in Tennessee, and a multi-county coalition organized around gas and oil taxes and drilling practices in West Virginia.

Hall (1984) and others also have pointed out the unique purpose for participatory studies to unmask the myth of science and to validate the knowledge of people. Some authors, however, identify what seem to be contradictions about participatory research (Couto, 1987). In practice it is very difficult to conduct research of this type without qualified persons outside the community. The role of the expert is needed, but difficult to integrate into participatory research practice.

The problems associated with conducting participatory research are identified in a study conducted by the Yellow Creek Concerned Citizens (YCCC), a community organization in Bell County in eastern Kentucky. The research was conducted in response to pollution of Yellow Creek coming from a tannery in the neighboring community of Middleboro, Kentucky. The community decision was to survey people along the creek to confirm illnesses related to creek contamination. The survey was largely determined to be successful; local residents were able to get 98% cooperation. The survey provided YCCC citizens with new anecdotal information about the pollution problem. It also allowed people to share their views and to explore possible action with their neighbors.

However, there were some limitations to the methodology in achieving the ultimate purpose of terminating the dumping of raw waste products into Yellow Creek. First, the survey instrument constructed with outside assistance was very long and difficult to code and analyze. Special subgroups within the total number of citizens surveyed, such as smokers and people in various age ranges, were not represented completely enough to provide an adequate analysis. The nuisance of appearance and smell of wastes in Yellow Creek dominated the survey results. The link between creek water exposure and illness was weak in the analysis. Another problem existed with variations in coding techniques used. The use of many different volunteers to gather and analyze data led to both incorrect coding and numerous errors, which had to be revised in the final report.

Couto (1987) cautions persons engaging in participatory research that there are risks, if care in planning and conducting a study of this type is not exercised. The political goal of Yellow Creek citizens, as an example, could have been jeopardized through use of faulty data gathering and analysis. Persons who have the power to change things within the community typically need to be persuaded by definable factual data.

Other criticisms regarding participatory research are advanced by some individuals who represent the more conventional paradigms of social science research. For example, Griffith and Cristarella (1979) suggest that "the term participatory research is a misnomer, applied idiosyncratically to activities not conducted primarily to advance knowledge, but rather to promote community development" (p. 18).

Participatory research does not, in their opinion, contribute to a body of knowledge, which conventional social science researchers see as the single most important function of the research process.

The strengths and weaknesses of participatory research are much the same as those for action research. The results can be applied directly to practice, but are not easily generalized to other situations. Greater involvement by participants in the research may ensure better application of research results. Greater involvement without expert assistance, however, also brings the potential of technique variations that may be counter to the overall objective for doing the research.

CRITICAL RESEARCH

Another form of research also intended to empower people is critical research, developed from a more definite Marxist reform philosophy. In his discussion of critical theory and adult learning, Welton (1993) explains how Habermas departed from the Marxist tradition as a second generation critical theorist. Critical research, as described through the words of Marx (1967), is critical in the sense that,

> we do not anticipate the world dogmatically, but rather wish to find the new world through criticism of the old; for all times is not our task, what we have to accomplish at this time is all the more clear; relentless criticism for all existing conditions, relentless in the sense that the criticism is not afraid of its findings and just as little afraid of conflict with the powers that be. (p. 212)

Habermas did not fully accept Marx's viewpoint that the "natural scientific" way of learning was the only source of knowledge. In his seminal work, *Knowledge and Human Interests* (1972), Habermas provides a means to understand the relationship between knowledge, learning, and the human condition. Knowledge is represented in three ways: technical, practical, and emancipatory. In the way of example, Welton (1993) points out that "a philosophy of adult learning influenced by Habermas starts with the affirmation that human beings are *material* and *historical* beings who have the potential to learn about nature, others and self" (p. 83). However, conditions of human life block us from gaining the competencies to develop our "many-sided potentialities." Critical reflectivity allows us to examine the cultural and psychological assumptions we hold, and thus, to move toward a more emancipated state through our learning (Mezirow, 1991).

Kemmis (1988), who readily interchanges critical research with action research, explains that critical education research exists in practice within the margins of the culture and technology of educational policy and practice. The tension created by a demand for self-awareness, on one hand, and threats of institutionalization on the other, forms the dialectic on which critical research is based.

A critical researcher assumes an oppositional stance in four distinct ways—epistemologically, cognitively, culturally, and politically. Epistemologically critical research practitioners reject empirism and idealism, also positivism and interpretivism. This translates into rejection of most foundations upon which much social and educational research is based. Cognitive opposition—the second way of being critical—is in the form of acknowledgment of and struggle against interpretations of the world as they are decoded and structured through language, culture, and traditions. This type of cognitive opposition is demonstrated by how the researcher treats familiar ways of understanding human activity and social relationships as problematic. This method questions such phenomena as human rationality, values associated with productive activity, and justice of social relationships.

The third mode of opposition in critical research practice, that of cultural opposition, is closely linked to cognitive opposition. It brings to focus the possibilities of how culture can sustain irrationality, unfulfilling lifestyles, and social injustice, revealing the degree to which certain ways of life within a culture are strategically organized to preserve the interests of some members of society at the expense of others.

Cognitive and cultural criticism together form the fourth way, or sense of opposition, termed political opposition. Critical research creates conditions within which individuals can work cooperatively as knowing human beings, as both products and producers of history who help "to find the new world through criticism of the old" and act together in bringing a new world into being (Carr & Kemmis, 1986). This pattern of critical research practice becomes more than opposition, Kemmis emphasizes; it is a form of resistance, by awakening people to the critical sense of what is possible and organizing them into action.

The following classification of alternative views of educational research, based upon the work of Carr and Kemmis (1986), provides synoptic descriptions of critical education research methodology and its comparison with other forms of research (see Table 7.1).

Table 7.1 Alternative Forms of Educational Research

	POSITIVIST (Empirical-analytic)	INTERPRETIVE (Historical-hermeneutic)	CRITICAL
Presumed nature of education as an object of research	Education as a 'phenomenon': schooling as a delivery-system (technology)	Education as a developmental process; schooling as lived experience	Education as a social project; schooling as an institution for social and cultural repro-duction and transformation.
Research methods	Natural-scientific; experimental; 'quantitative'	Historical inter-pretive; 'qualita-tive'; ethno-methodological; illuminative	Critical social science; emancipatory action research
Form of research knowledge	Objective; nomological; causal explanation	Subjective; idiographic; interpretive understanding	Dialectical; reflexive understanding aimed at critical praxis
Examples of substantive theoretical forms	Functionalist psychology; structure-functional soci-, ology, anthro-pology	Structuralism in psychology, sociology, anthropology	Ideology-critique; critical curriculum theorising by collaborating teachers
Human interest	Technical	Practical	Emancipatory
Practical purpose and form of reasoning	Improvement of the 'technology' of schooling; instrumental (means, ends) reasoning	Enlightenment of practitioners; practical-deliberative (informs judgement)	Rational transformation of education; critical reason-ing (i.e., practi-cal reasoning with emanci-patory intent)
Theory of human nature	Deterministic	Humanistic	Historical-materialist
Educational philosophy	Neo-classical, vocational	Liberal-progressive	Socially-critical, democratic

Table 7.1 (continued)

Educational values	'Moulding' metaphor. Individuals prepared for a given form of social life	'Growth' metaphor. Self-actualisation of individuals within meritocratic form of social life	'Empowerment' metaphor. Individuals collectively producing and transforming existing forms of social life through action in history
View of educational reform	Research, development and dissemination; bureaucracy, corporate management	Enlightened action; liberal-individualist, reconstructionist	Contestational, communitarian; reproduction and transformation through collective action

Kemmis, S. (1988, May 5–6). *Critical Theory*. Paper presented at the Critical Education Research Conference, Calgary, Canada.

Five formal requirements characterize a critical social or educational science, according to Carr and Kemmis (1986). They emphasize that any adequate approach to educational research and theory must:

1. Reject positivist notions of rationality, objectivity, and truth.
2. Accept the need to employ the interpretive categories of teachers and other participants in educational processes. The approach must be based upon the self-understandings of practitioners.
3. Provide ways of distinguishing ideologically warped interpretations from interpretations that are not, and provide explanations of how to overcome those distorted self-understandings.
4. Address identification and exposition of those aspects of the social order that interfere with pursuit of rational goals and provide theoretical explanations to practitioners that raise awareness to how these interferences may be eliminated or conquered.
5. Make a practical approach to educational theory and research, in the sense that the practice of criticism should always be directed toward transformation of ways that participants see themselves and their situations, so that obstacles that stand in the way of attaining their objectives can be identified and overcome.

An example of critical research being utilized is the study by Wilson (1993) of handbooks produced in the field of adult education. The purpose was to determine the extent to which adult education university researchers (handbook authors) rely on analyses typically associated with the natural sciences in their development of knowledge in an attempt to control the professionalization of the field. From his analysis of handbooks which are produced about every 10 years beginning in the mid-1930s, Wilson presents the argument that the content of handbooks edited by scholars in the field has changed. The author asserts that beginning with the 1948 edition, content has moved away from the original substance of providing reference to the institutional and programmatic existence of adult education in the United States. From the 1948 edition on, scientific empiricism is used instrumentally to produce knowledge that unifies and thus controls the development of the profession. Wilson asserts that "professionalization depends upon using scientifically-derived knowledge to standardize professional practice and training of practitioners in order to develop a market share in the service economy" (p. 1).

FEMINIST RESEARCH

A form of social science research that also focuses upon human equality is feminist research. Feminist researchers often embrace the tenants of action, participatory, and critical research methodologies. However, in a comprehensive review of feminist literature Reinharz (1992) points out that feminist inquiry is not necessarily distinguished by the type of methodologies used, but by the purpose for which the research is engaged—the study of phenomena from women's perspectives. The underlying purpose for feminist study is to discover and/or create new intellectual constructs other than those developed by men.

Historically, feminist research was closely associated with the women's movement. Throughout various stages of women's struggle for equality, feminist inquiry played an important role in raising public consciousness about social inequities. Early feminist inquiry, for example, began with discovering sexism in scholarship. This type of consciousness raising contributed to legitimizing feminist research and clarifying its purpose.

More recently, feminist researchers have included a broad range of issues related to human equality, such as concerns about racism and homophobia. Feminist inquiry can be represented by most of the research approaches discussed previously in this book. Experimental, ethnographic, cross-cultural, oral history, and action studies are examples of methods used by feminist researchers.

Feminist researchers also have contributed original elements to social science inquiry. Studies of special groups of women, such as upper-class women, farm women, women of unique cultural heritage, and women academics are original contributions from feminist research not found in most social science research (Glenn, 1986; Ostander, 1984; Simeone, 1987; Stall, 1985). Other original social science research contributions are studies of particular behaviors among women experienced in day-to-day life, such as how women care for their families and function within their communities. Also, the distillation of new types of information about the "subjective self" drawn from the personal reflections of women is an example of original social science research.

Other unique qualities of some feminist research are the manner in which research is reported and the transdiscipline approach to inquiry. Authorship of some studies, for example, is attributed to an entire group of individuals who helped to conduct the study, rather than to only principal researchers as is often the custom in academic circles. Everyone engaged in the research is considered an active contributor, even those who type the final report. Examples of studies with multiauthorship are the Boston Women's Health Book Collective (1971, 1973, 1976), the Combahee River Collective (1979), and Hull-House Maps and Papers (Addams, 1981) produced by persons who resided at Hull-House.

The transdiscipline or multidiscipline approach and integration of information not typically found in academic literature are other contributions to social science research. Feminist researchers do not limit themselves by the boundaries of academic organizations. They are also creative with the invention of descriptive terms and metaphors to better represent issues related to the struggle for equality. "Herstory," "mother work," "animal queendom," and "Ms." are terms invented by feminist scholars. Depicting the research process as "organism" (female) rather than "mechanism" (male) and redefining the research process as "recreation" or "play" are examples of how feminists doing research have developed the field of study metaphorically.

An explanation of feminist theory applied in the field of adult higher education is provided by Tisdell (1993a). The author presents two models of feminist theory (liberatory model and gender model) in her description of how feminism is related to adult learning. The liberatory model of feminism focuses on power relationships and systems of oppression based on gender, race, class, age, etc. Gender-oriented feminist researchers, on the other hand, concentrate more directly on "women's socialization as nurturers" (Tisdell, 1993a, pp. 96–97). The liberatory model has a sociological orientation, while the gender model focuses on the psychological aspects of feminism. In her synthesis of implications feminist theories have for adult learning in higher education settings, Tisdell outlines three pertinent areas for consideration. First, feminist literature suggests that women have different learning needs from men; second, the study of sociocultural context and existing power relationships merits attention; and finally, adult learning can be informed through the application of feminist theory by "direct discussion of how to deal with power issues in the learning environment that affect the learning process" (pp. 98–99).

Tisdell's (1993b) own research study of the interlocking systems of power, privilege, and oppression in adult higher education classes is based in the liberatory model. In intensive case studies of two adult higher education classrooms, she uncovered numerous ways in which professors and students both resisted and reproduced the structured power relationships of society.

In a meta-inductive analysis of feminist research literature Reinharz (1992) identifies 10 themes. In this attempt to thematically describe feminist research in its current state, we are provided with a type of working definition:

1. Feminism is a perspective, not a research method.
2. Feminists use a multiplicity of research methods.
3. Feminist research involves an ongoing criticism of nonfeminist scholarship.
4. Feminist research is guided by feminist theory.
5. Feminist research may be transdisciplinary
6. Feminist research aims to create social change.
7. Feminist research strives to represent human diversity.
8. Feminist research frequently includes the researcher as a person.
9. Feminist research frequently attempts to develop special relations with the people studied.
10. Feminist research frequently defines a special relation with the reader. (p. 240)

SUMMARY

In summary, each of the research designs discussed in this chapter departs in some way from the conventional modes of social science research. They represent less conventional approaches to inquiry that have contributed concepts and procedures to the education and training of adults.

These less conventional methods differ from more traditional approaches in how validity of research is understood. In research designs intended for human empowerment, validity is not judged by external and internal measures solely, but the researcher and participants are instrumental in the process of "knowing." Action, participatory, critical, and feminist research are characterized by the immediate impact of research results. Each of the methods discussed here contributes to the concept "knowledge of practical interest"; that is, knowledge that helps participants in the research more fully understand themselves and their circumstances.

REFERENCES

Addams, J. (1981). *Twenty years in Hull-House (1910)*. New York: New American Library.

Argyris, C. (1993). *Knowledge for action: A guide for overcoming barriers to organizational change*. San Francisco: Jossey-Bass.

Bogdan, R. C., & Biklen, S. K. (1992). *Qualitative research for education: An introduction to theory and methods*. Boston: Allyn & Bacon.

Boston Women's Health Book Collective (1971, 1973, 1976). *Our bodies, ourselves: A book by and for women*. New York: Simon & Schuster.

Carr, W., & Kemmis, S. (1986). *Becoming critical: Education, knowledge and action research*. London: Falmer

Combahee River Collective (1979). Why did they die? A document of black feminism. *Radical America, 13*(6), 41–50.

Couto, R. A. (1986). Appalachian explanations for America's new poverty. *Forum for Applied Research and Public Policy, 2*, 101–110.

Couto, R. A. (1987). Participatory research: Method and critique. *Clinical Sociology Review, 5*, 83–90.

Cunningham, J. B. (1993). *Action research and organizational development*. Westport, CT: Praeger.

Freire, P. (1974). *Education for critical consciousness*. New York: Seabury Press.

Froiland, P. (1994). Action learning: Taming real problems in real time. *Training 31*(1), 27–34.

Garratt, B. (1991). The power of action learning. In M. Pedler (Ed.), *Action learning in practice*. 2nd edition. Brookfield, VT: Gower.

Gaventa, J., & Horton, B. D. (1981). A citizens' research project in Appalachia, USA. *Convergence, 14*, 30–42.

Glenn, E. (1986). *Issei, nisei, war bride: Three generations of Japanese American women in domestic service.* Philadelphia: Temple University Press.

Griffith, W. S., & Cristarella, M. C. (1979). Participatory research: Should it be a new methodology for adult educators? In John Niemi (Ed.), *Viewpoints on adult education research* (pp. 43–70). Columbus, OH: ERIC Clearinghouse on Adult, Career and Vocational Education.

Habermas, J. (1972). *Knowledge and human interests.* Portsmouth, NH: Heinemann Educational Books.

Habermas, J. (1974). *Theory and practice.* (John Veirtel, Trans.). London: Heineman.

Hall, B. L. (1981). Participatory research: An approach for change. *Convergence, 14* (3) 6–19.

Hall, B. L. (1984). Research, commitment and action: The role of participatory research. *International Review of Education, 30,* 289–300.

Isaac, S., & Michael, W. B. (1981). *Handbook in research and evaluation* (2nd ed.) San Diego: EDITS Publishers.

Kassam, Y., & Mustafa, K. (1982). *Participatory research: An emerging alternative methodology in social science research* (Series No. 2). Khanpur, New Delhi: Society for Participatory Research in Asia.

Kemmis, S., & Fitzclarence, L. (1986). *Curriculum theorizing: Beyond reproduction theory.* Geelong, Victoria: Deakin University Press.

Kemmis, S., & McTaggart, R. (1990). *The action research planner.* Geelong, Victoria: Deakin University Press.

Lewin, K. (1947). Group decision and social change. In T. M. Newcomb & E. L. Hartley (Eds.), *Reading in social psychology.* New York: Holt, Rinehart & Winston.

McTaggart, R. (1991). Principles for participatory research. *Adult Education Quarterly, 41* (3), 168–187.

Marx, K. (1967). *Writings of the young Marx on philosophy and society.* (L. D. Easton & K. H. Guddat, Eds., Trans.). New York: Anchor Books.

Mezirow, J. D. (1991). *Transformative dimensions of adult learning.* San Francisco: Jossey-Bass.

Ostander, S. (1984). *Women of the upper class.* Philadelphia: Temple University Press.

Reason, P., & Rowan, J. (Eds.). (1981). Issues of validity in new paradigm research. In *Human inquiry: A sourcebook of new paradigm research* (pp. 239–250). Chichester: John Wiley & Sons.

Reinharz, S. (1992). *Feminist methods in social research.* New York: Oxford University Press.

Sanford, N. (1981). A model for action research. In P. Reason & J. Rowan (Eds.), *Human inquiry: A sourcebook of new paradigm research* (pp. 173–182). Chichester: John Wiley & Sons.

Simeone, A. (1987). *Academic women: Working towards equality.* South Hadley, MA: Bergin & Garvey.

Stall, S. (1985, Spring). *What about the non-feminist? The possibilities for women's movement coalition building in small-town America.* Paper presented at the 35th Annual Meeting of the Society for the Study of Social Problems. Washington, DC.

Status Report on the Participatory Research Project International Meeting, 1977.

Tisdell, E. J. (1993a). Feminism and adult learning: Power, pedagogy and praxis. In S. B. Merriam (Ed.), *An update on adult learning theory* (pp. 91–103). New Directions for Adult and Continuing Education Series, No. 57. San Francisco: Jossey-Bass.

Tisdell, E. J. (1993b). Interlocking systems of power, privilege, and oppression in adult higher education classes. *Adult Education Quarterly.* 43(4), 203–226.

Welton, M. R. (1993, Spring). The contribution of critical theory to our understanding of adult learning. In S. B. Merriam (Ed.), *An update on adult learning theory* (pp. 81–90). New Directions for Adult and Continuing Education Series #57. San Francisco: Jossey-Bass.

Wilson, A. L. (1993). The common concern: Controlling the professionalization of adult education. *Adult Education Quarterly, 44* (1), 1–16.

Wright, L. E. (1988). Participatory research: A study of empowerment in public housing through resident management. Unpublished doctoral dissertation, Northern Illinois University.

CHAPTER 8

DATA COLLECTION PROCEDURES AND TECHNIQUES

The collection of data, though interesting and inspiring at times to the researcher, can also be tedious and boring. Consequently, the "reward" of doing research is seldom considered to be data collection; it is more often what results from the collection. The routine and sometimes monotonous steps necessary to conduct research effectively may lead the novice researcher or casual consumer of research to lose interest. The experienced researcher, however, accepts the tedium, knowing that dedication to thoroughness in the process is necessary to produce supportable results. The process of conducting research is simply the deliberate choice and use of means that best answer research questions. Techniques and procedures for conducting research are to the researcher as the chisel and hammer are to the stone sculptor or a well-made musical instrument to the virtuoso; their careful and consistent use brings new images of reality.

The technique or procedure chosen for collecting data is derived from the particular research method. Depending upon the emphasis of the study (e.g., rational/empirical, intuitive, historical, or philosophical), appropriate procedures and techniques merge during the planning of the research. If the study is planned to test hypotheses deductively, for example, rational and empirical techniques such as questioning and observing may be used. Or, if the inquiry is of a historical nature, internal and external criticism of research documents through content analysis may be most appropriate.

For purposes of discussion in this chapter, the term *procedure* refers to the steps or activities that describe the general way data are gathered. For example, the use of questions for research participant response before and after an experience is a general procedure for gathering data. A *technique*, on the other hand, refers to the specific device or means of recording the data, such as an interview, a test, or a projective inventory.

THE NATURE OF RESEARCH DATA

The researcher gathers data—facts, impressions, beliefs, and feelings—that are related to the phenomenon being studied in order to systematically reach conclusions. Research data is an elusive term which, to the beginning researcher, may seem analogous to an answer to the research question. In fact, research answers come from the comparison of data; the data are relatively meaningless without such a comparison, and they cannot provide answers to research questions all by themselves.

Data gathered as a sample of the phenomenon under study are chosen to represent accurately those behaviors, perceptions, and events that are part of the phenomenon. The task of the researcher is to cull from the many bits of data those that are representative, and to shape accurate and meaningful conclusions. In many research studies, the researcher is limited by the amount of data that can be gathered. This limitation results from inaccessibility of data, or the sheer volume, which make collecting all pertinent data unrealistic. Therefore, one judgment that the researcher must make in designing and conducting the study concerns validity—how accurately do the data represent the phenomenon? The researcher must also recognize that a sample of research data is only an approximation of the phenomenon being studied and, in a sense, can never be completely accurate. Even data collected systematically provide only a partial glimpse of the total picture.

Accurate approximations of the larger picture being researched require some type of measurement procedure: *a technique for collecting data, plus a set of rules for using these data.* The purpose of any measurement procedure is to produce trustworthy evidence relevant to the research question being asked. For example, if we wanted to know the attitudes of black adults in the ghetto of a metropolitan city about a training program offered in their neighborhood, we might use a type of attitude scale that yields a score. Using this score, we could place individual responses on a continuum from unfavorable to favorable for comparison. This technique provides a way of gathering the data and also a guide for use: one individual can be compared with another by the position of each on the scale. But another way to gather the same kind of data is by using an unstructured interview. General questions about attitudes toward the training program could be asked of the same adults as before. However, a coding system, a set of rules for using the data, is necessary to approximate the participants' degree of favorable or unfavorable attitude.

The choice of which of these two techniques to use should be based upon the research problem, characteristics of the black adults, and conditions within the research environment. The following planning questions might be asked: Is the attitude scale valid for use with this sample population? How easily is it administered? Are norms based upon the population available for comparison? All of these questions must be considered in deciding whether or not to use the scale. If the participants are sensitive to filling out forms, or if the researcher is not certain about all the data needed, the unstructured interview may be more productive.

Data coded and represented by numerical scores are typically referred to as *quantitative* or *statistical* data. Data not transferable to statistics are called *qualitative* data. In the previous example, the scores produced from the attitude scale are quantitative data, while the unstructured interview produced qualitative data. Both types of data are useful in the process of systematic inquiry related to adult education and training.

The researcher has three major ways of collecting data: by asking questions through a survey, by observing, or by testing. Each procedure also includes choices of various research techniques. The choice of technique used for collecting data depends upon the type of research method already selected and conditions surrounding the research phenomenon. Primary techniques for gathering data are discussed in the following sections.

CONTRIBUTIONS OF SURVEY RESEARCH

Numerous research methods are effectively used to study the education and training of adults. However, descriptive research has made a significant contribution in the early development of these fields. The first major adult education survey was completed in England in 1851 (Hudson, 1969). Since that time several extensive surveys to study adult participation have been conducted (e.g., Boshier & Collins, 1985; Dimmock, 1985; Johnstone & Rivera, 1965; Tough, 1979, 1982). Interest in why adults participate in education appears to be a perennial source of descriptive survey research.

Dickinson and Blunt (1980) indicated that 86% of research reported in *Adult Education* during the 20-year period (1950–1970) used the survey technique as a basis of the study. Also, a review of graduate student scholarship revealed wide use of the survey technique (Grabowski, 1980). In looking to future trends for the field, Dickinson and Blunt (1980) forecast that because of persistent needs of an evolving discipline of social practice (adult education), the survey will continue to be the major means used in conducting research.

SURVEYING

Of all data-gathering techniques available to the researcher, the survey, either written or oral, is used most extensively. The term *survey* represents a broad category of techniques that use questioning as a strategy to elicit information. Written forms of survey are referred to as questionnaires; surveys conducted orally are interviews. Although they serve similar purposes in gaining information, each provides unique advantages to the researcher.

Construction and Use of the Questionnaire

Questionnaires vary in design according to the purpose suggested by the research problem. Two general types of questionnaires are the open questionnaire and closed (or forced-choice) questionnaire. An open questionnaire has items that allow greater freedom of response, whereas with a closed questionnaire, the person is forced to choose one of the alternatives provided. Responses from closed questionnaires are more easily analyzed because data essentially have been categorized prior to beginning the data gathering. Items on a closed questionnaire represent factors surrounding the research phenomenon that are the focus of the investigation. The researcher, anticipating alternatives, simply has the research participant choose from information, attitudes, etc., provided within the instrument. Thus, analysis and statistical manipulation are made easier for the researcher after the data are gathered.

The following are examples of items used in a closed questionnaire:

Example 1. The HRD training program offered at Benx Industries serves members of the Metrocity community by:
    a. providing more jobs
    b. making members more aware of positions in industry
    c. teaching specific transferable job skills
    d. upgrading the educational level of the community

Example 2. The methods used in the program at Paulson Community College to prepare students for the General Education Development (GED) Test are:

    a. effectively meeting the needs of all participants
    b. meeting the needs of most participants
    c. meeting the needs of a few participants
    d. ineffectively meeting the needs of participants

The open-ended questionnaire, being less structured, requires time for coding and developing categories after the responses to the instrument are made. Since the researcher does not preconceive appropriate answers, variation in response means more work in the analysis and identification of categories. For example, those responding to the questionnaire might be asked:

Example 3. What is your opinion of the effectiveness of the HRD program at Benx Industries?

Example 4. What is your opinion about the effectiveness of the Paulson Community College program for General Education Development (GED) Test preparation?

Another advantage of the closed form is that it allows the researcher to guide participants along pertinent lines of thought associated with the phenomenon. The open-ended questionnaire, on the other hand, has the advantage of eliciting a wider latitude of possible responses from participants, and, consequently, information may result that is unanticipated by the researcher. The open-ended questionnaire is also less threatening and frustrating to certain special populations of participants—e.g., undereducated, culturally different, or marginally literate.

Generally it is preferable to design questionnaires in a closed form, if the research problem permits. However, an open questionnaire may be useful if the researcher cannot determine appropriate items for a closed questionnaire. Responses from an open questionnaire can assist the researcher in developing a more focused, closed-form questionnaire later on. Construction of both becomes easier with experience and practice. Kerlinger (1986) suggests the following preparation guidelines:

    1. Is the question related to the research problem and objectives?
    2. Is the type of question appropriate?
    3. Is the item clear and unambiguous?
    4. Is the question a leading question?

5. Does the question demand knowledge and information that the respondent does not have?
6. Does the question demand personal or delicate material the respondent may resist?
7. Is the question loaded with social desirability? (pp. 444–445)

In addition to the basic criteria for developing questions—focus, clarity, and supplying appropriate alternatives—it is important to be aware of the general socioeconomic and cultural backgrounds of participants.

Borg et al. (1993) use the following questions to evaluate the closed questionnaire:

1. Was the questionnaire pretested?
2. Did the questionnaire include any leading questions?
3. Were any psychologically threatening questions included in the questionnaire?
4. Were the subjects who received the questionnaire likely to have the information requested?
5. What percentage of subjects responded to the questionnaire?
6. What steps were taken to contact nonrespondents, and how many ultimately responded? (pp. 112–113)

All the questions raised here reflect upon the validity of the questionnaire and ultimately upon the data collected through its use. Pretesting an instrument helps work out problems that may arise after the data have been collected. Also, previewing the questionnaire for leading and threatening items will guard against bias and weak reliability of results.

Researchers who distribute questionnaires through the mail face another problem. Mass mailing sometimes results in limited return. Low return rate, in turn, affects the degree to which the researcher is assured of a representative sample. A return of 60% or higher is acceptable, but 75% or over is desirable. A well-constructed and pretested questionnaire will assist in getting an adequate number of responses from participants.

Because the questionnaire is self-administered, a well-constructed questionnaire always includes precise and detailed instructions. Physical appearance and size will contribute to legibility and clarity. The way items are sequenced is another factor for the researcher to consider. Questionnaire items usually are sequenced in the following way: items appearing first focus on identifying the respondent; the next items, upon demographic information; and finally, the focus is upon substantive questions. Figure 8.1 (Hauser, 1980) is an example of portions of a well-planned questionnaire.

PROFESSIONAL DEVELOPMENT INVENTORY

The following inventory is designed to provide information about the needs of trainers for continuing professional development. Such information is useful in designing professional programs.

Please answer the following, and *return this survey* in the enclosed envelope. *Thank you* for your professional cooperation.

1. *Age*: __21–32 __33–44 __45–56 __57 & over

2. *Sex*: __Male __Female

3. Number of *years* in the training profession:

   __ 0–4 __5–10 __11–24 __25 or more

4. Please indicate your highest level of education:
   __High school   __ B.A. or B.S. degree plus grad hours
   __ Associate degree   __ Master's or equivalent
   __ College, no degree   __ Master's plus grad hours
   __ B.A. or B.S. degree   __ Doctorate

5. Indicate the *major* area of study in which your degree(s) were earned:
   Associate: _____
   B.A./B.S.: _____
   Master's: _____
   Doctorate: _____

6. How many *hours per week* would you estimate you spend on professional development (reading journals, attending classes, seminars, workshops, study groups, etc.)?

   __ 0 __ 1–5 __ 6–10 __ 10 or more

7. Check EACH CATEGORY within which you have received professional development assistance in the past *TWO* years:

   __ College or university   __ In-house program (internal staff)
   __ Community   __ In-house program
      college   (external consultant)
   __ Professional   __ Other: _____
      organization

8. Please indicate what percentage of your *time* is spent in each of these roles, for example, 20%, 30%, and 50%.

   __ Learning Specialist   __ Administrator   __ Consultant

Figure 8.1 Sample questionnaire.

PROFESSIONAL DEVELOPMENT NEEDS ASSESSMENT

You may feel the need for new or additional professional development. Your needs are probably higher in some areas than in others. Below, please indicate your level of need for additional professional development in each of the competencies listed. *CIRCLE* the number that *best* corresponds to your need.

Level of Need

	High need					No need
1. Developing material resources—scripts, artwork, other instructional materials	5	4	3	2	1	0
2. Determining appropriate training approaches—evaluate alternatives, commercial and in-house.	5	4	3	2	1	0
3. Needs analysis and diagnosis—construct and administer instruments, analyze and interpret data.	5	4	3	2	1	0
4. Group and organization development—apply techniques of team building, role playing, simulations, etc.	5	4	3	2	1	0
5. Job-related training—analyze job requirements, performance problems, programs for.	5	4	3	2	1	0
6. Conduct classroom training—lecture, lead discussion, operate equipment, evaluate, etc.	5	4	3	2	1	0
7. Individual development planning and counseling—career, development needs, plans, programs.	5	4	3	2	1	0

Figure 8.1 Sample questionnaire. (continued)

8. Manage internal resources—obtain, train supervise, and evaluate instructor personnel.	5	4	3	2	1	0
9. Professional self-development—attend seminars, conferences and keep abreast of training practices,concepts, and theories.	5	4	3	2	1	0
10. Training research—design and implement studies interpret data in reports, influence future trends	5	4	3	2	1	0
11. Manage working relationships with managers—establish/ maintain good relations, explain recommendations.	5	4	3	2	1	0
12. Program design and development—design content, select methods, develop materials, evaluate, etc.	5	4	3	2	1	0
13. Manage training and development function—budget, plan, organize, staff, lead, and control.	5	4	3	2	1	0
14. Manage external resources—external instructors, materials, program logistics, consultants, etc.	5	4	3	2	1	0

Figure 8.1 Sample questionnaire. (continued)

Each item should pertain to a corresponding factor in the research phenomenon being studied. Avoid trivial or unrelated questions, no matter how interesting they may be. Problems identified by Wiersma (1986) that lessen the validity of the questionnaire are:

1. There is excessive nonresponse.
2. Items are poorly constructed or organized.
3. Respondents are not truthful in their responses.
4. Questions deal only with trivial information.

5. Data from different questions are difficult to synthesize. (p.186)

Use of the Interview

The interview adds a dimension to the gathering of survey data that is not provided by the questionnaire—namely, the interview ensures a face-to-face encounter with the research participant. Like questionnaires, interviews have two major types of formats: structured and unstructured. The researcher who uses a structured interview format, rather than a questionnaire, has the advantage of becoming an extension of the schedule of questions. Clarification, restatement, and explanation are all available for use in eliciting responses from participants. On the other hand, the researcher essentially becomes the research instrument when using an unstructured interview. The unstructured interview only guides the researcher through areas for investigation. The validity of results, however, rests more with the interviewing skill of the researcher than with the interview format. It is the responsibility of the interviewer to elicit pertinent information in the investigation.

Increasing the structure increases the consistency from one interview to the next. When large numbers of people are being interviewed, for example, a highly structured format or schedule is necessary so that data can be compared later. One purpose of using an unstructured interview, on the other hand, is to explore all possibilities regarding the information sought. This type of interview helps identify and define important areas of information that might be studied through other techniques at another time.

Interviews are often useful in gathering data when the topic to be explored is complex and emotionally loaded. Interviews are also helpful when the chance for observation is limited; gathering opinions and facts from participants while observing their personal characteristics gives an added dimension to the observational data.

Choosing the documentation method is an important part of the planning. Data can be recorded in writing or electronically recorded on audio or video tape. When possible, electronically recorded interviews are preferable. Note taking may result in missed information and thereby reduce the validity of the interview results. On the other hand, some research participants are sensitive to electronic recording devices and may resist, not respond authentically, or even refuse to participate.

Direct interaction with research participants, a characteristic of the interview technique, is both an advantage and a disadvantage.

Adaptability of the technique is the primary advantage of interviewing. "The well-trained interviewer can make full use of the responses of the subject to alter the interview situation. As contrasted with the questionnaire, which provides no immediate feedback, the interview permits the research worker to follow up leads that show up during the interview and thus obtain more data and greater clarity" (Borg et al., 1993, pp. 113–114). The interview technique also permits greater depth than other techniques. By using deliberate encouragement and establishing good rapport, a researcher can obtain information participants would reveal in no other way.

An example of this use of the interview technique is the focus group interview (Lederman, 1990). This technique is utilized when in-depth/qualitative data are needed to study a specific situation or phenomenon. Focus group participants are selected because of their interest or expertise in a particular area being researched. Rather than totally representative of a given population, the focus group is selected because it is a purposive sampling focused on a given topic (Patton, 1990). The concept of focus group interviewing is based on the therapeutic assumption that people will respond more freely in the security of a homogenous group concentrating on a single problem or phenomenon.

The interviewer must have skill and knowledge in order to gather valid and reliable data. An adequate amount of training is necessary; the specific amount is related to the complexity and sensitivity of the data to be gathered. More training is usually necessary for those who conduct unstructured interviews. A researcher doing focus group interviews must be sensitive to group dynamics, thus requiring some different skills than those needed in conducting single interviews. Interviewing can be learned through role playing, peer critiquing, use of videotape, and observation of experienced interviewers. However, skill comes only with practice and feedback on one's performance (Sommer & Sommer, 1986).

The interview starts with simple and interesting questions to engage the interviewee and to obtain a good response. If the interview entails several subsections or topics, each section or topic should flow from the simple to the more complex. Questions are introduced in a logical progression and asked completely and slowly. The full intent of the question should be made clear to the person being interviewed. Care should be taken not to interrupt the interviewee's train of thought. The interviewer must understand the response before moving on to the next question. Let the interviewees articulate their answers rather than assume what the response will be. The fundamental principle of qualitative interviewing, Patton (1990) emphasizes, is to provide a framework within which respondents can express their own understanding in their own terms.

From the foregoing discussion of techniques, the reader probably recognizes that not all pertinent research data can be gathered by surveying. Other procedures and techniques may be needed to complement or replace the questionnaire or interview. The following section discusses observation, another major way of gathering data.

OBSERVATION

Viewing events and behavior of people is not just an alternative method of getting the same type of information that research participants could give in response to an interview or questionnaire. Observational data is directly related to typical behavioral situations; that is, people are seen in action. Because participants are frequently unaware of their behavior, having to recall or recount the past is not as productive as observing their behavior directly. Social scientists, for instance, in observing various cultural groups, often note facts that their best local informants would never have reported (Kidder & Judd, 1986).

Observation can serve several purposes. Since it can range from highly unstructured to highly structured, a great deal of flexibility is possible. In an exploratory study, for example, the technique of observation may be unstructured: the researcher observes while participating in a group activity related to the research. In contrast, when the research design calls for a comparison of events, a systematic rating scale is frequently used. The rating scale allows the researcher to concurrently observe the events and assess the degree to which an attribute, such as collaborative learning behavior, is exhibited by an individual or group. This makes comparison and analysis easier.

Observational techniques can be effective when participants in the research are unable or unwilling to respond in written or oral form. People who are physically handicapped, limited in their use of language, or highly sensitive to questioning or testing may have to be observed in order for the researcher to gather needed data.

Two problems associated with use of observation are the unpredictability of events the researcher wishes to sample and the "present" orientation of observation. Because forecasting all pertinent events the researcher needs to observe is difficult, the researcher may not be able to gather all needed data through observation. For example, following the activities of a group over several months in order to observe the point at which a gathering of individuals actually became a group may not be feasible. The technique of observation is also limited to sampling only the present; the story of a person's life, for instance, would be impossible to observe.

Planning the Observation

In planning the type of observation technique to fit the research problem, researchers may ask themselves the following questions:

1. What should be observed?
2. How should the observation be recorded?
3. What procedures should be used to try to ensure the accuracy of the observation?
4. What relationship should exist between the observer and the observed, and how can such a relationship be established?

Accuracy is the key to making the technique effective. Special training is needed to move from casual observer to systematic observer. Given the erratic nature of casual observation, that is, responding to any stimuli and to the impulse of motives unique to the observer, this training is of utmost importance. Through training, the observer seeks to gain uniformity with other observers also attempting to describe accurately the same phenomenon.

In using structured observation techniques, the researcher typically is searching for the relationship of independent variables to a dependent variable. The independent variable may be a method of teaching used in the instruction of adults, or it may be the learner's behavior in pursuit of a learning project. In either example, the independent variable is defined in terms that make observation possible. If the teaching method is to be observed, a description of the method in behavioral terms is needed. Only after the events to be observed have been described precisely can the observation technique be a. useful tool for gathering data. According to Kerlinger (1986), with structured observation "the fundamental task of the observer is to assign behaviors to categories" (p. 489).

A major concern of researchers planning structured observation is a balance between the "molecular approach" and the "molar approach" (Kerlinger, 1986, p. 490). This means choosing units of behavior that are small enough to ensure reliability in observation (molecular), while not reducing the size of units so much that they bear no resemblance to the context of human activity (molar). In the molecular approach to observation, verbal interaction, for example, is broken into words or phrases, whereas the molar observer first defines the variable broadly and then proceeds to identify several behaviors that fall into that one category. The molar observer "depends on his experience, knowledge, and interpretation of the meaning of the actions he is observing. The molecular observer . . . seeks to push his own experience and interpretations out of the observational picture. He records what he sees—and no more" (p. 490). A variety of rating scales can be used in observation, such as checklists, forced-choice inventories, category rating scales, numerical rating scales, and graphic rating scales. Each is somewhat different in format. Checklists, for example, are used as a guide in the observation and simply include a list of behaviors of events that potentially could be viewed by the observer. The observer checks those things on the list that are actually seen.

The following is an example checklist, randomly arranged, that might be used to observe the interaction within an adult learning group:

__ collaborative
__ consensual
__ apathetic
__ goal-oriented
__ congenial
__ hostile

The observer checks all the descriptions that apply to the group during the observation period, if any.

Forced-choice scales, on the other hand, provide a limited number of alternatives (generally 4 to 6) from which the observer chooses just one. A forced-choice scale using some of the same items for the same purpose, that is, to observe the interaction of a learning group, might be ordered in the following way:

__ collaborative
__ goal-oriented
__ consensual
__ congenial
__ apathetic
__ hostile

In this case, the observer is to choose only one alternative—the one that best represents the group. The descriptions on this scale are arranged in an order from bottom to top that represents increasing degrees of positive group interaction (collaborative being most positive and hostile being least positive).

Category, numerical, and graphic scales are arranged in a continuum or in an ordered series of categories with numerical values attached to each individual item as shown below.

hostile	apathetic	congenial	consensual	goal-oriented	collaborative
1	2	3	4	5	6

The observer rates the group by checking a point on the continuum that best represents what is being observed. The alternatives on a scale describe the degree an individual or group possesses certain traits. In the case of the adult learning group, the trait to be observed is group cohesiveness. Of the observation scales available, graphic scales are the most easily used and, therefore, are used frequently.

Problems of validity exist with use of rating scales. Raters tend to make "halo effect" errors; that is, they overlook specific characteristics due to the overall good impression made by the individual being rated. Other errors in rating judgment, according to Ary, Jacobs, and Razavich (1985) are generosity errors—to give the benefit of the doubt; severity errors—to rate very low in all categories; and errors of central tendency—to avoid extremes in rating, thus placing all individuals in the middle of the scale. Once again, rater training is important in order to reduce errors and ultimately increase reliability. Another procedure that increases reliability is the use of multiple raters. As the number of raters increases, so does reliability.

The following discussion focuses on a particular type of structured observation—content or document analysis.

Content Analysis

Content analysis is the systematic analysis of communications, whether it be in visual, aural, or printed form. It is defined by Holsi (1969) as "any techniques for making inferences by objectively and systematically identifying specific characteristics of messages" (p. 14). Patton (1990) describes this type of analysis as "the process of identifying, coding, and catagorizing the primary patterns of data" (p. 281). Guba and Lincoln (1981) point out four major characteristics of content analysis about which most research methodologists agree.

1. It is a rule-guided process in which certain steps are adhered to in the analysis.

2. It is systematic; the steps are completed routinely and consistently.
3. It is a process that aims for generality (application to other contents).
4. It deals with manifest or apparent content (what can be seen).

Both quantitative and qualitative approaches are used in content analysis. However, it is primarily a quantitative technique, generally used to determine and quantify what is emphasized in a document—for example, the incidence of propaganda, sexism, or racism. But the technique may also be used for a qualitative purpose, such as to determine how the learning process occurs by studying autobiographical material from a number of accomplished learners. Content analysis can also be used for studying the "mechanics" of the message in a document, such as reading difficulty, format, and style.

The researcher chooses units of content as the first step in the process of content analysis. Berelson (1954) gives five units of content: words, themes, characters, items, and space-and-time measures. Typically, the smallest unit of content is the word, although a smaller unit, such as a letter, is possible. By simply counting the number of times a word is used, it is possible to infer the preferences or values of the one who produced the material. Most often a theme, a phrase, or sentence is the unit of content for analysis. For example, looking for the number of sentences that contain reference to "training" rather than "education" might suggest a predisposition toward the type of learning the producer of the material is, or wishes to be, engaged in. The third type of content analysis is character analysis. This refers to studying the personification of individuals portrayed in material, such as a story, film, or play. The study of Eleanor Roosevelt as she is portrayed in film is an example of character analysis. Item content analysis, the fourth unit of analysis, is the study of an entire production, such as a book, play, or autobiography. Effective use of item content analysis is made in studying the learning activities of special persons in the past to determine motivation and style of learning. A study of the autobiography of Malcolm X, for example, that analyzes his motivation for education is content analysis. Space-and-time analysis refers to actual physical characteristics of content: the number of words, paragraphs, column inches of written material or number of minutes, frames, scenes, etc., in visual and aural media. The ultimate goal in content analysis is to quantify the content for purposes of comparison.

Duncan (1989) emphasizes the importance of content analysis in health education research. Unobtrusive techniques such as observing defacement of posters or bumper stickers can be used to study attitudes toward controversial health issues. Other examples of how content analysis may be used to research adult health issues are analyses of popular magazines, advertisement of cigarettes, or frequency of references to human sexuality in textbooks related to the handicapped.

Broad application is one of the advantages of content analysis as a technique for research data gathering. It is also efficient, economical, and can be done with a great deal of objectivity and reliability.

Qualitative Observation

Observation is particularly suited to gathering qualitative data. Qualitative data are the detailed descriptions of situations, events, people, interactions, and observed behaviors; direct quotations from people about their experiences, attitudes, beliefs, and thoughts; and excerpts or entire passages from documents, correspondence, records, and case histories (Patton, 1990). Where quantitative measurement uses objective and standardized instruments to limit data collection to prescribed categories of response, qualitative data are open-ended in order to find out what people's lives, experiences, and interactions mean to them in their own terms and in their natural settings. Qualitative measures add depth and detail to data gathered from objective techniques, such as descriptive surveys or objective tests. Bogdan and Taylor (1975) describe qualitative methods by saying that "they allow us to know people personally and to see them as they are developing their own definitions of the world" (p. 4).

Participant observation is a frequently used and effective technique for gathering qualitative data (Merriam, 1988). This technique allows for data to be "systematically and unobtrusively collected" (Taylor & Bogdan, 1984, p. 15). Use of this technique requires the observer to take the role, at least partially, of a participant. The researcher participates but does not become totally absorbed in the activity because one must simultaneously stay sufficiently detached to observe and analyze. Furthermore, one has to be conscious of how the act of observation may change what is being observed. It is also assumed that the observer's views of what is being observed change as the research progresses.

Unobtrusive observation measures are those techniques of observation not inducing response or reaction from participants (Webb,

1981). Unobtrusive observation techniques assess behavior or behavior patterns without the knowledge or awareness of those who are being observed (Guba & Lincoln, 1981). The observation of traffic patterns in a museum and usage wear of books in a library are examples. Examining the content of publications for references to such topics as AIDS is an example of unobtrusive observation. Another is sampling data from ongoing documents that record human events, such as minutes of meetings or birth and death records.

As with the use of the interview techniques, the reliability of results rests to a great extent with the observer. Care in designing devices and scales does improve reliability. However, observers trained and practiced in coding and recording and aware of the potential biases they bring to research contribute significantly to the reliability of results.

TESTING

A third category of data-gathering techniques is the objective test. Basically, a test is a systematic procedure for obtaining from an individual a set of responses that may be converted to a numerical score. The test score represents the degree to which the individual possesses the characteristic(s) being measured. A major difference between a test and a scale is the idea of competition associated with the test; that is, on a test one achieves a certain mark as a indicator of progress or success. Essential to the concept of testing is objectivity, or the degree to which agreement can be reached between scorers of the test. Knowledge of the characteristics and methods of test construction is important to the researcher who wishes to use tests as means of gathering research data.

Test Validity

A major consideration for the researcher gathering quantitative data is the matter of content and construct validity. If a test or another scaled instrument for gathering data is used, the question arises: Does the instrument measure the attitude or characteristic it is intended to measure? The content validity of the research instrument represents the extent to which items on a test or scale match the behavior, skill, or effect the researcher intends them to measure. Judgment of content validity is done through a critical assessment of the test by the researcher to determine how representative sample items are.

Content validity has two forms, concurrent validity and predictive validity. Both are of concern to the researcher if a comparison of the performance of participants is important in the analysis of data. Concurrent validity and predictive validity are sometimes referred to as criterion validity because they both are estimated through comparing performance with some criterion external to the test. Concurrent validity estimates the degree to which the performance scale or rating concurs with achievement. An example is the score on a preparatory examination for the GED test that concurs with the actual GED score an individual would achieve. Predictive validity estimates the extent to which performance on the test forecasts such things as achievement or job success. How well, for example, does passing the GED preparatory examination predict future success on the actual GED test?

Construct validity is established by both logical and empirical means. A construct is a theoretical explanation of an attribute or characteristic created by scholars for purposes of study. Constructs are abstract and, having not been observed directly, are not considered actual behaviors or events. Therefore, construct validity is first estimated logically by how well the various attributes, characteristics, and behaviors represent the particular construct. For example, the degree to which mental agility and physical dexterity actually represent intelligence is a question of construct validity. Then, an empirical analysis is done, comparing performance on the test that represents the construct—intelligence—with other tests measuring the same construct. Thus, construct validity is estimated both logically and empirically. For a detailed explanation of tests, the reader is referred to authoritative sources of measurement and evaluations, such as Buros (1992) *The Eleventh Mental Measurement Yearbook*.

Types of Objective Tests

Objective tests available to researchers are numerous, but all the various types of tests can be subsumed within five general categories: "intelligence and aptitude tests, achievement tests, personality measures, attitude and value scales, and miscellaneous objective measures" (Kerlinger, 1986, p. 451).

Intelligence, Aptitude and Achievement Tests

The tests in the intelligence and aptitude category measure potential for achievement, whereas achievement tests, the second category, indicate present proficiency or knowledge within specific areas of content. Some tests are professionally developed and use scores based upon norms developed through field testing. Scores that are related to group norms make comparison for research purposes easier. These types of tests are typically called standardized tests.

Occasionally instructor-made or researcher-made tests are developed for measuring aptitude or achievement in specific content areas. This is very time consuming and should be done only when professionally developed instruments are unavailable. Since validity and reliability of the latter are the result of meticulous construction and field testing, they should be used whenever possible. The researcher will be more assured of valid results with much less time expended. Some aptitude and intelligence tests used in adult education and human resource development research are the Graduate Record Examination (aptitude) and the Wechsler Adult Intelligence Scale.

Personality Measures

The third type of objective test, personality measures, is one of the most complex areas of psychological testing. These tests measure personality traits in which the term *trait* is used to signify an organization of behaviors representing a personality pattern. The difficulty with measuring personality is being certain of how valid the measures really are. Personality based upon multiple traits, interactions, and influences of one trait upon another is so elusive that it defies precise measurement. Personality is measured through attitude inventories, rating scales, and projective techniques.

In a personality inventory, the participant is supplied a host of statements describing various behavior patterns. By responding "yes," "no," or "uncertain" to each statement on the list of behaviors, the participant indicates which are self-descriptive. A score is derived by summing the responses associated with a trait being measured. Personality inventories are simple and inexpensive to develop, but the problem with them, as with most personality measures, is lack of validity.

Another widely used technique to measure personality is the rating scale. The rater is instructed to place the person being rated on a continuum or in a category that is characteristic of the behavior that person exhibits. The graphic scale is one of the most commonly used scales for measuring personality.

Attitude and Value Scales

In addition to intelligence and aptitude, achievement, and personality tests, a fourth category of objective tests includes attitude and value scales. This type of test attempts to elicit opinions from the participants that reflect their attitudes or values about a given topic or situation. When measuring attitude, the researcher is measuring "a predisposition to think, feel, perceive, and behave toward a referent or cognitive object" (Kerlinger, p. 453). An attitude is a set of beliefs that causes an individual to act selectively toward such things as ethnic groups, races, institutions, religious sects, political issues, and personal and constitutional rights. Values, on the other hand, are the preferences one has for all those things as influenced by culture.

Several attitude and value scale techniques are available to the researcher; the most commonly used is the Likert technique. The examples in Figure 8.2 use the Likert technique to investigate attitudes of women returning to school. Individuals are asked to indicate one of the five responses ranging from Strongly Agree (SA) to Strongly Disagree (SD). The scale is scored by adding the corresponding numerical weights below each response. Other types of scales are Thurstone scales—based upon equal appearing intervals; Guttman scales, which use a cumulative technique in rating; and semantic differential scales, which are constructed around denotative and connotative meanings, measuring only one variable. Scales used to measure attitude, such as the Kuder Preference Inventory and the Strong Inventory, are examples of standardized tests that use the Likert technique. (For a detailed description of scale construction, the reader is asked to refer to authoritative sources in test construction and evaluation procedures such as Kerlinger, 1986.)

Projective and Sociometric Techniques

A fifth major grouping of objective tests includes projective and sociometric tests. These methods are most commonly used in the fields

	SA	A	U	D	SD
Starting back to school as an adult was no different from starting as a child.	(−2)	(−1)	(0)	(1)	(2)
Returning to school was most difficult because of lack of support from my family	(2)	(1)	(0)	(−1)	(−2)

Figure 8.2 Likert scale items.

of psychology, social psychology, psychiatry, and sociology to indirectly elicit feelings of clients. When projective techniques are used to study personality, an unstructured stimulus such as an ink blot (Rorschach Test) or a picture (Thematic Apperception Test) is introduced. The individual respondent is asked to supply a story that interprets the blot or picture. The purpose of the technique is to get a sample of behavior from which influences can be drawn about personality, emotions, needs, internal conflicts, and self-images.

Projective techniques most applicable to research in adult education and training are (1) word association, (2) sentence completion, and (3) the open-ended question. Through these, the participants share feelings, attitudes, and thoughts that they might not share through direct means such as a questionnaire or an interview. Projective techniques are useful in determining the learning needs of adults.

Whereas projective techniques are used to study characteristics of individuals, sociometric techniques are used to study the organization of social groups. Sociometric techniques ask individuals to select first, second, and third choices of companions in some social situation, such as a team of workers or a learning group. Results of individual selections are then organized into a graphic figure called a sociogram. The sociogram visually represents the pattern of interpersonal relationships and can be quantified for use in research.

SUMMARY

In summary, data collection in the research process is the use of an intricate set of procedures and techniques aimed at getting the best information available (see Table 8.1). Procedures and techniques are selected on the basis of what is suggested by the chosen method of research, e.g., experimental, grounded theory, historical, or action. In turn, the choice of all three—method, procedure, and technique—results from the researcher's perception of the world and from the researcher's judgment of how best to address the research problem or concerns, given that perception.

A rational/empirical perception of reality, for example, usually leads to describing and proving things external to the researcher. Therefore, the trustworthiness of data is dependent upon the validity and reliability of the instruments used to gather the research data. A phenomenological perspective, on the other hand, suggests an intuitive method; thus, the researcher becomes more the instrument of data collection, and validity is an internal matter to the researcher.

Table 8.1 Summary of Research Data Gathering Techniques

TYPES	USES	ADVANTAGES	LIMITATIONS
Survey: Closed/Forced-Choice Questionnaire	Assessment of facts, attitudes, or opinions from research participants when the range and type of response generally can be anticipated by the researcher.	Easy to administer and decode data; a large group of participants may complete concurrently; may be administered through the mail and reach participants over a wide geographical area.	Provides little opportunity for divergent response or for in-depth material from participants; requires a great deal of preparation in instrument construction and validation prior to conducting the study.
Open-Form Questionnaire	Assessment of facts, attitudes, or opinions from research participants when the range and type of response cannot be anticipated, or the researcher does not wish to anticipate responses.	Allows participants to diverge, reflect, and respond in a more unique way than through structured formats (forced-choice questionnaires or interview schedules).	Focus is sometimes lost in response in relation to the purposes for the study; difficult to record, code, and analyze.
Structured Interview	Assessment of facts, attitudes, and opinions from research participants who cannot or will not respond to a written survey instrument (questionnaire).	Researcher interacts directly with the research participant, which permits assessment of nonverbal communications and encourages participation by the subjects; data easy to code and analyze.	Provides little opportunity for participants to diverge in response; more time consuming for the researcher and participant, as well as less convenient.

Table 8.1 (continued)

TYPES	USES	ADVANTAGES	LIMITATIONS
Unstructured	Assessment of facts, attitudes, or opinions from participants in research that requires data to be elicited through self-initiation or intuitive introspection.	Responses initiated by the research participants in most instances, which contributes to greater authenticity; allows the researcher to probe for the full meaning of response and typically results in more in-depth response and "richer" data.	Researcher has less control of the interview; data difficult to record, code, and analyze, more time consuming than the structured interview; requires training; can be threatening to participants.
Observation: (Structured) Checklists	Documentation and itemization of events, behaviors, or conditions.	Data easily coded and analyzed.	Requires training of the researcher; limits observation to predetermined list of descriptions or terms.
Rating Scales	Documentation and rating of degree that a particular characteristic, condition, or behavior is present in the observation.	Use of equal-interval scale adds power to researcher's ability to measure; indicates degrees of values being observed, thus more discriminating.	Requires intense and accurate observation; training is required in use of the scale.
Content Analysis	Documentation and quantitative analysis (primarily) of content in printed, aural, and visual media.	Few time constraints on the observation; the researcher can work at his or her own speed.	The researcher is limited to what is in print, recorded, or photographed; does not allow for interpretation beyond the material being analyzed.

Table 8.1 (continued)

TYPES	USES	ADVANTAGES	LIMITATIONS
(Unstructured) Unobtrusive Measures	Systematic observation of patterns of behavior or events in natural settings that does not induce response or reaction from subjects of the research.	Research subjects are not influenced by the research process; the researcher is not affected by extraneous factors that are presented while observing human interaction in progress.	The researcher does not interact with subjects of the research, and therefore may not detect the full depth of meaning in the data gathered.
Participant Observation	Comprehensive investigation of events or behavior in their natural setting.	Can combine the advantages of unstructured interview with observation to produce qualitative data; participants may be encouraged to respond more naturally in greater depth.	Influence of the researcher's presence as a participant may result in limited or unauthentic response; time consuming; effective use requires training and experience.
Tests (Objective) Intelligence and Aptitude	Quantitative assessment of research participant's potential for achievement in areas such as education.	Relatively easy to administer and score; gives quantitative data that assists the researcher in making comparison of individual abilities.	Tests are limited by lack of knowledge of what actually constitutes human intelligence or aptitude; narrow in scope and tend to represent a limited aspect of potential for achievement.

Table 8.1 (continued)

TYPES	USES	ADVANTAGES	LIMITATIONS
Achievement	Appraisal of participant's proficiency or knowledge in given content areas (e.g., math or manual skills).	Easy to administer and score; gives an approximation of progress for comparison.	Limits measurement of achievement to what is performed on the test.
Personality	Assessment of traits possessed by an individual that reflect an organization of behavior.	Quantitatively separates various human behaviors for study.	Some tests lack validity.
Attitude and Value	Assessment of an individual's predisposition toward an object or situation.	Quantitatively separates affective dimension of human experience for comparison.	Some tests lack validity.
Projective and Sociometric	Sampling of behavior that results from an unstructured stimulus, from which inferences about needs, feelings, self-concept, etc., can be made.	Absence of structure may elicit more natural response and "richer" data.	Lacks validity; relies heavily on subjective judgment.
(Informal) Researcher Prepared	Instrument developed for assessment of knowledge, attitudes, or skills to provide data required in conducting the study, when a standardized test is unavailable.	Serves the need for special data that could be gathered in no other way.	Time consuming; may lack validity without substantial field testing; may be of limited value for comparison without norms.

No matter what perspective guides the process, a plan of procedures and techniques is essential in conducting quality research. Sometimes the plan cannot be completely formulated at the beginning of a project because of the intuitive and/or inductive nature of the research. However, systematic inquiry requires the documentation of how data were gathered as well as what was concluded from the data. A plan that is thoughtfully developed before the research project begins and that considers data sampling, types of intervention by the researcher, and ways the data are to be analyzed by the researcher in drawing conclusions, is well worth the amount of time invested.

REFERENCES

Ary, D., Jacobs, L. C., & Razavich, A. (1985). *Introduction to research in education*. (3rd ed.). New York: Holt, Rinehart and Winston.

Berelson, B. (1954). Content analysis. In *Handbook of social psychology*, (Ed.). G. Lindzed. Reading, MA: Addison-Wesley.

Bogdan, R., & Taylor, S. J. (1975). *Introduction to qualitative research methods: A phenomenological approach*. New York: John Wiley & Sons.

Borg, W. R. (1981). *Applying educational research: A practical guide*. (2nd ed.). New York: Longman.

Borg, W. R., Gall, J. P., & Gall, M. D. (1993). *Applying educational research: A practical guide*. (3rd ed.). New York: Longman.

Boshier, R., and Collins, J. B. (1985). The Houle typology after twenty-two years: A large-scale empirical test, *Adult Education Quarterly*, 35, 113–130.

Buros, O. K. (1992). *The eleventh mental measurements yearbook*. J. J. Kramer & J. C. Conoley (Eds.). Lincoln, NE: The Buros Institute of Mental Measurements of the University of Nebraska-Lincoln.

Dickinson, G., and Blunt, A. (Eds.) (1980). Survey Research. In H. B. Long, R. Hiemstra and Associates (Eds.), *Changing approaches to studying of adult education* (pp. 50–62). San Francisco: Jossey-Bass.

Dimmock, K. H. (1985). Models of adult participation in informal science education. Unpublished doctoral dissertation, Northern Illinois University.

Duncan, D. F. (1989, December). Content analysis in health education research: An introduction to purpose and methods, *Health Education*, 20 (7).

Grabowski, S. M. (1980). Trends in graduate Research. In H. B. Long, R. Hiemstra and Associates, (Eds.), *Changing approaches to studying of adult education* (pp. 119–128). San Francisco: Jossey-Bass.

Guba, E. G., & Lincoln, Y. S. (1981). *Effective evaluation: Improving the usefulness of evaluation results through responsive and naturalistic approaches.* San Francisco: Jossey-Bass.

Hauser, J. G. (1980). A study of professional development and self perceived needs for continuing professional education among selected training specialists (pp. 143–144). Unpublished doctoral dissertation, Northern Illinois University.

Holsti, O. (1968). Content analysis. In G. Lindzey and E. Aronson (Eds.), *Handbook of social psychology.* Reading, MA: Addison-Wesley.

Hudson, J. (1969). *The history of adult education.* London: Woburn Press.

Johnstone, J. W. C., and Rivera, R. J. (1965). *Volunteers for learning: A study of educational pursuits of American adults.* Chicago: Aldine Company Publishing.

Kidder, L. H., and Judd, C. M. (1986). *Research methods in social relations.* New York: Holt, Rinehart & Winston.

Kerlinger, F. N. (1986). *Foundations of behavior research* (3rd ed.). New York: Holt, Rinehart & Winston.

Lederman, L. C. (1990, April). Assessing educational effectiveness: The focus group interview as a technique for data collection, *Communication Education, 38.*

Merriam, S. (1988). *Case study research in education: A qualitative approach.* San Francisco: Jossey-Bass.

Patton, M. Q. (1990). *Qualitative evaluation methods.* Beverly Hills: Sage Publications.

Sommer, R., & Sommer, B. (1986). *A practical guide to behavioral research* (2nd ed.). New York: Oxford University Press.

Taylor, S. J., & Bogdan, R. (1984). *Introduction to qualitative research methods: The search for meaning* (2nd ed.). New York: John Wiley & Sons.

Tough, A. (1979). *The adults' learning projects.* (2nd ed.) Toronto: Ontario Institute for Studies in Education.

Tough, A. (1982). *Intentional changes.* Chicago: Follett Publishers.

Webb, E. T. (1981). *Nonreactive measures in the social sciences.* Boston: Houghton-Mifflin.

Wiersma, W. (1986). *Research methods in education* (4th ed.). Boston: Allyn and Bacon.

CHAPTER 9

WRITING UP YOUR FINDINGS

Many people think of the research process as a matter of designing a study, collecting and analyzing data, and interpreting the results. But the process is incomplete without the very important final step of *reporting* the results. Unfortunately, much good research goes unnoticed because many investigators underestimate the time and discipline it takes to write up their findings. For most, doing almost anything else is preferable to sitting down at a word processor and writing! Transforming the information and insights gleaned from an array of notebooks, tapes, or computer printouts into a written format that others can understand often becomes an insurmountable task. However, if the research is going to contribute to the knowledge base of a field or enhance practice in some way, this important step cannot be avoided. There are some things you can do to ease the agony of writing up your findings. First, acquaint yourself with the standard format of a research report. Next, consider how to maximize the time you do spend writing.

THE STANDARD RESEARCH REPORT

A standard format for reporting research has evolved from the logical progression of steps in an actual investigation. The inherent logic of this format has resulted in its repeated use, which in turn has led to its being *required* by some journals and other publication outlets. While no doubt some researchers feel constrained by the format and not all types of research can be made to fit, there are several advantages. First, the format offers the writer a readymade outline for writing the research findings; no time is wasted devising an outline for each piece of research. Second, readers can easily extract desired information from any number of studies because the same type of information is found in approximately the same location in every report. Third, a uniform format allows for easier and faster distribution of work and supervision of those assisting in writing the results

169

of a large-scale investigation. Overall, the standard format is flexible enough for writers to delete sections that are not needed and to add or change items that will contribute to the report's clarity. It might be noted that even historical, philosophical, qualitative, and emancipatory/critical forms of research can generally follow this format. For regardless of the research design being used, nearly all reports of research identify the problem, refer to pertinent literature, discuss sources of data and how data were analyzed, and present and interpret findings (see Becker, 1986; Van Maanen, 1988; and Wolcott, 1990).

The underlying structure of the standard research report can be divided into halves, and each half can be further divided into several sections (Fox, 1969). The first half represents "the thinking and action that occurred before the point at which the data were collected" (p. 771). Fox more fully describes this basic dichotomy as follows:

> Before we report *any* of the data relevant to the hypotheses tested or questions studied, we must present all of the material on our thinking about the problem which structured the study, about the literature, about how we actually did the study, and any descriptive data about the people who comprised our sample. All of this must be out of the way so that the section reporting the data themselves can be free of this pre-data-collection information. (p. 711)

The first or "pre-results" half can be subdivided into the introduction of the research problem, the review of the literature, and data collection procedures. The second half of the report can be broken into three sections covering the results of the study, interpretation of the results, and conclusions and suggestions for further study. The structure of the report can be visualized in Figure 9.1. This subdividing, then, reveals the six sections that form the body of a research report; typically, a report also includes some standard introductory

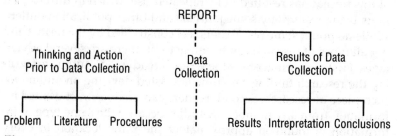

Figure 9.1. Structure of a research report.

and closing material as well. A brief description of the various parts of a research report follows.

Introductory Materials

Depending upon the audience for whom the report is being written and the length of the report, preliminary materials might include a title page, preface and acknowledgments, table of contents, and a list of tables and/or figures. In most cases an abstract of the study is offered on a page prior to the report itself. Abstracts are brief summaries of the study presenting a statement of the problem, the procedures used to study the problem, and the results of the study. The purpose of an abstract is to help readers decide whether to read the report, to assist other researchers who scan great amounts of literature for information pertinent to their own work, or to provide a framework or advance organizer to someone intending to read the full report. Abstracts for journal articles rarely exceed 200 words; in longer, self-contained publications, such as a monograph or in-house report, abstracts may be one to two pages in length.

Presentation of the Research Problem

This section of the report tells the reader the purpose of the research, the nature and scope of the problem under study, and the need for the study. It is also important to discuss the theoretical framework from which the problem was derived or has emerged. This discussion helps to anchor the study in a larger context and usually reveals the significance of the particular aspect under study. It should also be clear from the introductory section what variables are being isolated for study and how these variables logically and reasonably relate to concepts and the problem area already identified. In short, the reader is given a clearly stated rationale for the problem. That is, one will know after reading this section, why the study is being done at all and why it is being done in the way the investigator has chosen. The reader also needs to be convinced that the problem is sufficiently important to be investigated, yet narrow enough to be treated in a thorough manner. After finishing the introductory section, the reader should know (1) what the problem area is; (2) how (generally) the problem is being approached in this study; (3) what the principal variables (if known) of the study are; and (4) why it is being undertaken at all.

The Literature Review

The several functions of the literature review are discussed in detail in Chapter 3. Briefly, the literature review acquaints the reader with the history of the problem under consideration, establishes the fact that existing findings do not answer the questions related to the problem, and helps establish a conceptual framework for the immediate study. While the literature review usually comes after the introduction of the problem, in some highly theoretical or philosophical studies it may make more sense to reverse the two sections. In this way, the literature review leads to the conceptualization of the problem rather than to supporting a problem already formulated. In grounded theory studies, the literature can be integrated with the emerging theory rather than set off by itself (Glaser, 1978).

Research Procedures or Methodology

The purpose of this section is to tell the reader how the study was done. As is discussed in Chapters 4 through 7, each methodology— whether it is an experimental design or a historical inquiry or a case study—has systematic procedures for collecting and handling data. It is these procedures and how they have been used to solve the research problem that are detailed in this section. For example, a research question about how adult nonreaders cope in our society would require an explanation of a field-based methodology such as grounded theory or case study.

In general, this section of the research report presents a detailed explanation of the techniques and tools used to deal with the research problem such that another researcher could replicate the study. Regardless of the methodology, it is important to present the following information: the type of data used and reasons for its use; the way in which the data were selected; how the data were analyzed after being collected; and precautions the investigator has taken to ensure that the data and its analysis will justify inferences drawn from them.

Depending upon the type of study, methodology may include the following items:

1. *Definition of terms.* While a conceptual discussion of terms is sometimes offered in the introduction section, a functional definition—how the researcher is defining terms for this particular study—usually evolves from the literature review and so is found in this section of the report.

2. *Research design.* In general, the type of design used and a rationale for its selection are included here. Hypotheses or research questions used to guide the investigation follow the design discussion, if appropriate.
3. *Sample selection.* A detailed description of the nature of the sample and how it was selected is included. This "sample" may be people, inanimate objects, events, etc.
4. *Data collection procedures.* A discussion of how the data were obtained may also include a discussion of a pilot study. All types of studies, including historical and philosophical, look at data. A discussion of how they were accumulated for analysis is thus an important section regardless of methodology.
5. *Data analysis.* This part discusses how the data were processed in order to answer the questions raised by the study.
6. *Assumptions and limitations.* The writer should make it clear what is being assumed and what the limits or weaknesses are of the particular methodology being used, with particular reference to how it is being applied to the problem under investigation.

Findings or Results

This section describes what the researcher has found as a result of the investigation. Findings may be presented in narrative form, in tables, graphs, charts, pictures, numbers, or formulas. In general, factual data are kept separate from inferences and interpretation, which usually, but not always, follow presentation of the actual findings. In historical, philosophical, case study, ethnographic, or grounded theory studies, interpretation may be interwoven with the factual results. If this is the case, it should be clear to the reader what is a finding and what is an interpretation of the finding. For example, to say that "17 percent of those interviewed were married" is a finding. To say that "only 17 percent of those interviewed were married" indicates surprise on the part of the investigator. Inherent in saying "only" is a value judgment that may be linked to interpretation as in "only 17 percent of those interviewed were married, which may explain why . . . "

Discussion and Interpretation of Results

If not already integrated with the reported findings, the discussion and interpretation section allows the researchers to explain why the study produced the results that it did.

> The discussion is a much freer section than the results. Where the results are data-*bound*, the discussion is only data-*based*. This means that in the discussion the researcher is free to take off from the data and discuss what he believes they mean and how he believes they came about. Notice, however, that while the researcher has considerably more freedom in the discussion section, it is nevertheless based on the data. (Fox, 1969, p. 742)

In the discussion section, findings are tied back to the theory and rationale presented for the study in the first part of the report. Insights gleaned from the literature review may also be referred to in interpreting the results of the study.

Summary, Conclusions, Recommendations

The entire study should be briefly summarized at the beginning of this section. Generalizations or conclusions safely supported by the study might also be presented here for the first time or succinctly summarized from the discussion section. Finally, the investigator may want to include recommendations for implementing the findings or suggestions for further research. Suggestions for further research can be particularly helpful to other researchers in that the investigator of the present study has learned much about the problem, including what procedures or techniques were helpful or problematic, whether the question itself needs to be refocused, and what related questions might be worth pursuing.

References and Appendix

A list of the references used in the literature review and elsewhere in the report follows the body of the work. The style and arrangement of the reference section should reflect the audience for whom the report was written. A report for the general public will have few if any references, whereas a scholarly journal article will have a complete and accurate documentation of all references. The same is true for material in an appendix. Depending upon the audience, such material might include tests or survey forms, personal communications, charts or graphs in addition to those found in the results section, raw data such as transcribed interviews, or historical documents.

Reporting one's research findings is made easier by becoming familiar with the standard format. Other areas of importance to the re-

search writer are: editorial style and documentations, writing and reviewing guidelines, tables and figures, and the use of statistics.

EDITORIAL STYLE AND DOCUMENTATION

Editorial style refers to the mechanical details of putting together a
research report. How one does footnotes, references, spacing of lines
and paragraphs, headings, placement of tables and figures, and other
mechanical aspects of a report depends upon the style used. There
are many editorial styles, each providing "roughly the same information, which is sufficient to allow the reader to check the original
sources of quotations, opinions, and facts used in the paper: the name
of the author, the title of the publication, the facts about the publication—place of publication, publisher, date, pages" (Maimon et al.,
1981, p. 110). Four of the more commonly used editorial styles are:

1. *Publication Manual of the American Psychological Association.* 4th ed.
   Washington, DC: American Psychological Association, 1994.
   This style is used by over 200 journals in the social sciences
   and education.
2. *MLA Handbook for Writers of Research Papers, Theses and Disser-
   tations.* 2nd ed. New York: Modern Language Association of
   America, 1984.
3. *A Manual for Writers of Term Papers, Theses, and Dissertations,*
   Kate L. Turabian. 5th ed. Chicago: University of Chicago
   Press, 1987.
4. *The Chicago Manual of Style.* 14th ed. Chicago: University of
   Chicago Press, 1993.

What and when to footnote are sometimes a problem for writers,
especially with the recent confusion over copyright laws. The copyright law protects the author's rights to his or her own work, whether
it is published or not. The copyright holder is the only one with authority or the right to sell, distribute, revise, or publish the work covered by copyright. The author of a published work, however, usually
assigns the rights to the publisher who then becomes the author's
agent for any further rights, sales, or permissions to reprint. When
quoting a long passage from a copyrighted work, or a complete unit
such as a graph or table, poem, or short story, permission must be obtained from the copyright holder. "Fair use" of copyrighted material
means that others may use short, incomplete sections of a copy-

righted work—with acknowledgment—in order to support a point in their writing. "Short" has come to be defined as a selection of 150 words or less.

In a book on writing in the arts and sciences, Maimon et al. (1981, pp. 107–109) outline four types of material that must be documented:

1. Direct quotations—used when the way someone said something cannot be improved upon, or when the authority of the person is important and a quotation from that person will add weight to your argument;

2. "Other people's judgements, ideas, opinions, and inferences, even if you rephrase their material"—if other people's ideas have had an impact upon your own thinking, or if you link your ideas or support your ideas with someone else's but don't use their exact words, you still need to acknowledge the source;

3. "Facts that other people have discovered and that are not generally known by the reading public"—facts about a topic that are common knowledge (they reappear in most of your sources) do not have to be documented; however, if you uncover what appears to be a new piece of information, the author of the information should be referenced. For example, it has become common knowledge that most adults continue learning into very old age. The fact that 90 percent of adults conduct at least one independent learning project a year, though, discovered by Allen Tough (1979), is not common knowledge and should be documented appropriately.

4. Research studies conducted by others—previous research studies referred to in your own research report should be documented so that others might refer to them if they desire.

TABLES AND FIGURES

Visual presentations can be dramatic and revealing in explaining important information to the reader. But care in the construction of tables and figures is necessary if they are to enhance and not confound the report of research findings.

Tables are used to display quantitative data in some logical pattern. The pattern of organization—chronological, alphabetical, numerical, or qualitative—must be readily apparent to the reader. The table should be understandable by itself without accompanying text. This is not to say that tables can supplant text; rather, tables offer detail that would be tedious to put into the text. Tables are never totally independent of text. Fox (1969) discusses the responsibility of the reader and the writer with regard to tables:

> This perception of the table as supplementary and yet independent means that in preparing the research report the researcher can place some responsibility for the full understanding of the data upon the reader. But he cannot place all of it there. That is, he cannot go to the extreme of presenting a table with no comment other than an introductory sentence . . . If we have nothing to say about the table, the chances are excellent that there is no reason to include the table in the report . . . Obviously then the researcher's problem is to hit the appropriate middle way in which he reports, in the text, the highlights of the data in the table. (p. 739)

Some general guidelines might prove helpful to those interested in constructing tables. To begin with, the "well-constructed table, like a well-written paragraph, consists of several related facts that are integrated to present *one main idea*" (Van Dalen, 1966, p. 428). A complex table showing numerous relationships or interactions needing many pages of explanation is self-defeating. The major focus of the table should be easily grasped by the reader. To test whether one's table is clear, ask someone unfamiliar with the study to take any item or number in the table and explain what it means (Fox, 1969). This will also check whether the horizontal and vertical axes have been clearly labeled.

Labeling is important. The title itself should contain four bits of information: "(1) the variable or variables for which data are being presented; (2) the groups on whom the data were collected; (3) the subgroups within the table; and (4) the nature of the statistic included within the table" (Fox, 1969, p. 720). For example, in a hypothetical table titled "Percent of Adult Men and Women Enrolled in Six Different Degree Programs at County Community College," enrollment is the variable for which data are being presented, adults are the group on whom the data were collected, men and women are subgroups, and percent is the statistic. In addition to a precise title, column headings and row labels should be accurate and as brief as possible.

Mechanically, there are several conventions for including tables in a research report. Some of the more common practices include the following:

- The table is placed immediately after it is first referred to in the text, or on the next page.
- Tables should fit within the page size of the text. Larger tables can be reduced or placed in the appendix.

- Capitalization and punctuation should follow a consistent format.
- Rulings or lines should be used sparingly and only to enhance readability.

As an alternative to presenting data in tables, many types of figures can be used. Figures include charts and graphs, diagrams, blueprints, maps, and photographs. Each of these categories can be subdivided; for example, there are pie charts, flow charts, organizational charts, line graphs, histograms, and bar graphs. Selecting the best type of figure to present data depends upon the type of data. In ethnographic research, for example, photographs are often used to convey culturally based results; in case studies, organizational charts are commonly used.

Figures are visual presentations and typically contain a minimum of numbers and words. A figure "is used only if it snaps important ideas or significant relationships into sharp focus for the reader more quickly than other means of presentation" (Van Dalen, 1966, p. 431). Figure 9.2 is an example of a bar graph that dramatically displays the rise in life expectancy since 1900.

The point being made by the graph—that life expectancy has been substantially increasing since 1900—is more easily grasped by this visual presentation than by offering the same explanation in words. It is also clearer than the table of vital statistics from which the data were derived.

Appropriate use of figures can do much to add interest to a research report. Several cautions about using figures are worth mentioning.

- Keep the figure simple, including only that information that is necessary to understanding the presentation. Too much information will clutter the figure; a complex figure can be divided into two simple ones.
- Fewer figures representing important ideas will draw attention to those ideas; keep the number of figures to a minimum.
- Integrate the figure with references to it in the text, keeping the figure as close to its discussion as possible.

In summary, by constructing tables and figures that are easy to read and interpret, you may enable the readers to understand the study results more easily and forcefully than they would by reading only the text itself. Tables and figures accompanied by brief explanations give the reader a double opportunity to understand what information the writer is trying to convey.

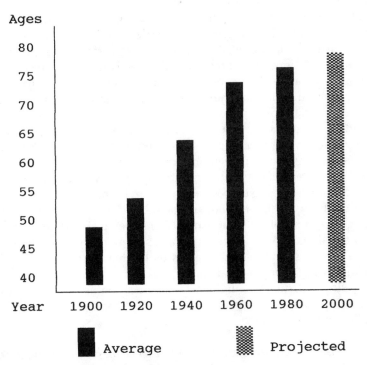

Figure 9.2 A sample bar graph.

REPORTING STATISTICS

Statistics are typically used in tables and figures to summarize and explain data economically. A statistic is a piece of data (fact, event, characteristic) converted to a numerical unit that permits uniform comparison of data. There are two types of statistics—descriptive and inferential. *Descriptive statistics* allow the researcher to summarize information or make simple comparisons of data. A descriptive statistic can summarize the distribution of a group of data, indicate the degree to which a particular score deviates from the average, or describe the degree to which one event or characteristic is related to other events or characteristics. *Inferential statistics* are used to test hypotheses as well as to estimate the parameters of the population used in the study. An inferential statistic is a more powerful statistic than a descriptive statistic. The researcher can say more about the individual data from which the statistic is derived, as well as speak to characteristics of the total population that the statistic represents. Inferential studies "have the purpose of drawing implications from data to some setting, subjects, or material other than those that were directly involved in the completed study" (Drew, 1980, p. 266).

In using either descriptive or inferential statistics to report findings, researchers should take care that their statistical presentation enlightens rather than confuses the reader. Nearly everyone at one time or another has had the frustrating experience of being unable to interpret a table or graph or statistical procedure in a research report. And nearly everyone can remember the satisfaction and feeling of power when the meaning of those numbers was finally revealed. These contrasting feelings represent, at least in part, the weaknesses and strengths of using statistics to transform raw data into meaningful concepts that are embedded in research findings. On one hand, we can be confused, misled, and possibly turned off by the foreign language of numbers. On the other hand, being able to comprehend relationships between several variables by glancing at a single page in a report is compelling. It gives us the feeling of being in command—a "master" of the data.

Using statistics to enlighten rather than confuse a reader means avoiding some common problems in the reporting of statistics. The following are four errors to be avoided:

1. *Use of descriptive statistics to infer beyond the present study.* Misuse of descriptive statistics is the result of not understanding the assumptions of inferential and descriptive procedures. It is a temptation, for example, to assume that two groups are significantly different if the means of the two groups appear to be very different. Without the test of an inferential statistic to see if the difference is significant, what *appears* to be a real difference could have happened by chance. Statistical significance cannot be assumed simply on the basis of descriptive analysis.

2. *Lack of consistency of selection in displaying statistical data.* It is helpful to the reader of research reports to have statistical tables or figures presented in a consistent pattern. Also, it should not be assumed that all statistical data generated in conducting a study must go into the final report. Only selected, essential data should be included if statistics are to make reporting more clear and concise as intended. Much may be deduced from a few carefully chosen and consistently displayed sets of statistics.

3. *Improper placement of statistics.* In a discussion of findings, statistical procedures should be subordinate to the findings themselves, even to the point of putting certain statistics in

parentheses at the end. For example, it is much clearer to say "the responses of the trained managers were correct significantly more often than the responses of those who had no training ($p = .05$)," than to write "the chi-square tests of differences between samples were calculated determining at the .05 level of significance that the trained managers' responses differed from those that had received no training." Highlight the findings by subordinating the statistics.

4. *Overuse of statistics.* Just because statistics are produced by and are available to the researcher does not mean that they have to be reported. An important contribution of statistics is helping the researcher better grasp meaning from raw data. Meaning is not the statement of a statistic, but what is inferred from the statistic. Therefore, a discussion may be more effective in conveying meaning than simply supplying numbers. Readers of research need assistance in understanding the essence of what has been discovered. This is particularly true in exploratory studies. For example, if a study is intended to develop theory about the concept of competency, well-documented lists of competencies from practitioners may be useful data to gather and include. But a discussion of findings, rather than a quantitative summary, is likely to be more helpful to the reader who is trying to understand the concept.

In summary, statistics, well chosen and properly handled, can bring clarity and understanding to the findings of a research study. They should not take the place of a verbal discussion of a study's results; rather, they should be used in support of the findings.

GUIDELINES FOR WRITING AND REVISING

Why is it so difficult to write up the findings of a research study when what we have found will surely be of interest to others and may even have a positive effect on practice? Graduate students, who are doing some of the best research, talk of being "burned out" or too sick of their study to want to revisit it to write something up. And busy practitioners who may have done some research to solve some immediate work-related problem, often find that once they've solved one problem, they are pressed to move on to the next crisis and have little time or inclination to record their study.

For those who are committed to sharing their work with others through publication, there are other barriers. Becker, in a humorous book titled, *Writing for Social Scientists* (1986), identifies two powerful obstacles. One is thinking that there is One Right Way; if we don't know the right way to write up research we can't do it. Becker writes,

> Some very common, quite specific writing difficulties have their origins in this attitude: the problem of getting started and the problem of "which way to organize it." Neither one has a unique solution to be discovered. Whatever you do will be a compromise between conflicting possibilities. That doesn't mean that you can't arrive at workable solutions, only that you can't count on finding the one perfect one that was there all along waiting to be found. (pp. 48–49)

A second barrier that Becker identifies, and perhaps the most powerful deterrent of all, is the risk one takes by writing up something for others to see. Fear of rejection, fear of criticism, fear of being thought of as unscholarly, fear of being found out, paralyze many a writer.

Assuming that a commitment to contributing to the knowledge base of your field and to improving practice is strong enough to allow you take the risk, there are some strategies you can employ to get on with the task of writing up your research.

First, determine who you intend the audience to be for this report. Is this for the general public? For practitioners who are in positions to apply the results? Policy makers? A funding source? Other researchers and academicians? The content, writing style, and even length of the report will be determined by the intended consumer of the report. Of the identified audience you can ask, "(1) *what* does this audience want or need to know about the study? and (2) *how* can this information best be presented?" (Selltiz et al., 1976, p. 501). Practitioners or the general public, for example, do not need to know why a particular statistical analysis was chosen, whereas for other researchers such a piece of information would be crucial to evaluating or replicating the work.

Second, get started, even if it is not at the beginning of the report. There is no rule that you have to start with an introduction, which in fact many writers find one of the hardest things to write. It might be easier to begin with the procedures section of the study. What you did and how you did it are concrete enough to help you get going. Once started, proceed to the next easiest part of the report. Mullins (1980) calls this approach the "block" method which is something of a compromise between the "beginning to end" and the "bits and pieces" method. In the "beginning to end" method, an outline is generally followed. In a research report, you would begin with the introduction of the problem and proceed to the literature review. The "bits and pieces" approach, on the other hand, is for those who "dislike any kind of formally organized procedure" (Mullins, 1980, p. 142). You begin with what you feel like writing at the moment and proceed by bits and pieces. This method is more time consuming than the others, but it is better than being stuck in an outline or not writing at all.

Other suggestions that might be helpful in establishing your own writing pattern or breaking through a writer's block include the following:

- Determine in what type of environment you are most productive.
- Determine the time of day when you write best; is it early morning, late at night, midday?
- Expect that there will be times when conditions are perfect but you still cannot write; do something else and try again later.
- "Talk" your way through. Describe to yourself or to others what you intend to write; this almost always helps to clarify what you will write next and may cause you to realize that more reading or thinking needs to be done.
- Before stopping for a day, list what you intend to do during the next writing session; this should reduce the time needed to get started again.
- Set aside what you have written to be reread after some time has lapsed.
- Don't let yourself get bogged down in the technical aspects of writing such as spelling and grammar; these can be corrected later.

Once a draft of the report has been completed, you are ready to revise. "To revise means literally 'to see again.' The key task during the revision process is to see your paper as others will see it" (Maimon et al., 1981, p. 14). Most writers consciously or unconsciously assume too much on the part of the reader. Readers are usually not that familiar with the topic, and they have not read the vast amount of material that the author has. Thus, readers are not capable of moving from point to point and of seeing how points connect in the way that the writer can. Readers "need to be reminded frequently of what you are talking about. If you want them to connect two ideas, you have to do the work of forming the connection" (p. 15). Neither can the writer become bogged down in unnecessary details—readers "want to know your point in writing, and they want to know this point as efficiently as possible. They do not want to wade through a chronological account of your research process" (p. 15).

The best way to determine if your report is clear and readable is to have several other people read it. This

> will help you see quite clearly the differences between writer-based and reader-based prose. You will find there is frequently a subtle battle going on between a writer and a reader, with each one trying to expend the lesser amount of energy. When you have a stake in getting your information or ideas across, you are entering a buyer's market, and you should learn all that you can about accommodating the needs of your buyers, your readers (Maimon et al., 1981, p. 14).

Readers who have to expend energy trying to understand what you have written will have no energy left to make use of your findings or may just give up reading your report altogether. The task in revising is to see that all obstacles that hinder the transmission of information from writer to reader are removed. Steps in the revision process might include: (1) checking the overall organization of your report by making an outline from your draft; (2) "interviewing" each paragraph by asking " 'What is the point of this paragraph?' " (Maimon, et al., 1981, p. 15); (3) cutting out repetitive sections and unnecessary words; (4) smoothing out clumsy sentence structures; and (5) checking for spelling, grammar, and typographical errors.

Occasionally it is necessary to shorten the report to satisfy certain journal requirements or to have an abbreviated form of the report available for newsletters or in-house publications. It is easier to pull together a shortened version of a longer draft than to create a shortened version from nothing. Once you have drafted a report, it can be cut in several places. The literature review may be eliminated and the crucial points summarized with reference to the supporting literature. The bare skeleton of the theoretical framework needs to be preserved, but a detailed discussion can be eliminated. Sample questions from data collection instruments can be given instead of inserting the entire instrument. Finally, findings can be stated without supporting tables or charts, or certain findings can be highlighted and separate articles written for other findings (Selltiz et al., 1976).

In summary, while there is no magic formula for writing and revising a research report, the task can be made easier by familiarizing yourself with the standard format for a research report, by determining who the audience is and writing to that audience, by starting at whatever point works for you, and by establishing a pattern of writing and revising that feels comfortable. Unfortunately, there are some who are able to write up their research, but for various reasons, the report ends up in a file cabinet or is shared with only a few trusted colleagues. Perhaps the risk factors are too daunting; or perhaps the manuscript is never considered "good enough" to send out. Becker (1986) in a chapter titled "Getting It Out the Door," speaks to the tension all writers feel between "making it better and getting it done" (p. 122). A manuscript can be indefinitely revised, updated, perfected. At some point it needs to be disseminated. Following is a discussion of why it is important to disseminate research and how one can go about doing it.

DISSEMINATING RESEARCH

The decisions an investigator makes when writing the research report depend upon (1) the audience for whom the report is intended and (2) the purpose of disseminating research results. While many researchers are content to add to the stock of knowledge in a field, others are also concerned with the implementation of their findings into practice. Since this text is intended for those in the applied fields of adult education and training, the issue becomes one of how best to disseminate findings to maximize their chance of being applied to practice. Answering this question involves taking into account the issue—whether real or imagined—of the gap between research and practice in an applied field of study.

Practitioners stereotype researchers as ivory-tower residents who investigate questions no one needs to answer. Researchers, on the other hand, characterize practitioners as naive about research and too tied to everyday concerns to see the larger questions. Such attitudes thwart advancements that could be effected through the close cooperation of researchers and practitioners in applied areas. Fortunately, efforts are being made in many fields to bring researchers and practitioners together on common problems. One method is to involve the participants of research in all aspects of the investigation from the conceptualization of the problem, to collecting and analyzing data, to disseminating the findings. This particular research approach is discussed in detail in Chapter 7 in the sections on action research and participatory research.

A second avenue for bringing practitioners and researchers closer together has been through graduate programs in which both groups become more sophisticated in doing and appreciating research. Practitioners working in master's degree programs usually complete a research component as part of their studies. And those who intend to be researchers and scholars receive advanced training in investigating the complex problems in the world of practice.

A third mechanism by which researchers and practitioners have become more aware of one another has been through structured activities, such as conferences, where researchers stress the practical implications of their work. Some large organizations have also created liaison positions or offices where research is collected and interpreted to appropriate audiences. Such a person or office is likely to be found in the research and development section of large corporations, government agencies, private foundations, and universities.

Undoubtedly there are other ways social science researchers and practitioners are working together to address the problems encountered in a society as complex as ours. The apparent lag in the adoption of new practices may also have less to do with the so-called "gap" between research and practice, and more to do with the cautious assessment of new discoveries or human nature's natural resistance to change:

> There are built-in aversive properties of any new findings. Any new idea or new practice, almost by definition, implies that the old idea was wrong and that the practitioner's current methods are ineffective or at least inadequate . . . In addition to being told one is wrong, anyone who accepts new findings and their implications for practice faces the arduous task of unlearning old ways of responding and of acquiring a newly organized repertory of behaviors. (Helmstadter, 1970, p. 402)

Thus the "why" of disseminating research in applied fields of study is to improve practice. This is not to suggest that contributing to knowledge alone in one's field is not a worthwhile goal. But it is only through dissemination that knowledge is accumulated and practice has a chance of being improved.

HOW TO DISSEMINATE FINDINGS

There are many ways to transmit research results to relevant audiences. Three of the more common ways are journal articles and books, sponsored publications, and conferences.

Most researchers strive to publish their research in refereed journals. Depending upon the journal, this can be the most prestigious and the most difficult method. *Refereed* means that the report is sent to editorial consultants who critique the article and determine whether it is appropriate for publication. The review is usually done blindly; that is, neither author nor reviewer knows the identity of the other. Many people assume, erroneously, that only recognized authorities in a field are allowed to publish in major journals. While an important person might be invited to write an article on occasion, most journals consider all submissions regardless of who the author is. Other criteria—such as the appropriateness of the content, the significance of the problem, and the clarity of presentation—determine the acceptability of the manuscript.

Prior to submitting an article for publication, the researcher should determine which journal most closely matches the article's content area. A copy of the journal should then be studied for style, format, and procedures for submission (usually found on the inside cover). Most journals follow the standard format for reporting research. If one is not sure which journal would be appropriate, there are guidebooks available that detail such information. *Cabell's Directory of Publishing Opportunities in Journals and Periodicals* (1992), for example, has catalogued 3,900 journals in the humanities and social sciences. Each entry contains the following information: name of editor and address, when it was first published, how often it comes out and the annual subscription rate, circulation, an editorial description listing the subject matter and audience for whom the journal is intended, and complete information for the submission of manuscripts. In addition to comprehensive directories, each discipline has its own directory of periodicals. The *Guide to Periodicals in Education and Its Academic Disciplines* (Camp & Schwark) lists over six hundred education-related periodicals in the United States with the same information as above. Specific to adult and continuing education is a resource compiled by the Office of Research and Evaluation in Adult and Continuing Education at Northern Illinois University (1991). *RE/ACE Journal Index for Adult and Continuing Education Research* gives pertinent information about several hundred journals that adult educators might consider for publishing outlets.

Typically, research results are not disseminated in book form unless the research was a large-scale undertaking with significant results appealing to a wide audience. Often these books are produced by presses associated with the university or organization where the study was done. Occasionally a commercial press will publish research results that have wide appeal (Sheehy's book *Passages: The Predictable Crises of Adult Life*, 1976, for example). The individual researcher might consider publishing results in a monograph form if the study is too big for a journal article and too small for a book. Monographs are similar to books, but smaller and more focused. Some academic presses, private agencies, and foundations publish monographs. As with journal articles, there are directories of publishers that give the necessary information on how to submit a manuscript.

A second major means of disseminating research is through publications sponsored by organizations that have some interest in the research problem. Such groups might include professional associations, foundations, social service agencies, and community organizations. Perhaps such a body has contributed to the funding of the project or collaborated by providing other forms of support such as personnel or computer time. The organization may want to disseminate the study's results through a newsletter, monograph, in-house journal, audio-visual tape, or oral presentation. Such research is likely to be action oriented with highly practical applications for the sponsoring agency or institution. Professional journals (already discussed) and conferences offer avenues for the researcher who desires to disseminate findings beyond the collaborating and related agencies.

Conferences are sponsored by professional organizations, institutions, and agencies. They can be designed for anyone interested in the topic, for certain professional groups such as nurses or trainers, for employees of certain agencies, and so on. Any conference is potentially a forum for disseminating research results. There are, however, conferences that have as their sole purpose the presenting of research. Information about conferences and procedures for submitting research proposals can be found by consulting recent journals and newsletters in the appropriate field. If a proposal is accepted for presentation, it is common practice to prepare a paper to be distributed at the conference. Such papers usually follow the traditional format for reporting research. The oral presentation itself is less formal than a journal article and may be a report of research in progress rather than completed work. Conference presentations often result in the formation of networks of people interested in the same problem area. Such networks facilitate the accumulation of knowledge in a field and result in greater dissemination of recent research findings.

SUMMARY

Conferences, sponsored publications, and refereed journal articles are three common means of disseminating one's research findings. The method chosen depends upon the audience one is trying to reach and to some extent the type of research that has been conducted. In any case, reporting and disseminating are a crucial part of the research process and demand a commitment on the part of the researcher from the outset of the project. Not to make this effort deprives the field of a potential contribution and brings into question the importance of the undertaking in the first place.

REFERENCES

Becker, H. S. (1986). *Writing for social scientists*. Chicago: University of Chicago Press.

Cabell, D. W. E. (Ed.). (1992). *Cabell's directory of publishing opportunities in journals and periodicals* (3rd ed.). Beaumont, TX: Cabell Publishing.

Camp, W., & Schwark, B. L. (1975). *Guide to periodicals in education and its academic disciplines* (2nd ed). Metuchen, NJ: Scarecrow Press.

Drew, C. J. (1980). *Introduction to designing and conducting research*. St. Louis: C. V. Mosby.

Fox, D. J. (1969). *The research process in education*. New York: Holt, Rinehart & Winston.

Glaser, B. G. (1978). *Theoretical sensitivity*. Mill Valley, CA: The Sociology Press.

Helmstadter, G. C. (1970). *Research concepts in human behavior*. New York: Appleton-Century-Crofts.

Maimon, E. P., Belcher, G. L., Hearn, G. W., Nodine, B. F., & O'Connor, F. W. (1981). *Writing in the arts and sciences*. Cambridge, MA: Winthrop.

Marquis Academic Media (1981). *Directory of publishing opportunities in journals and periodicals* (5th ed.). Chicago: Marquis Academic Media.

Mullins, C. J. (1980). *The complete writing guide*. Englewood Cliffs, NJ: Prentice-Hall.

Office of Research and Evaluation in Adult and Continuing Education. (1991). *RE/ACE Journal Index for Adult and Continuing Education Research*. DeKalb, IL: Northern Illinois University, Office of Research and Evaluation in Adult and Continuing Education.

Selltiz, C., Wrightsman, L. S., & Cook, S. W. (1976). *Research methods in social relations*. New York: Holt, Rinehart & Winston.

Sheehy, G. (1976). *Passages: The predictable crises of adult life*. New York: E. P. Dutton.

Tough, A. (1979). *The adult's learning projects*. (2nd edition) Toronto: Ontario Institute for Studies in Education.

Van Dalen, D. B. (1966). *Understanding educational research*. New York: McGraw-Hill.

Van Maanen, J. (1988). *Tales of the field: On writing ethnography*. Chicago: University of Chicago Press.

Wolcott, H. F. (1990). *Writing up qualitative research* (Qualitative Research Methods Monographs, Vol. 20). Newbury Park: Sage.

CHAPTER 10

ETHICAL DILEMMAS IN DOING RESEARCH

Each step in the research process—from shaping the problem through disseminating findings—is fraught with potential ethical dilemmas. Consider what you would do, for example, if:

- In a case study of an adult literacy program reputed to have an unusually high retention rate, you discover in tracking some of the students that attendance and graduation records have been tampered with.
- You notice that a particular training program, the effectiveness of which you are testing with treatment and control groups, cuts the time needed to learn a new procedure in half for some, but actually impedes learning for others.
- The head administrator of the hospital where you've just completed a study of patient education withdraws permission for you to publish the results.
- In observing a volunteer CPR training session you observe what appears to be inappropriate physical contact between the instructor and some participants.

The above dilemmas were generated from actual situations. While some problems can be anticipated and accounted for ahead of time, most of the dilemmas arise unexpectedly in the process of collecting, analyzing, and disseminating findings; some are inherent in the design of study. In this chapter we will address ethical concerns embedded in the various components of the research process from selecting the topic to disseminating the findings.

SELECTING WHAT TO STUDY

As is discussed in Chapter 2, the decision about what to study is shaped by more than just a desire to contribute to the knowledge base of adult education and training. What one studies is also a function of interest; practical considerations such as time, money, and access; social and political contingencies, and the personal values of the researcher. As Robinson and Moulton (1985, p. 52) observe, "The questions and the problems studied are the ones considered interesting, worthwhile, and important. The criteria that determine what is interesting, worthwhile, and important are often based on ethical values." No longer is there such a thing as value-free research which produces "neutral" knowledge, even in the "hard" sciences. In applied social sciences such as education and training where practice involves the social world and people in it, research is particularly value-laden, hence potentially ripe for ethical conflicts.

Take, for example, the correlation between research and currently fashionable topics. In the 1960s job training was a social priority; in the 1970s and especially the 1980s literacy was in the forefront; for the 1990s multiculturalism and ethnic diversity are hot topics. For each of these concerns there has been government and private support for research. To what extent is the selection of a research topic driven by social concern, political ideology, or financial exigency? To what extent should it be?

Research directly related to social interventions, and much of adult education and training research is intervention-related, is particularly problematic. Teaching adults to read is an intervention; retraining workers in computerized line work is an intervention; teaching patients to monitor their diabetes is an intervention; forming interdisciplinary teams and training professionals to function in them are interventions. Kimmel (1988) points out the ethical problems inherent in studying interventions:

> Research often represents an attempt to change patterns the scientist believes are potentially damaging to specific individuals and threatening to society in general . . . Values inevitably enter into intervention studies at all stages of the research process, beginning with the decision that there is a social problem and a need for intervention . . . The ethical question that emerges as a result centers on the extent to which a scientist has the right to impose his or her values—to set goals and select methods in an attempt to affect the lives of those who perhaps do not wish to change their behavior and life experiences or are not aware of what happens to themselves in the process. (p. 125)

An example of ethical dilemmas inherent in the selection of a research topic that illustrates Kimmel's point, is in literacy research. Policy makers, funding agencies, educators, and the public generally view literacy as a good thing and support efforts that assist adults in becoming literate. A ground-breaking study by Fingeret (1983) revealed that adult illiterates are in well-established social exchange networks where their literacy needs are met by others *in exchange* for services they supply in return. Becoming literate would likely disrupt this network, isolating the illiterate from important support and requiring the adjustment or formation of a new network. What right does an educator have to intervene in this case? What implications are there for designing a research inquiry on the topic of illiteracy?

Robinson and Moulton (1985) link the establishment of priorities in research to the issue of academic freedom. Should researchers have the right to investigate any topic, no matter what? "Unpopular truths are truths nonetheless," they write. "If God does not exist, if sexual promiscuity increases longevity, if mental ability is related genetically to some ethnic, sexual, or racial groups, it can be argued that we should know these things" (p. 58). But should we? They concede that "there may be some truths that can cause more harm than good." The ultimate problem, they note, which "seems especially dangerous is the possibility that a few people hold the power to decide what knowledge is to be sought" (p. 58).

Thus, there are numerous ethical considerations in merely selecting a topic for investigation. Our position is that it is not possible to be value-free in defining the problem. What is seen as an important problem to be investigated is defined by the value system of the researcher in conjunction with sociocultural, political, and practical realities. Ultimately, "the choice of a research topic involve[s] a balance between practical concerns, theoretical issues, interests of the participants, and curiosity of the researcher" (Kimmel & Moody, 1990, p. 492).

SELECTION AND PROTECTION OF PARTICIPANTS

Concern for the well-being of participants in research studies dates back to the uncovering of brutal medical experiments conducted in Nazi concentration camps. Scandals related to several other studies—the Tuskegee syphilis study in which 399 black men were injected with syphilis and not treated, the Millgram studies of obedience, and Humphreys's study of gay men (Kimmel, 1988)—gave rise to codes and guidelines for conducting research with human beings. While social science research does not typically endanger participants to the extent that biomedical research might, nevertheless there are risks whenever people are studied. Kimmel (1988) lists five:

(1) actual changes in their characteristics, such as physical health, attitudes, personality, and self-concept; (2) an experience that creates tension or anxiety; (3) collection of "private" information that might embarrass them or make them liable to legal action if made public; (4) receiving unpleasant information about themselves that they might not otherwise have to confront; and (5) invasion of privacy through the collection of certain types of damaging information. (p. 37)

At the heart of the issue is society's right to know and an investigator's right to inquire *versus* a person's right to safety and privacy. Guidelines for dealing with the competing values center around protecting participants from harm, preserving their right to privacy, making sure that their consent to participate is informed, and eliminating or minimizing deception. In particular,

1. Respondents should be told the purpose of the research and how the data they are being asked to provide will be used.
2. Respondents should be informed of the nature of the research before data are collected and should be allowed to withdraw at any given point.
3. There should be no unpleasant or damaging effects on the individual, the setting, or others close to the participant either during or subsequent to the research.
4. The investigator must respect the privacy of the respondents and, whenever possible, ensure anonymity or confidentiality.
5. There should be no unprofessional behavior required of the participants.
6. The participants should be given an opportunity to learn from the research. (Fox, 1969, pp. 384–386).

Each of the six areas mentioned above is to some extent problematic when the guidelines are put into practice. For example, informed consent involves providing a full explanation of the purposes and procedures of the study, as well as outlining potential risks and benefits. However, informing participants of the purpose of the study may in some cases obscure the purpose of the study. If managers were told that they were being studied to determine the extent to which the sex of an employee determined promotability, their behavior may well be different from the way it would be if they were unaware of the purpose of the study. Further, how is consent obtained when participants may not be capable of understanding the potential risks involved? Or when doing research within an organization such as a school or business, how necessary or practical is it to obtain consent from all members of the organization?

Even the implementation of the third guideline—that there be no unpleasant effects or damage to participants—can be problematic. It is not always possible to determine ahead of time whether there will be unpleasant effects or the extent of those effects. If an experimental study were designed to test a new method of teaching adults to read, for example, it certainly would be difficult to say whether or not those receiving the treatment would be set back or would advance in their reading progress. If the method were tremendously successful, one might also wonder how ethical it is to deprive the control group of the benefits of the method.

Likewise, ensuring for anonymity or confidentiality may be easier to promise than to carry out. For example, while the site and the participants in a case study of a unique program may be given pseudonyms, people in the area or aware of the program will know its true identity and perhaps those of the participants. In a different sort of example, a study of how an intensive pastoral counseling program affected the marriage of participants presented problems of confidentiality in that spouses who had been interviewed separately and given pseudonyms were able to recognize each other in the data (Carse-McLocklin, 1992).

Diener and Crandall (1978, p. 43) suggest that investigators should reveal what a " 'reasonable or prudent person' would want to know. This legal term captures the essence of a commonsense approach to the problem." In addition, participants "have an *unconditional right* to know of any potential danger or of any rights to be lost during the study." Approaching the problem of the ethical treatment of research participants from a commonsense position suggests at the very least that reasonable measures be taken to ensure the safety of participants, that participants be treated by the researcher as if the researcher were also a participant, that the respondents give their consent to participate, and that all information be kept confidential.

DATA COLLECTION

Research in applied fields such as adult education and human resource development nearly always involves collecting data from human beings. Thus, issues of informed consent, privacy, deception and protection are important concerns regardless of the design of the study. These concerns manifest themselves somewhat differently depending upon whether data are collected in an experiment, through observations or interviews, or through surveys. At issue is the amount of control the investigator has versus the participant.

Experiments, either in the field or in a laboratory, create the greatest power differential between researcher and participant. The very essence of an experimental design (see Chapter 4) is control and manipulation. In order to assess cause and effect, experimental researchers manipulate variables and intervene in the natural process of events. As Reynolds (1982) points out, "the same research techniques that provide the greatest confidence that a causal relationship between variables can be established also maximize the investigator's responsibility for the impact on participants" (p. 156). Ethical dilemmas arise in deciding how "informed" participants need to be, how much deception is necessary so as not to contaminate the behavior being studied, and the extent to which potential risks outweigh potential benefits. Negative effects in experimental designs "may include being deceived, physical discomfort, psychological stress, or unpleasant self-knowledge" (p. 30).

Studies that rely upon observations as the major source of data present ethical problems of their own. Observations can range from those that are totally unobtrusive (such as in a public place, or through a one-way mirror) to those where the researcher is an active participant in what is being observed and whose role is known to the other participants. Thus the range of control that a participant has varies from none, as when the observation is unknown, to a great deal. Invasion of personal privacy is the most obvious problem, but public exposure of information gained in this manner could also lead to embarrassment, if not harm, to those involved. In considering observation as the primary data collection technique, Diener and Crandall (1978) recommend the following safeguards:

1. Deceive as little as possible.
2. Enter private spheres with the maximum informed consent consonant with the research goals. Consider obtaining informed consent post hoc whenever possible.
3. Plan procedures that absolutely guarantee subject anonymity, especially in published reports and where sensitive information is reported.
4. Review the potential influences of the observers on the group and rework the study if any negative consequences are foreseen.
5. Fully inform research assistants about the research, giving free choice whether to participate.
6. Consider whether the study could cause indignant outrage against social science, thus hampering other research endeavors.

7. Consult colleagues and request their suggestions for minimizing ethical problems. If possible, consult representatives from
the group to be studied. (pp. 125– 126)

Perhaps more than other forms of data collection, observations
can lead to unanticipated ethical dilemmas for the researcher in that
troublesome behavior may be observed as part of routine data collection. In a study of mental institutions, Taylor and Bogdan (1984) witnessed physical abuse of patients. In a study of women in outlaw
motorcycle gangs (Hopper & Moore, 1990) researchers witnessed not
only abuse of the women by the men, but criminal activity. Bringing
this concern within the realm of adult education and training, what
if in an observation at a place of business blatant sexual harassment
of a worker by a supervisor is witnessed? Or in studying interaction
patterns in classrooms of adults, incompetent or demeaning teacher
behaviors are observed? For any of these situations, the researcher
must decide whether to intervene, and if so, how and when. And, as
Taylor and Bogdan (1984, p. 71) point out, failure to act is itself "an
ethical and political choice" that researchers must come to terms with.
Data collected through interviews, whether highly structured or
open ended, afford participants more control in that they can refuse
to answer troublesome questions. Ethical concerns arise when respondents feel their privacy has been invaded, when they are em-
barrassed by the questions, or when disclosure of certain information has negative effects. Furthermore, in-depth interviews common in qualitative research may have unanticipated long-term effects. What if, in the study mentioned above focusing on the effects
of an intensive training program on the marriage, one partner artic-
ulates a growing dissatisfaction with the marriage? What if, in a
study of how being retained in school as a youth has impacted one's
adult life, painful, perhaps debilitating memories are brought to the
surface? Not all long-term effects of interviewing need be negative,
however. Many people enjoy being sought out to share their experiences, opinions, or expertise. Often there is satisfaction in knowing
one has contributed to the knowledge base in a particular area
through research. In applied fields, there may be satisfaction in
thinking that the knowledge contributed could lead to improved
practice. Some gain valuable self-knowledge; for others an in-depth
interview is therapeutic.
The data collection technique where the participant has the greatest control is in paper-and-pencil surveys or questionnaires. Whether
mailed or by telephone, respondents simply need not respond. Ethical concerns with this type of data collection have to do with "mis-

representing the purpose of research, pressuring individuals to respond through indirect means or coercion of any form, and not providing true confidentiality in protecting individual or subgroup responses" (Payne, 1987, p. 51). Of most discomfort to participants is the oftentimes not-so-subtle pressure to respond to a survey or questionnaire. Pressure can be exerted through a cover letter from a respected colleague, through supervisor "encouragement," through relentless contacts and followups, and so on. Nevertheless, this form of data collection is probably least intrusive among the above mentioned methods.

DATA ANALYSIS

Rarely in social science research does anyone track down the original raw data of a reported study to check the accuracy of the findings. There is thus a rather high potential for unintentional to deliberate distortion of data and almost no risk of being detected. Pressure to publish (and studies having significant findings are more easily publishable), passionate commitment to a particular theory, incompetence or inexperience in research design and analysis can result in unethical practices with regard to data analysis. There are, in fact, some famous cases of blatant fabrication of data such as the "Piltdown man," "where modern parts were added to an ancient skull to suggest the existence of a human 'missing link' " (Robinson & Moulton, 1985, p. 63). Other examples are Cyril Burt's twin studies in which data were fabricated to show intelligence is genetically rather than environmentally determined; fake diaries of Hitler; and plagiarism in Haley's *Roots*.

In an article on ethics in data analysis, Kromrey (1993) discusses seven questionable practices with regard to quantitative data analysis that can result in the distortion of findings. The first is **selectivity of data** in which researchers "tend to bury results that do not support their hypotheses" (p.25). The second, **use of data-driven hypotheses**, occurs when researchers look for patterns in the data and then decide what hypotheses to test, rather than deriving hypotheses from theory. A third questionable practice is the **use of post-mortem analyses**. This is the proverbial fishing trip where a researcher relentlessly searches the data for a significant effect. **Probability pyramiding and selective reporting**, the fourth item, suggests that "if enough different statistics are computed, some will indicate structure in the data that are merely artifacts of the intensity of the search" (p. 25). The fifth practice, familiar to students of statistics, is failure to recheck calculations for **Type I and Type II errors**. Also rather technical is practice number six, **confusion of probability level and the strength of relationships**, in which inappropriate statistical tests are used with the data. Finally, Kromrey identifies **confusion between exploratory and confirmatory approaches to analysis** as a potential source of unethical practice. This is similar to the second item of looking through the data and then posing hypotheses.

Several strategies are recommended by Kromrey for improving ethical practice in quantitative data analysis. He suggests incorporating more ethical training in graduate education, valuing the outcome of a research study as a contribution to the knowledge base *whether or not* null hypotheses were rejected, using multiple working hypotheses, and "explicitly describ[ing] analyses that were conducted" (p. 26).

Two of these strategies, more ethical training and explicitly describing analyses, are equally appropriate recommendations for those involved in qualitative data analysis. Since statistical procedures are rarely used in qualitative data analysis (or in much historical research), the possibility for unethical behavior is great. In qualitative data analysis, the researcher works from interview transcripts, field notes, and documents attempting to build an interpretation of the data that is derived from and is in turn supported by the data (Merriam, 1988b, Miles & Huberman, 1994). How easy it would be to ignore data that fail to support or that perhaps contradict emerging findings. As in quantitative research, there are strategies the researcher can use to ensure the validity and reliability of the findings. These are discussed in Chapter 6. The most common are member checks, triangulation, and an audit trail, which is the explicit detailing of data collection and analysis (and thus similar to Kromrey's suggestions above).

In addition to the data analysis itself, distortion or misrepresentation of findings can occur in the discussion section of a research report. "This occurs when a researcher fails to specify the limitations of a study, especially in those cases where such limitations may seriously affect the interpretation of the findings, and where such limitations may not be self-evident to the reader" (Campbell, 1987, p. 72).

In summary, data analysis is a part of the research process particularly amenable to unethical practices, intentional or otherwise. While the above listed strategies can be employed to minimize error or misinterpretation, the bottom line, according to Jackson (cited in Campbell, 1987, p. 73), is that the researcher "has a moral obligation to minimize the possibility of error by checking and rechecking the validity of the data and the conclusions that are drawn from the data."

DISSEMINATION OF FINDINGS

An important part of the research process is the dissemination of findings. As with other parts of the process, there are ethical considerations in releasing the findings of a study, whether it be through publication or other forms of presentation. Thus, the *consequences* of making one's findings known need to be considered. What is the potential for misunderstanding or misapplication of knowledge generated through research? This concern is easily illustrated by published reports of medical studies. Should we take aspirin to guard against heart attacks? Is coffee dangerous to our health, and if so, in what quantities? Should we drink more red wine? What about the report of correlation between creased earlobes and heart disease?

The worry is present in social science as well. In the 1960s some research was reported that "proved" that blacks were intellectually inferior to whites. How much damage was done before subsequent research contradicted these findings? Likewise, to what extent or at what point should practitioners in adult education and training change their practice as the result of new research in an area? Unfortunately there are no guidelines for assessing when and how to apply research findings. As Sigel (1990) points out, "consumers of research are free agents to do as they wish with the results of research. The only constraints utilizers of research findings have are their own professional standards" (p. 134).

When public policy that draws upon research is affected, stakes are even higher. Suppose, for example, that Tough's (1979) findings that 90% of adults are engaged in learning projects on their own were used by legislators to reduce or eliminate funding for more formal adult education. On the other hand, research into the numbers and status of illiterates has prompted national attention and funding in this area. Kimmel (1988) comments on the "subtle" effects of ethical dilemmas at the societal level: "Members of a society might experience a reduced sense of personal autonomy as knowledge of phenomena increases, and questions about the trustworthiness of those responsible for applying new knowledge might emerge" (p. 38).

The extent to which researchers are responsible for the consequences of their research is a debatable issue in the literature. Certainly there is always the possibility that research findings will be used to promote special interests, be misinterpreted, or be misapplied to practice. Researchers cannot possibly foresee all the potentially inappropriate (and appropriate) uses of their work. What they can do, and what many writers recommend, is that (a) "research should be undertaken only after careful consideration of its plausible consequences," (b) results should be presented "in a way that promises the least potential for distortion and the greatest opportunity for social gains," and (c) special care should be taken, "when publicizing the research, to state conditions pertinent to the usefulness of the research in applied contexts" (Kimmel, 1988, pp. 117–118),

GUIDELINES FOR THE ETHICAL CONDUCT OF RESEARCH

As mentioned earlier, ethical codes can be traced back to Nuremburg military tribunals in the mid 1940s. The Nuremberg Code of 1947 is a 10-point code that outlines limits for experimentation; its major contribution is articulating the concept of informed consent—a concept central to all subsequent codes and guidelines. When abuses in biomedical research came to light in the 1960s and 1970s, government agencies responded by establishing rigorous reviews of any research funded by the government.

Following the federal government's lead, most agencies and institutions, public and private, have established institutional review boards (IRB) for reviewing proposals for research that will be conducted within or under the auspices of the institution. For example, institutions of higher education where research takes place have IRBs from which faculty and students must obtain approval before beginning a research study. Such reviews are designed to protect both the researcher and the institution by ensuring informed consent, minimal risk to the participants, confidentiality, and so on.

Professional associations are another major source of guidelines for ethical behavior. Through graduate training and the monitoring of who is admitted to a profession, as well as review committees that can revoke a member's right to practice, professional associations themselves are able to exert some control over the ethical behavior of their members. Several associations have codes of ethics that specifically address research concerns. Anthropology's code addresses relations with those studied, responsibility to the public, responsibility to the discipline, responsibility to students and sponsors, and responsibility to one's own government and host government. Items in psychology's and sociology's codes deal with weighing the costs and benefits of an investigation, with safeguards to protect the rights of participants, and with ethical considerations in the presentation of research findings (Diener & Crandall, 1978; Kimmel, 1988). To date, the fields of adult education and human resource development have no codes of ethics that cover research, although general codes of ethics are being considered (Brockett, 1988; Karp & Abramms, 1992; McDonald & Wood, 1993). Practitioners and researchers in these areas will have to look to one of the disciplines mentioned above or to other related fields such as health, social work, and counseling for guidelines.

Ultimately, of course, government regulations and professional association guidelines will be attended to by researchers who are already concerned with conducting research in an ethical manner; no regulation or guideline will prevent abuses by unethical researchers. Guidelines can help researchers think through the study design a *priori* and consider ways to reduce risk and deception. However, for the ethical dilemmas that emerge in the execution of a research study, what is operative is the value system of the individual researcher. Take, for example, any one of the four dilemmas sketched out at the beginning of this chapter. What makes them dilemmas is there is no easy or right answer; rather, "acting ethically, or making an ethical decision, is the operationalization of what one considers to be the correct, right, or best way to behave" (Merriam, 1988a, p. 146). The researcher ultimately has to look to her or his own set of values in deciding the correct, right, or best way to behave.

To conclude, Kimmel (1988) offers five recommendations for ensuring, as best any individual researcher can, that the conduct of the research has been as ethical as possible. First, Kimmel suggests that we try to achieve "a more balanced relationship between investigator and research participants" (p. 139); that participants' views be included in the design of the research; that they be considered as another " 'granting institution,' granting us their valuable time in return for our generation of valuable scientific knowledge" (p. 139). A second recommendation is that in assessing the cost and benefits of doing the research, we also assess the cost and benefits of *not* doing it, and/or "the possibilities of doing the research in another manner" (p. 140). The third recommendation is that researchers be required in all published work to give a detailed account of the ethical procedures used in the study. Fourth, Kimmel recommends that the social sciences strive for "a mutually monitoring scholarly community that stays in close communication on shared scientific questions and issues, while still vigorously criticizing one another" (p. 144). Kimmel's final recommendation is that researchers be aware of the ethical context of society, its shifts, emphases and current concerns, for it is within a particular context that ethical behavior is defined.

SUMMARY

In summary, this chapter has delineated some of the ethical concerns inherent in doing research. Beginning with formulating a problem, it was pointed out that even this part of the process is value-laden and open to ethical considerations. The selection and protection of participants center on acquiring informed consent, minimizing risk and deception, and protecting individuals' privacy. But as was seen in the discussion of participants, there is a fair amount of ambiguity, even in normal circumstances, in dealing with these concerns. The next section of the chapter dealt with ethical dilemmas characteristic of the various methods of collecting data including experiments, observations, interviews, and surveys. Data analysis, whether quantitative or qualitative, presents many opportunities for unethical conduct. These were discussed as were some strategies for dealing with inadvertently less-than-ethical practices. As the final step in the research process, ethical concerns in the dissemination of research findings were reviewed. Finally, sources of guidelines for the ethical conduct of research were discussed.

REFERENCES

Brockett, R. G. (Ed.). (1988). *Ethical issues in adult education*. New York: Teachers College.

Campbell, D. J. (1987). Ethical issues in the research publication process. In S. L. Payne & B. H. Charnov (Eds.), *Ethical dilemmas for academic professionals* (pp. 69–94). Springfield, IL: Charles C. Thomas.

Carse-McLocklin, S. (1992). The effects of a clinical pastoral education upon the marital relationships of its students. (Doctoral dissertation, The University of Georgia, 1992). *Dissertation Abstracts International, 53*, 1021A.

Diener, E., & Crandall, R. (1978). *Ethics in social and behavioral research*. Chicago: University of Chicago Press.

Fingeret, A. (1983). Social network: A new perspective on independence and illiterate adults. *Adult Education Quarterly, 33*, 133–146.

Fox, D. J. (1969). *The research process in education*. New York: Holt, Rinehart & Winston.

Hopper, C. B., & Moore, J. (1990). Women in outlaw motorcycle gangs. *Journal of Contemporary Ethnography, 18*(4), 363–387.

Karp, H. B., & Abramms, B. (1992). Doing the right thing. *Training & Development*, 46(8), 36–41.

Kimmel, A. J. (1988). *Ethics and values in applied social research.* Applied Social Research Methods Series, Vol. 12, Newbury Park: Sage.

Kimmel, D. C., & Moody, H. R. (1990). Ethical issues in gerontological research and services. In J. E. Birren & K. W. Schaie (Eds.), *Handbook of the psychology of aging* (pp. 490–502) (3rd ed.). San Diego: Academic Press.

Kromrey, J. D. (1993). Ethics and data analysis. *Educational Researcher*, 22(4), 24–27.

McDonald, S. K., & Wood, G. S., Jr. (1993). Surveying adult education practitioners about ethical issues. *Adult Education Quarterly*, 43(4), 243–257.

Merriam, S. B. (1988a). Ethics in adult education research. In R. G. Brockett (Ed.), *Ethical issues in adult education* (pp. 146–161. New York: Teachers College.

Merriam, S. B. (1988b). *Case study research in education.* San Francisco: Jossey-Bass.

Miles, M. B., & Huberman, A. M. (1994). *Qualitative data analysis: An expanded sourcebook* (2nd ed.), Newbury Park, CA: Sage.

Payne, S. L. (1987). Concern for academic research participants. In S. L. Payne & B. H. Charnov, (Eds.), *Ethical dilemmas for academic professionals* (pp. 47–68). Springfield, IL: Charles C. Thomas.

Reynolds, P. D. (1982). *Ethics and social science research.* Englewood Cliffs, NJ: Prentice-Hall.

Robinson, G. M., & Moulton, J. (1985). *Ethical problems in higher education.* Englewood Cliffs, NJ: Prentice-Hall.

Sigel, I. (1990). Ethical concerns for the use of research findings in applied settings. In C. B. Fisher & W. W. Tryon, (Eds.), *Ethics in applied developmental psychology* (pp. 133–144). Norwood, NJ: Ablex.

Taylor, S. J., & Bogdan, R. (1984). *Introduction to qualitative research methods* (2nd ed.). New York: Wiley.

Tough, A. (1979). *The adult's learning projects.* (2nd ed.) Toronto, Ontario, Canada: Ontario Institute for Studies in Education.

CHAPTER 11

GRADUATE STUDENT RESEARCH

Professionals in applied fields are typically more concerned with the daily tasks of administration, planning, teaching, or counseling than with doing research. While a few practitioners and some professors engage in research, much more is conducted by students pursuing graduate degrees. And even though graduate research is primarily a learning experience for those involved, it is one way in which significant contributions to the theory and practice of a field can be made. Students, after all, especially those supported by assistantships or grants, have time to devote to their research. Also, students who are practicing professionals or those on temporary leave from their jobs are in positions both to detect important problems that need investigating, and to access sources of data to deal with those problems. Finally, graduate students do not work in a vacuum: they are guided by experienced researchers whose job it is to ensure that a study is well conceptualized and well planned. Rarely do professionals who want to do research have such support once their formal academic preparation is complete.

In an undergraduate program a student is introduced to and acquires the basic knowledge of a field; at the graduate level more is learned about a particular field, and a student is introduced to the methods by which knowledge is tested. Graduate programs in such fields as engineering, education, business, and nursing have the additional goal of preparing people to make an impact upon the practice of their specific vocation. The standard requirements of graduate programs have been adjusted by most institutions to fit this applied emphasis. Course work often includes internships (work experience in the field); computer or statistics courses may take the place of the more traditional foreign language requirement; and research projects tend to evolve from practice.

All doctoral programs and some master's programs require students to conduct research as part of their graduate preparation. The difference between research at the master's level and research at the doctoral level is one of degree. Theoretically, doctoral research involves a problem of greater magnitude, the significance and ramifications of which will have a potentially greater impact on the field:

> Because the problem is more complex, the candidate must draw upon a greater breadth of understanding in his field in solving it; and because he must demonstrate that he can perform independent research, he must exercise his own initiative and demonstrate professionalism to a greater extent than is expected in a MS project. (Davis, 1980, vi)

In practice, however, some master's research is as rigorous as that conducted at the doctoral level. Differentiating between the two is further obscured by the fact that the term *thesis*, while usually applied to master's research, is sometimes used to refer to doctoral research. *Dissertation* is the more appropriate term for the latter. This chapter will focus upon doctoral-level graduate research with the realization that most of the information presented is equally applicable to master's level research. Specifically, this chapter will deal with the practical aspects of selecting a topic, forming a committee, writing a proposal, carrying out the research, and defending the research.

SELECTING A TOPIC

Selecting a topic is the first step in the dissertation process (Long et al., 1986). Many students find this a difficult task because so much is involved. To begin with, you have to be relatively certain that no one is investigating precisely the same problem or concern. You must also be prepared to make a mental, emotional, and perhaps financial investment in the topic—an investment that will take at least a year's time. Finally, all the members of your committee must agree that the topic is worth investigating.

Often students engage in practices that appear to speed up the selection of a topic, but actually hinder the process. Some students have an area of interest in mind and expect that a topic will present itself or be handed to them by someone else; however, no one should expect to focus on a topic without first reading widely in the problem area and reviewing all the previous research. Other students are hindered in topic selection because they first decide to use a particular instrument, methodology, population, or data set, and then try to find the problem. The problem should come first, followed by a selection of the best means of approaching it. Another block occurs when a student settles on a topic but fails to anchor it in a concep-

tual/theoretical framework and, as a result, finds it difficult to articulate the significance of doing the study.

There are ways a student can facilitate the selection of a topic.
First, no later than halfway through course work, you should begin
thinking about a problem or area of concern in terms of its potential
for producing a suitable dissertation topic. Papers and presentations
in courses can then be used to explore the topic, to learn what has
and has not been done, and perhaps to test an idea on a small scale.
Second, you should be attuned to the multitude of sources from
which ideas can be generated, such as current journals, class work,
dissertations, newspapers, conversations, media events, or research
agendas. Keeping an ongoing list of tentative topics from various
sources provides a starting point when the time comes to decide
upon one topic.

Basically, a research problem is something you wonder about,
something that puzzles or confuses. Determining more exactly what
you are puzzled by, curious about, or confused about will help focus the study further. For example, wondering if something works
leads to an experimental or evaluation study; needing to understand a process involves exploratory research such as case study;
and asking about the variance of a phenomenon necessitates a descriptive approach.

Martin (1980) suggests that problems arise out of four circumstances:

1. Little or no research exists on a particular topic. How entry
   level people in applied fields become "professionalized" is an
   example where there is little data-based research.
2. "There is some research, but it has not been applied to enough
   samples or in enough situations to be considered a reliable
   phenomenon . . . the limits of the extent to which the phenomenon can be generalized are unknown" (p. 39). Much of the research on adult development has been done with male,
   middle-class samples. How the findings apply to other groups,
   such as women or lower-class males, is not known.
3. There might be a great amount of research, but the results of
   some studies are inconsistent with those from other studies.
   This is characteristic of the research on group versus self-
   directed learning.
4. There are two theories that explain the same phenomenon but
   that recommend or predict different outcomes of a common action. At one time, for example, the disengagement theory pre-

> dicted the withdrawal of older people from social interaction after retirement; another theory predicted a changing pattern of interaction, but not withdrawal. (pp. 39–40)

Whatever the source of the research topic, at least three criteria need to be applied to the final selection: the interest of the student in the problem, the feasibility of actually carrying out the study, and the significance of the problem itself. A person who is about to invest a year or more in a research endeavor should be vitally interested in the topic. In the long run, genuine interest is more motivating than the desire to finish and get the degree. Also, this interest may carry over into professional life after formal study is completed and perhaps lead to further work in the area. Feasibility is a consideration; Is the population accessible? Is there money for mailing? Does the project demand extensive travel? How much must other people be depended upon? Does the library have the necessary documents? and so on. It is not enough to be personally interested in a topic—the study must also be manageable.

The third criterion, that of significance, is more complex than the other two, for there is some debate about what constitutes a significant research topic. Significance is related to the original purpose of research—to contribute to knowledge. This raises the question of what constitutes a contribution to knowledge. According to Allen (1973),

> A contribution represents some advancement in the state of the art; a breakthrough in some theory; formulation of a new theory; refutation of an existing theory; addition to an existing theory; new insights into human, physical, or natural sciences; establishing of new relationships; or a creative accomplishment. (p. 2)

Many years before Allen, Almack (1930) dealt with the same question. For him, research was significant if it contributed to the fund of knowledge (by adding a new principle, law, or historical information), if it contributed to both knowledge and technique, or if it made available to many what only a few had before (translating a book, for example) (p. 281).

In applied fields significance typically answers the question "How is getting an answer to this problem going to make some difference in the world?" The results of a significant study should have some implication for practice. To get thinking along these lines, the student might try to answer these questions: Who will benefit from the findings? In what way(s) will they benefit? Of what value is it to them to know the answer to this problem?

A helpful aid to students in the process of selecting a thesis or dissertation topic is the thesis/dissertation generator shown in Figure 11.1. Students can use it as a worksheet to bring their topic into focus.

The Thesis/Dissertation Generator

1. State in two sentences or fifty words, a question, issue, activity, or situation that makes you curious, angry, or enthusiastic. (For example: "What is the process people go through who make career changes?" or "Why do so many adults drop out of Adult Basic Education programs?)"

2. You have just written a problem statement. Now complete the following: "The purpose of the proposed study is to . . . "

3. You have just written a purpose statement. Now explain in fifty words or less why you think the problem is worth solving.

4. Without being overly technical, state how you might go about solving the problem.

5. You have just developed a strategy for approaching the problem. What research methodology most nearly reflects your approach?

Figure 11.1 The thesis/dissertation generator.

In summary, the selection of a dissertation topic need not be an overly anxious or time-consuming undertaking. The emphasis should be on delineating a topic that is both interesting and feasible and that contributes to either knowledge or practice in a field. Avoiding what appear to be the shortcuts (selecting a methodology and then looking for a problem, for example) will also facilitate the selection of an appropriate topic.

FORMING A COMMITTEE

A faculty person with some expertise and interest in the problem area you are pursuing will most likely become the director of your dissertation and chair of your committee. Your director is likely to be the most important person on your dissertation committee (Long et al., 1986). In addition to advising on specific matters concerning the preparation of your dissertation, this person may have previously helped you to focus in on your topic and will later guide you in developing and presenting a proposal to your committee.

Procedures and criteria for the composition of dissertation committees vary among universities. Usually the student works closely with the major advisor in selecting members of the committee. There are several criteria you can use in deciding whom to invite to serve on the committee. First, you should look for highly qualified persons:

> Successful and qualified people rarely have "insecure egos" that need to be fed by putting others down. The "tougher" your committee (meaning the more qualified) the "easier" it will be. First, they are capable of recognizing an "outstanding" proposal. On the other hand, they will have little patience with a poorly thought out proposal. If you have a good committee, they can make suggestions based on their own experience in doing research that can be very helpful to you. (Gardner and Beatty, 1980, p. 81).

Successful people are usually busy people, however, and so it is important to consider the availability of prospective committee members. A nationally recognized researcher may not be around enough to be of any real assistance.

In addition to being qualified and available, a prospective committee person should be interested in your topic. This is probably a more important consideration than the time availability criterion. "If a faculty member is truly interested in a particular topic, she/he will usually find the time to help a student investigate that topic" (Martin, 1980, p. 32).

Finally, there is the personality factor to consider in the selection of a committee. You should feel that you can work with each member of the committee and that the committee members can work with one another. In theory, committee members are professionals who can separate personal concerns from their academic pursuits. In practice some people cannot work with certain other people. Personality traits, biases, private agendas, and so on may interfere with getting the task accomplished. With most committees there is a strong tendency

> toward negotiation and compromise. This process breaks down when one committee member is clearly more expert in the topic area of the student's research than the chairperson and when the chairperson does not acknowledge this in making decisions. The process can also break down in cases where two "experts" with different approaches to a problem, e.g., persons having different theoretical orientations, are on the same committee. To avoid this problem, the student should choose as the committee chairperson the faculty member with the

most interest and expertise in the area of the proposed research and ask for suggestions from this chairperson when selecting other members. (Martin, 1980, p. 33)

The extent of the contact a student has with the advisor and committee during the dissertation process is determined by the working styles and wishes of those involved. In some cases, after the committee has accepted a proposal, students will work almost exclusively with their advisor until a draft of the dissertation is ready to present to the entire committee. Other committees may want to see each chapter as it is written, or certain members may want to review particular chapters during the process. The procedure is usually established at the time the committee approves the proposal.

How to work best with an advisor is an individual matter, but it is helpful if each person's expectations are communicated to the other. At the very least, students should remember that advisors are also teaching, doing research, and advising other students. Students can maximize advisement time by seeking their advisor's help only for the problems of their study and by summarizing the work they have accomplished to date at the beginning of each conference. "Nuts and bolts" type questions can be answered by a graduate school manual or by more experienced graduate students. Students, however, have the right to expect reasonable access to their advisor and a reasonable turnaround time on the work they submit for their advisor's review.

PRESENTING A PROPOSAL

The dissertation proposal presents an overview of the research you are "proposing" to do. It should tell the reader what your specific problem is, how you intend to do the research, why it is significant, and how it is different from other research on the same topic. There are two major reasons why a proposal is a valuable component of the dissertation process. First, it forces you to structure the entire project. The proposal serves "as a 'road map' for your research, always letting you know where you have been and where you are going" (Allen, 1973, p. 34). Second, it protects both the student and the committee. It is a type of contractual agreement in which the committee endorses the study as proposed, and the student agrees to carry out the investigation in the manner stipulated in the proposal.

The format of a proposal differs from one institution to another. You can learn the form expected at a particular school by referring to that school's doctoral handbook, by reviewing proposals that have been accepted there, or by consulting your advisor. In most cases, the proposal addresses, in abbreviated fashion, the same areas that will be treated in depth in the dissertation. Proposals can be divided into three sections that reflect the content of the first three chapters of the dissertation. Most proposals are at least twelve pages in length and most (in the experience of the authors of this text) average twenty pages. Figure 11.2 outlines the parts of a typical proposal. Of course not all the parts shown here are appropriate for all investigations.

The proposal may also include a timeline that projects when different phases of the research will be conducted, a bibliography of literature to be reviewed in the Review of the Literature section, sample

---

Proposal

A. Introduction and Problem (Chapter 1 of dissertation)
   Introduction to the study
   Background of the problem
   Statement of the problem (What is the problem, the
      area of concern?)
   Purpose of the study (specific purposes and/or objectives)
   Rational or theoretical basis for the study
   Hypotheses or questions to be answered
   Importance or significance of the study
   Definition of terms (operational definitions)
   Assumptions and limitations of the study
   Organization of the remainder of the study

B. Review of the Literature (Chapter 2)
   Introduction and organizational structure of the chapter
   An abbreviated review of pertinent literature, grouped around
      major topics or themes

C. Methodology (Chapter 3)
   Introduction reviewing purpose of the study
   Description of methodology to be used (e.g., experimental,
      case study, historical)
   Design of the study (operationalize variables)
   Sample and population or source of data
   Instrumentation
   Data collection and other procedures
   Data analysis (how you expect to analyze the data once they
      are collected)

Figure 11.2. A typical proposal outline.

letters of introduction and/or permission, sample interview questions, data collection instruments, and any supporting material that will be involved in the study.

Just as the format for a proposal is likely to differ among universities, so too is the system for getting a proposal approved. Committee members may approve a proposal on an individual basis with the chair signing a form or the proposal itself. Some universities require that the proposal be defended before the committee as a whole. In this case a formal committee meeting is held, at which time the student presents a brief synopsis of the proposed research and defends it in response to questions asked. Gardner and Beatty (1980) list six areas most often questioned in a proposal hearing:

1. Why the subject should be studied
2. Reliability and validity of instrumentation
3. Length and type of treatment (or survey procedures)
4. Population
5. Research design
6. Data analysis procedures (pp. 85–86)

In summary, the research proposal sketches out the entire project. It offers an overview of the problem, justifies the need for doing the research, relates the study to other literature, delineates just how the study is to be carried out, and proposes how the data are to be analyzed. Spending the time to be thorough in developing the proposal will save the student time in completing the dissertation because the structure of the proposal mirrors that of the dissertation. So if the proposal is approved, the student not only has committee support for the study itself, but also has an outline of the first three chapters of the dissertation.

COMPLETING THE RESEARCH

The thesis or dissertation has come to connote a formal paper detailing the process and results of a research investigation. More precisely, it is "a substantial paper that is submitted to the faculty of a university by a candidate for an advanced degree that is typically based on independent research and that if acceptable usually gives evidence of the candidate's mastery both of his own subject and of scholarly method" (*Webster's Third New International Dictionary*, 1981). The format for the organization of the dissertation has also become fairly standardized. In addition to the three chapters already discussed, the typical dissertation has two concluding chapters. The fourth chapter presents the findings of the study. It is a nonevaluative reporting of data, including tables, figures, and charts. If hypotheses or research questions guided the study, data are reported relative to each question or hypothesis. Depending upon the topic and type of data used, conclusions may also be interwoven with the results of this chapter.

The purpose of the fifth chapter is to present an analysis and interpretation of what was found in the study and to recommend ideas for additional research. This final chapter can be divided into three major sections:

1. Summary. The summary should contain an overview of the entire study: a brief description of the problem, the research methodology, the findings, and the conclusions. It should be thorough enough to allow someone to get the gist of the research without reading the entire dissertation in detail.
2. Conclusions and/or Discussion. If conclusions were not integrated with the findings in the fourth chapter, they may be presented here. The discussion of the findings goes beyond the data in an attempt to place the findings in a broader perspective. Such a discussion should also tie in some of the pertinent literature reviewed in the second chapter. Creativity is allowed in interpreting the data as long as the implications are suggested by the data.
3. Recommendations. This section should specify areas of additional needed research and may suggest a different procedure that would bring about more substantive results.

The closing material in a dissertation includes a complete bibliography and appendixes. Appendixes contain all information not immediately germane to the body of the paper, but of interest to the reader such as data-gathering instruments, survey forms, and supplemental data analysis. Although some dissertations or theses may have six or seven chapters, depending upon the type of analyses and volume of narrative required for a given study, the sequence, general content, and organization of chapters of the research report are similar.

The dissertation, with its stylized format, has not always been so prescribed or research-focused. "To dissertate" originally means to discuss a topic in a learned and formal manner. The meaning underwent gradual change over the centuries, until today a dissertation has come to signify "an original research project that contributes to knowledge"—quite an imposing image and intimidating to many students. The Carnegie Foundation for the Advancement of Teaching expressed its concern with this emphasis:

> Some graduate departments have magnified the thesis beyond reason, both in size and in emphasis upon it as an original contribution. There is no demonstrable relationship between the size of the dissertation and its quality. Some believe that the emphasis on an original contribution to knowledge is the most important factor in forcing students into more and more abstruse and narrow topics.
>
> The important thing to keep in mind is that it is not so much what the individual can "prove" or "contribute" that counts in a dissertation; it is what the individual shows of how his mind works, of his literacy, of his quality of thought . . . Published contributions are only one desirable consequence of research training. Other consequences are scholarly judgement, critical acuity, knowledge in depth, and the capacity to teach in an inspired fashion. (quoted in Koefod, 1964, p. 94)

Nearly half the students who begin doctoral study fail to finish. For some, adult responsibilities to family and work have to take precedence over school. Sometimes those who have entered programs to change, upgrade, or prepare for a job find that the right job comes along before completing the degree and the new position leaves little time for a major research project.

These practical barriers are accompanied by motivational problems. There are few, if any, rewards or reinforcements once students have passed comprehensive exams until the degree is awarded, and so they must set their own schedules of reinforcement. Once students finish courses and turn their attention to a dissertation, they enter a different world. No other people are structuring their work, setting their deadlines, or providing them various forms of support. They rarely have contact with fellow students or faculty other than their advisor. Many students cannot cope with the lack of structure and the loneliness of the task.

There are several ways to deal with these motivational barriers. The problem of being overwhelmed by the complexity of the task can be alleviated by dividing the task into many smaller, manageable units. Set deadlines for the completion of each unit and reward yourself when the deadline is met. It might also help to remind yourself that you would not have been admitted to the program or not have gotten this far if you were not capable of completing the dissertation. A dissertation requires perseverance, not brilliance. In a discussion of self-control techniques and the dissertation, Martin (1980) offers five ideas to help students complete their dissertation:

1. The student must schedule regular and frequent work periods. Try being possessive of your time and setting aside certain periods each week. The longer the time elapses between sessions, the harder it is to begin again.
2. Work periods should take place in the same spot each time and the place should be conducive to work. "Behavior analysis has documented the fact that if a behavior is carried out repeatedly in one setting, the setting will come to be associated with that behavior and will tend to foster the continual occurrence of that behavior."
3. "A goal should be set for the amount of work to be produced each day or each week and a record should be kept of the amount of work accomplished in order to determine if the goal has been met." This technique will both motivate and reinforce your efforts.
4. Set up reinforcements or punishments if needed. Martin recounts the example of a person who gave a friend money to send in five dollar amounts to a proselytizing church "that the subject disliked" if she did not complete five or more pages in a week.
5. "Anticipate lower rates of production after a large segment of work has been completed." Stronger reinforcements can be established for anticipated periods of low production. (pp. 73–79)

DEFENDING THE RESEARCH

The final step in the dissertation process is the oral defense. The oral defense is a vestige of the European tradition of graduate education. In medieval Europe, students desiring to become masters, doctors, or professors (the terms were synonymous) demonstrated mastery of a subject through a public examination or series of lectures (Davinson, 1977). Except for Scandinavian countries where the rigorous public examinations of doctoral students still exists, contemporary dissertation defenses are private affairs. Present are the student and the committee, perhaps a few additional faculty members who may examine the candidate, and possibly other doctoral students who are merely observing the process.

Most oral defenses begin with the chair introducing the session and laying out suggested procedures for questioning the candidate. At this point the student is usually asked to review briefly how interest in the topic developed, what the purpose of the study was, how it was carried out, and the major findings. Since everyone present has read the entire study, it is important that this overview be kept brief and to the point. The chair then invites questions from committee members, sometimes suggesting where the questioning might begin.

Students, perhaps because they are more expert in content than methodology, anticipate and prepare for difficult methodological questions. Unless there are blatant methodological problems, committee members are most likely to ask questions related to significance and generalizability. Allen (1973) lists several questions that a student might expect, none of which deals directly with methodology:

> (1) A dissertation is supposed to be a contribution to the literature. What is your contribution? (2) Who, in your area of study, would agree with your findings? Why? Who would disagree? Why? (3) What questions were you unable to answer with your research? (4) What areas for further research did you uncover? (5) How did you reduce your biases and prejudices? (6) What additional work do you intend to undertake as a result of your study? (7) Where could you publish your findings to reach the audience that could profit most from your work? (8) What did this exercise in research teach you? (9) How do you intend to use your findings? (p. 86)

Once the questioning has been completed, the committee must decide whether or not the student has passed the oral exam. Typically, the student and other visitors are asked to leave while the committee deliberates. Depending upon the university, the committee may exercise one of several options: the student can pass, fail, pass on condition that certain revisions are made, or if major revisions are needed, a committee may have the option of postponing a decision and rescheduling a hearing. The student is informed immediately of the decision. A student who passes is considered a holder of the doctoral degree even though formal graduation ceremonies are still to come. It is a rare dissertation that survives the defense without some revisions being needed. These revisions are often handled by the advisor and the candidate, but on occasion other members of the committee may want to approve them.

A student can prepare for the defense in several ways. Anxiety can be reduced by realizing that the committee cannot challenge you on the basic structure of the study because they approved it at the proposal stage. Secondly, no one else knows as much about the study as you do at this time—you should be able to defend it. Finally, most advisors will not take a candidate to the oral defense unless the advisor is satisfied with the product. More often than not, an advisor who has approved your work will be supportive of you during the hearing. Other suggestions for preparing are:

1. Carefully read through the dissertation the night before.
2. Check the room where the defense is to be held and make sure any necessary aids are there.
3. Practice your introductory remarks with a friend.
4. Check—or have your advisor check—with the other committee members ahead of time for serious or major concerns.
5. Attend a few oral defenses prior to yours in order to familiarize yourself with the process.

The oral defense culminates a person's career as a doctoral student. It can be a stimulating experience in which you feel a great sense of achievement. It offers an opportunity to discuss your research with interested faculty. Finally, the defense signals a rite of passage from student status to professional colleague.

SUMMARY

The process of graduate research is not unlike doing research in other contexts. In community settings, in business and industry, in education, the person who engages in research must first focus the problem or concern and then select a strategy for investigation. In many instances a proposal is presented to a funding source, and a committee may be formed to guide the research. Finally, the research needs to be carried out followed by a "defense" in the form of a journal article, conference presentation, or final report to the funding source. Most of these aspects have been covered in other chapters of this text. This chapter has concentrated on the practical aspects of graduate research. For students interested in more detailed discussions of the research process, Table 1.1 in Chapter 1 lists the parts of the graduate research process and the corresponding chapter discussions.

REFERENCES

Almack, J. C. (1930). *Research and thesis writing.* Boston: Houghton Mifflin Company.

Allen, G. R. (1973). *The graduate students' guide to theses and dissertations.* San Francisco: Jossey-Bass.

Davinson, D. (1977). *Theses and dissertations.* Hamden, CT: Linnet Books.

Davis, R. M. (1980). *Thesis projects in science and engineering.* New York: St. Martin's Press.

Gardner, D. C., & Beatty, G.J. (1980). *Dissertation proposal guidebook.* Springfield, IL: Charles Thomas.

Koefod, P. E. (1964). *The writing requirements for graduate degrees.* Englewood Cliffs, NJ: Prentice-Hall, Inc.

Long, T. J., Convey, J. J., & Chwalek, A. R. (1986). *Completing dissertations in the behavioral sciences and education.* San Francisco: Jossey-Bass.

Martin, R. (1980). *Writing and defending a thesis or dissertation in psychology and education.* Springfield, IL: Charles Thomas.

Webster's third new international dictionary of the English language, unabridged. (1981). Springfield, MA: G & C Merriam Company.

GLOSSARY

ABSTRACT. A brief summary of a research study presenting the problem statement, the procedures used, and the results of the study.

ACTION RESEARCH. A type of research that aims to solve a specific and current problem.

APPLIED RESEARCH. A type of research that is directed toward solving immediate and practical problems.

A PRIORI THEORY. A mode of inquiry in which a theory is proposed and hypotheses are developed in advance of gathering data about a specific phenomenon (also called hypothetical-deductive theory).

BASIC RESEARCH. A type of research that is motivated by intellectual interest alone and is concerned with knowledge for its own sake.

CASE HISTORY. An analysis that traces the past of a person, group, or institution.

CASE METHOD. An instructional technique whereby the major ingredients of a case study are presented to students for illustrative or problem-solving purposes.

CASE STUDY. An intensive description and analysis of a particular social unit that seeks to uncover the interplay of significant factors that is characteristic of that unit.

CASE WORK. The remedial or developmental procedures that are undertaken after the causes of maladjustment have been diagnosed.

CAUSAL/COMPARATIVE RESEARCH. A form of descriptive research in which the investigator looks for relationships that may explain phenomena that have already taken place (also called ex post facto research).

COLLECTIVE BIOGRAPHY. An application of quantitative analysis in which the historical researcher looks at biographical characteristics of a particular group of people.

CONCEPTS. Abstract ideas that develop from observation and are used to explain and describe the phenomena being studied.

CONCEPTUAL LITERATURE. *See* THEORETICAL LITERATURE.

CONSTRUCT VALIDITY. The extent to which a test measures the abstract, theoretical ideas (constructs) that it is designed to measure.

CONTENT ANALYSIS. A form of analysis in which the researcher establishes the frequency with which certain words, ideas, or attitudes are expressed in a particular body of material.

CONTENT VALIDITY. The extent to which items on a test or scale match the behavior, skill, or affect the researcher intends them to measure.

CRITICAL RESEARCH. A methodology that emphasizes the examination of epistemological, cognitive, cultural and political bases of policy and practice through dialectic intercourse, leading to knowledge of practical interest and "new world" perspectives by those engaged in the process.

CROSS-SECTIONAL RESEARCH. A design in which data are gathered from different groups (usually age groups) at a single point in time.

DESCRIPTIVE RESEARCH. A method used to describe systematically the facts and characteristics of a given population or area of interest.

DESCRIPTIVE STATISTICS. A set of procedures that can be used to summarize data or to make simple comparisons of data.

DIALECTIC METHOD. A type of philosophical inquiry in which disputes and contradictions are disclosed, examined, and reconciled.

DISSERTATION. Commonly used at the doctoral level to mean a formal paper that details the process and results of a research investigation.

ETHNOGRAPHY. A research methodology that includes both a set of techniques used to uncover the social order and meaning that a setting has for the people participating in it and the written record that is the product of using those techniques.

EX POST FACTO RESEARCH. *See* CAUSAL/COMPARATIVE RESEARCH.

EXTERNAL VALIDITY. The degree to which the results of a study are generalizable to other situations under similar conditions.

FACTORIAL DESIGN. A method used to study the effects of more than one independent variable on more than one dependent variable.

FEMINIST RESEARCH. Any investigation of phenomena from women's perspectives with the underlying purpose of discovering intellectual constructs other than those developed by men.

FUTURES RESEARCH. A methodology that frequently uses the past as a means of illuminating the study of possible futures.

GROUNDED THEORY. A research methodology that is characterized by inductive fieldwork and the goal of having theory emerge from the data.

HISTORICAL DEMOGRAPHY. An application of quantitative analysis in which the researcher studies the composition of a population by examining public records.

HYPOTHETICAL-DEDUCTIVE THEORY. *See* A PRIORI THEORY.

INFERENTIAL STATISTICS. A set of procedures that can be used to test hypotheses or to estimate the parameters of the population used in the study.

INTERACTIVE RESEARCH. A methodology in which the design is formulated while the research is in progress, the researcher serves as a facilitator for problem solving, and the results are intended for immediate application by those who participated in the research.

INTERNAL VALIDITY. The degree to which the research procedure measures what it purports to measure.

INTERVIEW SCHEDULE. A highly structured format of questions that will be asked of a research participant.

LITERATURE REVIEW. A narrative essay that integrates, synthesizes, and critiques the important thinking and research on a particular topic.

LOGISTIC METHOD. A type of philosophical inquiry in which knowledge is examined by understanding the elements of which it is composed.

LONGITUDINAL RESEARCH. A design in which data are gathered from the same sample on several occasions.

MOLAR APPROACH. A procedure used with structured observation in which the observer groups several behaviors into broadly defined categories.

MOLECULAR APPROACH. A procedure used with structured observation in which the focus is on units of behavior that are small enough to ensure reliability in observation.

PARTICIPATORY RESEARCH. A type of research that aims at the political empowerment of people through group participation in the search for knowledge.

PRIMARY SOURCES. Oral or written accounts by someone who was an eyewitness to the event.

PROBLEMATIC METHOD. A type of philosophical inquiry in which problems are solved one at a time and without reference to an all-inclusive whole or a simplest part.

PROCEDURE. The steps or activities that describe the general way data are gathered.

PROJECTIVE TECHNIQUES. A group of methods used for getting participants to share their feelings, attitudes, and thoughts.

PSYCHOSOCIAL HISTORY. An approach that uses modern psychological and sociological theories and concepts to interpret personalities, events, groups, or movements of the past.

QUALITATIVE DATA. Data that are not transferable to numbers and not comparable by statistical procedures.

QUANTITATIVE DATA. Data that are coded and represented by statistical scores (also called statistical data).

QUANTITATIVE HISTORY. An approach that analyzes a historical period or event by focusing upon phenomena that can be counted or measured.

RATING SCALE. A measuring instrument on which the researcher assigns observed behaviors to numbered categories.

RESEARCH AND DEVELOPMENT (R&D). A term used in business and industry to refer to applied research that is directed toward product development.

RESEARCH ETHICS. Policies and practices related to doing research that impact the protection of the research participants and governs the rights and responsibilities of researchers conducting research studies.

RESEARCH STUDIES. Writings that are based on the collection and analysis of data gathered from sources extraneous to the author.

SECONDARY SOURCES. Oral or written accounts by someone who did not witness an event.

SOCIOMETRIC TECHNIQUES. A group of methods used for studying the organization of social groups.

STATISTICAL DATA. See QUANTITATIVE DATA.

SUBSTANTIVE THEORY. An explanation that emerges from a grounded-theory study and deals with phenomena that are limited to particular real-world situations.

SURVEY. A broad category of techniques that use questioning as a strategy to elicit information.

TECHNIQUE. The specific device or means of recording the data.

THEORETICAL LITERATURE. Writings that are based on an author's experience or opinions (also called conceptual literature).

THESIS. Commonly used at the master's level to mean a formal paper describing a culminating research project.

INDEX